Jeffrey Dahmer

The Milwaukee Cannibal

Jeffrey Dahmer

The Milwaukee Cannibal

Brittany Ann Jones

PEN & SWORD
TRUE CRIME

An imprint of
Pen & Sword Books Ltd
Yorkshire - Philadelphia

First published in Great Britain in 2026 by
Pen & Sword True Crime
An imprint of
Pen & Sword Books Ltd
Yorkshire - Philadelphia

ISBN 978 1 03611 524 1

A CIP catalogue record for this book is available from the British Library.

Typeset in INDIA by IMPEC eSolutions
Printed and bound in England by CPI Group (UK) Ltd, Croydon, CRO 4YY

The Publisher's authorised representative in the EU for product safety is Authorised Rep Compliance Ltd., Ground Floor, 71 Lower Baggot Street, Dublin D02 P593, Ireland.
www.arccompliance.com

For a complete list of Pen & Sword titles please contact

PEN & SWORD BOOKS LIMITED
47 Church Street, Barnsley, South Yorkshire, S70 2AS, England
E-mail: enquiries@pen-and-sword.co.uk
Website: www.pen-and-sword.co.uk

or

PEN AND SWORD BOOKS
1950 Lawrence Rd, Havertown, PA 19083, USA
E-mail: uspen-and-sword@casematepublishers.com
Website: www.penandswordbooks.com

MIX
Paper | Supporting responsible forestry
FSC® C013604
FSC www.fsc.org

Contents

Acknowledgements

To my friends, my family and to my book club full of mothers. Thank you for your support, love and never-ending words of encouragement.

I would also like to thank those who contributed to this book and shared their expert insight, including Mandy Morris, Caitlin Weese, Jill Sitnick, Holly Keller, Alex Alvarez, Israel Reyes, Naomi Murphy, Fotoulla Menikou, Dr Manpreet Dhuffar-Pottiwal, Elreacy Dock, Dr Joel Frank, and Amy Bentley.

Without your contribution, this book would not have been able to dive into the psychological aspect of the case, nor the forensic process and legal proceedings.

Part I

Introduction

On the surface, Jeffrey Lionel Dahmer may not have been pegged as a nefarious figure. But he was far from a trustworthy neighbour. Pale, tall, shy and donning spectacles, Dahmer was an unassuming character who blended into the very fabric of American suburban life. To those who lived near him and casually knew about his life, he appeared to be a quiet young man, someone who may have been slightly odd to converse with, but he was certainly no killer. Right?

While his outward appearance created the image of an all-American man, he most definitely did not share the same values and morals as his peers. Beneath the timid façade lay a twisted mind entangled by desires so incomprehensible and dark that they would go on to shock the world. There are only so many crimes in the world which truly shock and sicken the general public, and this is arguably one of the most heinous. It was a series of crimes so sickening that the effects of the murders still send ripples throughout the world today. Decades on, many wonder why the victims were selected to be butchered, but only one person had the answers.

The case of the Milwaukee Murders began in 1978 and ended in 1991, resulting in the deaths of 17 men and young teenagers. The motive? It can only be speculated that it was for sexual pleasure and the need to demonstrate ultimate control over the victims. With victims ages ranging from 14 to 32, Jeffrey Dahmer's Modus Operandi was difficult to pin down.

Why did he choose the men and boys that he targeted? What was their similarity? Nobody can say for certain.

Born on 21 May 1960, Dahmer's Milwaukee, Wisconsin early life could hold the key to the mystery of his motive. His childhood was marked by an unsettling pool of isolation, neglect and an emerging obsession and fascination with death and the inner workings of living creatures. Dahmer's trajectory speaks volumes and in hindsight, he held all the hallmarks of a killer in the making. From dissecting roadkill in his teenage years, to the murders of 17 men and boys, the escalation proved to be increasingly depraved and brutal. His crimes were not merely acts of homicide, but they also bled into the realms of cannibalism and necrophilia, branching out into acts so grotesque that they could have been mistaken for the work of a horror film psychopath.

The story of Dahmer is not only a recounting of his heinous acts; it is also an exploration into the psyche of a man who seemingly rejected all semblance of conventional understanding of humanity and morality. What compelled him to commit such heinous crimes? Were his actions spurred by a mind so damaged that it could only be close to another human as long as they were incapacitated for good? Or was there something deeper at play? Perhaps a dark void that could not be filled, no matter the amount of societal intervention? These questions have been on the minds of criminologists, psychologists and the public alike for many decades.

When Dahmer was captured in the July of 1991, after one of his targeted individuals was able to escape his grasp and alert the authorities, the depth of his depravities was uncovered. His house of horrors was something that nobody could have been prepared for. Inside of his small Milwaukee apartment, law enforcement discovered a macabre collection that could shake even the stoniest of men. There were severed heads stored in the refrigerator, human remains floating in acid-filled vats within the living quarters, and polaroid photographs depicting his many grisly deeds. The discovery of evidence left the investigators stunned and the public were equally outraged and nauseous at the details which emerged.

This book unpicks the story of the infamous killer, Jeffrey Dahmer, the Milwaukee Cannibal, without sensationalizing his crimes. Within the pages you'll begin to understand how the trajectory occurred, the circumstances surrounding his upbringing and psyche, as well as how he was able to get away with his crimes for so long. Through painstaking research, analysis and interviews, the chapters examine the interplay of nature versus nurture, and the personal decisions made which created a killer who still stands as a grim reminder of the darkest potential humanity can achieve.

Why do we as people, return to figures like Dahmer to satiate our desires for morbid fascination? Perhaps it is because Dahmer represents an abyss in which we dare not to look into for so long, but cannot help but glance at every so often. His story challenges our fundamental understanding of what it means to be a human being. It also forces us to confront the uncomfortable truth about the fragility of our mortal being, our moral codes and the monsters that lurk in the most unassuming of places. As these pages look into the life and crimes of Dahmer, it is necessary to remember the victims whose lives were snatched away, and the families whose grief will never heal from the truth of what was done to them. Their stories, whilst often overshadowed when Dahmer's crimes are explored, deserve respect and remembrance. As to understand the darkness, you must never forget the flames which were extinguished by its horror.

This is the life and death of Jeffrey Dahmer – a man, a Milwaukee Monster, and a stark reminder of the depravities which do not lurk in the shadows.

They instead pretend to be your quiet neighbour.

Origins of a Milwaukee Monster

The Beginning

Jeffrey Dahmer was born on 21 May 1960, in Milwaukee, Wisconsin to parents Lionel and Joyce Dahmer and was then raised in Bath Township, Ohio, a middle-class suburb of Akron. Joyce, born Annette Joyce Flint, married on 22 August in 1959 and became pregnant afterwards. However, she suffered from nausea and muscle stiffness during her pregnancy with Dahmer. While tough, Joyce continued through her pregnancy and would soon welcome a little bundle of joy.

After the birth of her first son, the wife then went on to gain a master's degree in counselling but worked as a typist whist Dahmer was a child. As the first of two sons, he was the older brother to David, who was born after the family moved to Doylestown when Dahmer was 6 years old. Unfortunately, Joyce struggled with depression and Lionel's work schedule was the priority in the household, leading her to manage things at home on her own.[1]

There are many conflicting statements regarding how young Dahmer was treated as an infant, as some believe that he was a victim of neglect, whilst others say that he was perfectly contented and doted upon by his parents. According to one article, Dahmer was 'a normal, healthy child whose birth was the occasion of great joy'. It described him as a 'happy, bubbly youngster who loved stuffed bunnies and wooden blocks' and he also loved his dog named Frisky. However, he was 'thrilled by the sound' of bones.

Whether this was a true depiction of how Dahmer's early years truly developed or not, it was clear that something was amiss with the young child. Afterall, what toddler is excited by the prospect of the bones of critters? It could ultimately be explained away as the naivety and sensory exploration of any child. However, what would go on to transpire decades later may shine a more sinister light on his blossoming infatuation with death and anatomy.

What is known for certain was that Joyce struggled with her mental health during this time and even went on to attempt suicide, as per Lionel's memoir which accused her of struggling with addiction, and she was also allegedly dependant on prescription medications. After her second pregnancy with David, Joyce was also diagnosed with postpartum psychosis[2] which is characterized by the National Health Service as a 'serious mental health illness that can affect someone soon after having a baby', impacting around 1 in 1,000 mothers. Symptoms include hallucinations, delusions, mania, low moods and confusion. The Mayo Clinic described that this condition can also spur thoughts or attempts of harming the baby, or themselves.[3] It is a serious condition which requires treatment, whether this be in the form of medication, therapy or in-patient care. This terrible environment may have been the catalyst for Dahmer's future crimes.

According to crime expert Cheish Merryweather: "When we talk about a traumatic childhood, it doesn't have to be physical. It can be stressful events such as this. From a young age, he was retiring to this fantasy world to deal with what's going on around him."

These stressful events, while something that many people can empathise with and may have even experienced themselves, could have had an impact on his psychological development. This is an issue that psychologists have attempted to understand for decades. According to trauma-informed care practices, trauma 'results from an event, series of events, or set of circumstances that is experienced by an individual as harmful or life threatening'.

Mind[4], the mental health charity, shares how most of us 'will experience an event in our lives that could be considered traumatic', however, 'we won't all be affected the same way'. It states that 'trauma can happen at any age, and it can affect us 'a long time' afterwards. For Dahmer, one traumatic instance may have been his double hernia operation at the age of four, for which Lionel believes was the catalyst to creating the monster known as the Milwaukee Monster. According to the father, he was 'an energetic and happy child' until that day, and afterwards, he became reclusive.

"I think there were several events in his life starting with the hernia operation," his father said.

Lionel added that his son was concerned about having his penis cut off during the surgery and had asked Joyce if it had been amputated. According to the Cleveland Clinic: "A hernia usually happens in your abdomen or groin, when one of your organs pushes through the muscle or tissue that contains it. It may look like an odd bulge that comes and goes during different activities or in different positions."[5] Entertainment Daily reported that Dahmer's hernia was discovered in his scrotum after suffering from a string of ear and throat infections. The sickly child may have had his fears exacerbated due to his continuous downward health struggles.

"The operation may have been necessary to cure a birth defect, but the experience was so painful for the child that he 'asked Joyce [his mother] if the doctors had cut off his penis,'" the authors of the book *Mythologies of Violence in Postmodern Media* wrote.

According to research, their fears about his surgery impacting his mental health may not have been wrong. Research shows that there is a small risk of psychiatric disorders when children before the age of 5 are exposed to surgery and anaesthesia. This may also include dissociative identity disorder,[6] ADHD, developmental delays, and paediatric medical traumatic stress disorder (PMTSD).

Whilst, at the time, these fears of Dahmer's may have been simply the over exaggerated imaginations of a toddler who was put through a traumatic surgery and was unable to cope due to the lack of emotional support available, it could have had a far more profound impact on the way that he viewed his penis, and even his sexuality. Noticeably subdued, it was reported that Dahmer became increasingly withdrawn, which only heightened following the birth of his younger brother and the family's habitual location changes, particularly when the Dahmer's' moved to Ohio. Without friends and nobody to turn to, Dahmer sunk deeper into himself.

But at what cost? There is much conflicting information regarding the upbringing of Dahmer, which causes confusion as to how he could have become a person who would go on to commit such heinous crimes. A fantasy world of your own creation does not necessarily cause the need for alarm, and nor does it typically manifest into something dark and twisted.

According to Helen, who had briefly researched Dahmer's life whilst she was completing her higher education, the information did not lead her to believe that he would become a killer later in life.

She shared: "What I found interesting about the Dahmer case was that I didn't understand why."

"When I studied serial killers at sixth form there was normally a history of trauma [or] abuse in childhoods [whereas] in his, there didn't seem to be much. What drove him?"

Perhaps his own father could provide the missing piece to the puzzle. Or at least, paint a picture of the downward spiral of Dahmer's mental health. In his own words, he told all in his book *A Father's Story,* which was published in 1994.

He wrote in the book: "As a scientist, I wonder if the potential for great evil resides deep in the blood that some of us may pass on to our children at birth."

He also went on to do a series of televised interviews, such as the *Dahmer and Dahmer* special where he and his second-wife, Shari, shared their theories.

"When Jeff was born, the grandparents were not allowed to hold the baby," Shari said.

"Joyce didn't want anyone touching the baby, or breathing on it. She was afraid of germs."

As per a fictional television show reenacting the case, an actor playing Lionel shared during a vital scene: "She never even held him. She scared the shit out of him. And then she just left. She got in her car, and she drove away, and she left that kid in that house all summer."

As a young boy, it is believed that Dahmer suffered from a lack of emotional connection and attention at home and allegedly confided in friends that he was 'unsure of the solidity of the family.' But this sentiment was not echoed by his mother and father.

In an interview with Dr Kenneth Smail, Dahmer later admitted: "It just didn't seem like the parents really liked each other too much. Arguments, fighting, just made me feel on edge, unsure of the solidity of the family. I know she was in a hospital for about a month, a mental, you know, a ward and dad was busy working."

Dahmer's parents, whilst not on good terms, both agreed that he was not a monster per se, and that he was in dire need of help. However, while Lionel believed that he had had a good childhood, Joyce disagreed and many later blamed Lionel for being too naïve; he had his own theories as to the cause of his son's compulsions. In an interview with *Good Morning America,* Lionel shared that on top of his operation, 'a blow to the back of the head' and 'going around and getting roadkill' may have 'hooked into his sexuality at age 14 or 15'. But ultimately, 'there really were no overt signs'.

The father said: "There really were no overt signs. He wasn't foaming at the mouth or talking to himself in his sleep or acting in a weird fashion."

However, Dahmer developed an unhealthy obsession with animals as a child and would collect carcasses and dismember their bodies. This led to him decapitating a dead dog and nailing its skull to a tree. While gruesome, Lionel encouraged him and believed he had a scientific brain. Lionel helped him to clear the crawl space beneath the home where several dead animals lay, and Dahmer would later recall that he enjoyed listening to the bones rattle as they were dropped into a pail. Then, as a child, his father taught him how to bleach and clean bones.

Lionel recounted: "His small hands dug deep into the pile of bones. I can no longer view it simply as a childish episode, a passing fascination. This same sense of something dark and shadowy, of a malicious force growing in my son, now colours almost every memory."

Dahmer's obsession with animal bones didn't end with rodents, instead, he began collecting roadkill where he would either use chemicals to strip the bones bare, or would try to preserve them in jars of formaldehyde, as per the *Independent*. But this was just one of the things that may have culminated in warping the mind of young Dahmer. In the special feature about Dahmer called *Dahmer on Dahmer* where Lionel and Shari spoke of his compulsions, it was explained that he could have been impacted by his mother's alleged extreme fear of germs, or perhaps medications being injected whilst he was a foetus in her womb.

There are dozens of studies exploring the harm opiates can cause to the brain development of a foetus. Most interesting is one study which shows that 'opioid use alters the connectivity in the area in the brain responsible for emotions.' Barbiturates, another drug which Joyce is said to have taken during pregnancy, has been shown to cause learning disabilities, cognitive disabilities, and psychosocial maladjustment to children after birth. Scientifically, Lionel's blame may not be misguided, however, there is more that could have been prominent in his life which would have impacted his psyche as a child.

For example, in 1991, Lionel told probation officers that his son was molested by a neighbour when he was just 8 years old, according to the *Associated Press.* This claim apparently originated from a statement that Lionel gave to Dahmer's probation officer when he was an adult, but both Dahmer and Lionel later denied the claims. Though, this rumour could speak volumes about the way a child could internalise such trauma and even go on to become an abuser himself, which Dahmer did. A landmark study found that of all fifty convicted serial killers, 36 per cent of the group had suffered from physical abuse attacks and 26 per cent had suffered from sexual abuse. Another study found that abuse or neglect during childhood could lead a 'desensitised' child 'to future painful or anxiety-provoking experiences' and that this might make them 'less emotionally and physiologically responsive to the needs of others, to be callous and lack empathy, and to lack remorse or guilt.' On top of the extensive research on this topic, it is a widely held belief that molestation or physical abuse produces a negative person later in life, shaping how they go on to treat others.

Janice Englander Katz, Ph.D. HSPP, a clinical psychologist said of the molestation claims: "If there is sexual abuse, and a child doesn't feel like he has resources to go to, such as mom being emotionally unavailable and dad working a lot, then he doesn't have a good support system who can buffer and process the events with him."

That same year in 1968, he was given a chemistry set, which he used to experiment with animals, such as preserving insects in jars and then later impaling cats and frogs on sticks. Childhood friends confirmed that he was keenly interested in the insides of animals, specifically how things worked. Speaking on the *Dr Phil* show, Lionel said that his son would explore dead animals, stating: "[He] felt them, explored them – their insides, their entrails and terrible things like that. Although I've had friends who have told me they've done the same sort of thing, but that would have been a red flag."

While these may very well have been innocent thoughts and compulsions, there is a lot to be said about his early interests and the crimes that Dahmer would ultimately engage in. As his interests began to pick up in severity, as well as his tastes beginning to mature and manifest in different ways, Dahmer's formative years pique the interests of psychologists and psychiatrists alike. This is due to a range of reasons. For example, the trauma Dahmer may have suffered from after his hernia operation, could ultimately have changed his personality, resulting in his new excitement for the anatomy of bodies. Or perhaps the emotional neglect and physical neglect by his withdrawn parents played a role in creating an environment which paved the way for Dahmer to become the man he did. This theory is known as nature versus nurture, which explores the question of whether a person is born to become a certain way, or if environmental factors contributed to their disposition later in life.

In a university study, researchers from Teesside University talked to teenagers in Romania, and found that 86.3 per cent viewed homeless animals being abused or killed as 'normal', and they were found to later self-harm or have suicidal tendencies. Nearly all questioned had witnessed animals being poisoned or hanged.

Similarly, for Mandy Morris, LPC, EMDR Clinician & Trauma Expert, Dahmer's trauma is universally known to have been caused by his early childhood experiences.

She revealed: "The Case of Jeffrey Dahmer and Broader Research Childhood trauma has long been recognized as a critical factor in shaping an individual's mental and emotional development. According to trauma-informed psychologists, early adverse experiences—whether 'big T' traumas (e.g., physical abuse, sexual abuse, or life-threatening neglect) or 'small t' traumas (e.g., chronic emotional neglect, bullying, or repeated criticism)—can have profound and lasting effects on a person's sense of self, interpersonal relationships, and capacity for empathy.

"While not everyone who experiences childhood trauma becomes violent, research indicates that a significant number of serial killers' report histories of abuse, neglect, or other profound disruptions in early attachment. Jeffrey Dahmer's life story offers a stark illustration of how complex developmental factors, unmet attachment needs, and genetic predispositions can converge in tragic, violent outcomes."

Morris went on to share that work conducted by the 'renowned physician' and 'expert on trauma and addiction', Dr Gabor Maté 'highlights two fundamental needs humans have from the moment they are born'.

She explained that these needs are:

> "Attachment – the ability to connect with caregivers in a bond that ensures survival (physical and emotional safety).
>
> "Authenticity – the freedom to experience, express, and develop one's true emotions, needs, and sense of self."

According to Morris: "When a child grows up in an environment where emotional or physical safety is compromised, the child often must make a devastating choice between authenticity and attachment. To maintain the attachment bond with a caregiver who might be neglectful, abusive, or emotionally unavailable, the child may learn to suppress feelings, desires, or aspects of their personality to avoid further threat, abandonment, or rejection.

"When children repeatedly suppress their authentic emotional responses—because it is not safe to express them—they risk becoming disconnected from their own sense of self. This can lead to various psychological adaptations, which, in some extreme cases, manifest as violent or destructive behaviour later in life. While most trauma survivors do not become violent offenders, the common thread in cases of chronic emotional and/or physical abuse is a disconnection from empathy and from one's own emotional needs."

Regarding Dahmer's early years, the potential neglect and unresolved parental issues he may have faced, it would have been 'significant' to his life.

The expert continued that as per what is reported of his upbringing, he 'experienced significant disruption in his attachment relationships'. She broke it down into two different sections which set the groundwork for creating a person who may become stunted by the experiences. Morris stated that the 'emotional neglect' that he faced was proven by his own father's public words.

She stated: "His father, Lionel Dahmer, has publicly admitted that he was often absent—consumed with work and personal interests—leaving Jeffrey feeling isolated and overlooked."

Another aspect was Dahmer's 'parental instability' in his life.

Morris clarified: "Jeffrey's mother, Joyce, reportedly struggled with severe depression, anxiety, and obsessive-compulsive behaviours. She was described as a 'germaphobe,' avoiding physical contact with her infant son. Joyce also had multiple suicide attempts, creating an unstable and frightening environment for Jeffrey."

This 'frightening' upbringing potentially harmed the way in which little Dahmer was able to attach himself to those around him, develop relationships and more.

The expert continued: "From a trauma perspective, these issues suggest that Jeffrey did not develop a secure base or consistent emotional support. His parents' inability to resolve their own mental health struggles likely impeded their capacity to nurture his emotional well-being. When a child's need for both attachment and authenticity is continually threatened, the child may shut down critical parts of themselves, paving the way for maladaptive coping mechanisms—or, in extreme cases, deeply pathological behaviours."

There are varying arguments in the trauma worlds about whether there is a genetic predisposition or an environmental 'trigger' which could have set in motion the horrific events that rocked Milwaukee and continues to do so, even today.

This is what is known as the Nature versus Nurture debate, which explores whether a person is predisposed to become the adult that they grow up to be, or if their upbringing and experiences shaped their ultimate path.

As for Morris, her expert opinion points to Dahmer's later criminal notoriety being caused by his environment.

She explained: "The interplay of genetic and environmental factors is often summed up as: 'Genetics load the gun, but environment pulls the trigger.' In Jeffrey Dahmer's case, there may indeed have been a genetic predisposition toward obsessive-compulsive or anxiety disorders, potentially inherited from his mother. This predisposition, combined with severe disruptions in attachment and emotional neglect, created a context in which Dahmer's capacity for empathy and healthy relational development was profoundly compromised.

'Obsessionality' can manifest in multiple forms. In some individuals—like those with OCD—it manifests as repeated rituals or compulsions aimed at reducing anxiety. In others, it might breed a distorted, fixated fantasy life. Where caring adults fail to intervene or provide a safe container for a child's emotional world, these disturbing fantasies can escalate, ultimately leading to the violent, compulsive acts Dahmer committed."

As for the connection between Dahmer's childhood trauma and that of serial killers, she expressed how research insights and 'numerous studies underscore the prevalence of childhood trauma among violent offenders, including serial killers.'

Drawing upon evidence to support this, she explained that 'in interviews with incarcerated serial killers, former FBI profilers such as John Douglas and Robert K. Ressler consistently found a history of physical abuse, sexual abuse, severe neglect, or abandonment.' As well as interviews, academic reviews also highlighted key signs that Dahmer's childhood could have sparked a similar path in him which serial killers have also walked.

She said: "Reviews of serial homicide cases often highlight chaotic home environments, exposure to substance abuse, and parental rejection. In a 2005 study published in the Journal of Police and Criminal Psychology, researchers noted that many serial killers had experienced childhood abuse and neglect that contributed to emotional detachment and lack of empathy. Although somewhat controversial and outdated in its predictive power, the Macdonald Triad (bedwetting, cruelty to animals, fire-setting) correlates with early trauma and has been frequently observed in the histories of violent offenders. It underscores that disturbances in a child's environment can lead to the outward expression of suppressed rage or deviant behaviours.

"Collectively, these findings point to trauma as a central theme in the developmental histories of many serial killers. Where trauma is unacknowledged, unaddressed, and compounded by parental neglect or abuse, children may form rigid, maladaptive strategies for coping—some of which can manifest later as sadistic or homicidal acts. Importantly, it is not trauma alone that determines the outcome; many factors—social support, access to mental health resources, resilience, and personal constitution—can mitigate or intensify the impact of adverse childhood experiences."

Similar upbringings of notorious US serial killers can be compared with Ted Bundy, whose mother Louise Cowell, was rumoured to have been impregnated by her own father, who went on to tell a young Bundy that his mother was his sister and that his grandparents were his true parents. This type of early life confusion, betrayal and instability could have attracted the man to the idea of violent control, and to attack, rape and murder over 30 women with the same dark features as his mother—who had lied to him.

Another serial killer with a troubling childhood was that of Edmund Kemper, who had murdered his grandparents, and six hitchhiking women in the 1970s before turning his fury on his mother and her friend. According to reports, his mother was an overly critical alcoholic who he dreamed of one day murdering.

Ed Gein, another serial killer, also had a strange relationship with his parents, particularly his mother. His story was so shocking that it went on to inspire the character Norman Bates of the *Psycho* film. His father was an alcoholic, and his mother ruled the home with an iron fist and fanatic religious teaching. Gein murdered two women in the 50s, and once apprehended at his home, police made the shocking discovery that he had been stealing bodies from graves and turning them into pieces of furniture and clothing. He also preserved a shrine for his abusive mother.

The discovery that serial killers typically come from dysfunctional dynamics and backgrounds isn't surprising. According to Morris: "Jeffrey Dahmer's tragic case demonstrates the interplay of childhood trauma, unmet attachment needs, and potential genetic vulnerabilities. While genetic predispositions might contribute to obsessive or anxious tendencies, they are rarely the sole cause of homicidal violence. It is the repeated experiences of abandonment, emotional neglect, or abuse—combined with the absence of a stable, empathetic environment—that most significantly disrupt a child's ability to form healthy relationships and a stable sense of self.

"One can see how the lack of authentic emotional expression and secure attachment can breed a profound disconnection—both from oneself and from others' humanity. Although the majority of individuals with trauma histories do not become violent criminals, research consistently highlights the destructive potential of unaddressed childhood trauma. Ensuring safe, nurturing environments and providing early interventions for at-risk children can serve as a critical line of defence against the formation of violent, sociopathic, or psychopathic behaviours.

In summary, Jeffrey Dahmer's life path—like those of many other serial killers—reflects a confluence of early adversity, instability, and potentially inherited mental health vulnerabilities."

She added: "Understanding these factors through the lens of attachment theory and trauma research can guide more effective prevention, identification, and treatment strategies. I believe the path forward to break these patterns starts with individuals, especially parents, doing their own work towards healing. When we take responsibility for our own trauma we can work toward creating contexts where children's authentic emotional needs are met and their capacity for empathy and healthy development is supported."

Jill Sitnick, an author and the founder and CEO of the Journey Sage, who demystifies MDMA therapy for Post Traumatic Stress Disorder sufferers had a poignant expert opinion on Dahmer's childhood and the way in which it shaped his predisposition to criminal activity, as well as how his parents' rearing affected his development.

She explained that she can 'speak to not feeling loved' and 'how we learn about the world at a young age'.

As she works with many clients who are in need of her assistance, she is able to provide sound advice based on her professional expertise, as well as her own personal life experiences.

She said: "If at that young age we are neglected and harmed, it can leave an adult feeling empty and afraid. Filling that emptiness could manifest in a variety of ways. One thing I've learned is that my parents didn't evolve their trauma-laden choices in child rearing or life in a vacuum. It came from their upbringing. I can now see the generational trauma patterns in my own life that I could never see before. That means that sometimes, children don't have anyone in the family to turn to for love or validation. That is a very lonely place to be."

While she is unable to comment on the families of serial killers specifically, her opinion is 'there is probably a mix of nature and nurture'.

Sitnick shared: "People always ask me how I managed to succeed from how my life started and I always had some sort of motivation to be the opposite of my parents. I didn't learn that externally. So, somewhere along the line, an internal operating system (for lack of a better word) comes into play, along with the external abuse and the genetics from traumatised generations (Gabor Mate talks about this a lot - you should check him out). Now, that is my opinion. I'm not a doctor, and I don't play one on TV - this is my reflection on what I see in myself and when working with others who have trauma and have made different decisions."

When asked how do childhood experiences, such as emotional neglect or a lack of physical affection, typically impact psychological development in children, Sitnick replied: "When you consider that children learn about the world from their caregivers, it makes sense that a lack of physical affection can make them feel an emptiness that they might never understand. When I talk to people whose parents were unable to connect to them in loving ways, we have a lingering sense of 'I'm not good enough' or 'I'm too much' to love. These are the strategies young minds use to understand why a caretaker isn't caretaking.

"We can't understand at a young age that our caretakers are anything other than there to take care of us. So if the caretaker isn't providing affection, then it 'must' be something within us causing that behaviour. It is a deep wound that many people have. Trying to explain the emptiness a neglected child feels to people who were not neglected is very difficult. It is like you feel something is missing within you. I had to get it filled with some reparenting during a psychedelic-assisted therapy session."

From a psychological perspective, the potential long-term effects on a child who grows up with a parent struggling with mental health issues, such as suicidal thoughts or depression could lead to their own challenges seeping into the psyche of their children.

Speaking from her own experiences, the expert explained just how much her childhood struggles came to fruition as an adult.

Sitnick revealed: "I can only speak for myself as my mother was diagnosed with depression her entire life. Looking back now, I can see it was treatment-resistant depression. Additionally, she attempted suicide more than five times in her life. As a child I didn't see any of that. My father was a domestic abuser of women, and during my childhood, my mother was the safer alternative. By having the one parent figure that wasn't dangerous, I gravitated to her. I didn't know that her constantly depressed and scared of practically everything mindset was seeping into my mindset. I grew up with an unhealthy dose of unnecessary fear about everything.

"My PTSD attack's foundation, in my mid-forties, was the knowing I was going to lose everything even though I was working at Microsoft, had paid off my house, and had several safety nets. The irrational fear was overwhelming. That's what ultimately led me back to my therapist because I couldn't understand how my body was feeling when there was no reason to be scared."

The role that early childhood trauma and attachment issues play in shaping the future behaviour of individuals, particularly when they experience emotional neglect or lack of nurturing is significant, with Sitnick explaining that it colours their perspective of everything.

She shared: "Childhood trauma plays a vital role in how individuals view the world and interact with it as adults. As my therapist likes to say, most adults are simply children wrapped up in layers. It is the unravelling of those layers in therapy (whether talk therapy or psychedelic-assisted therapy) that helps people understand the origins of their adult patterns and behaviours. For instance, I received very little nurturing as a child. As an adult, after my partner's loss, I gravitated to relationships with avoidant men. My nervous system was very comfortable with this lack of emotional response from men, because that's how I grew up. My nervous system didn't seek out people like my partner, who were open and giving. My early imprinting took over.

"It took years of psychedelic trauma work to unravel the origins of why I never expected people to be emotionally available. Through psychedelic journeys I revisited pivotal childhood moments of neglect and could then see why I saw unavailable people as people to have in my life. That's what I grew up knowing so it made sense I was following that pattern. Understanding the origin of that behaviour pattern has made all the difference."

The relationship between early childhood trauma and the likelihood of someone becoming a serial killer or engaging in violent behaviour is quite an interesting one. For Sitnick, though she cannot speak to the serial killer part, has deep insights when it comes to violence.

The expert revealed: "In terms of violent behaviour, I think children repeat in adulthood what they learn unless they take the initiative to adjust their behaviour. There are a lot of adults, myself included, who would never harm a child because we know what it is like to be harmed. While other people pass forward that kind of behaviour because "that's how I was raised." I think there not only needs to be a bit of self-awareness but also exposure to different people who didn't grow up that way. There is research that one loving person in a young child's life can dramatically change the trajectory of that life. If a child learns from a caring adult that abuse does not have to be carried forward, that can dramatically shift the adulthood for that child."

She went on to explore how a child's emotional and psychological needs can be influenced when they grow up with parents who are not emotionally available or who have severe psychological difficulties, sharing: "A child can shut down their emotional and psychological needs to a certain extent, which breeds deep loneliness and disconnection. But when attempts in childhood to get needs met were ignored and produced abuse (my father loved to slap me across the face when I was already feeling down) a child can learn to shut down those feelings and live life automatically. Not a life of joy, a life of existing without understanding why life feels the way it feels."

There are a multitude of studies which look into the effect of negative childhood experiences and upbringings which could point to many reasons as to why a person becomes a killer. However, it is not to say that every person who experiences similar backgrounds will in fact go on to kill or commit a crime. The complexities surrounding the human psyche and how our 'nurture' impacts the way that we grow as a person has been of great interest to the psychology community for decades. But the answer is widely argued.

Of course, it is impossible to pinpoint one resounding denominator in all serial killers, but there are similar causations which can be grouped together which allows psychologists an overall explanation as to how serial killers are created: childhood trauma.

Sadly, while childhood trauma is often caused by a generational cycle of familial abuse, it does not mean that it is inevitable to be repeated time and time again.

Of course, there are many supportive measures which could be put in place to help children who are going through traumatizing situations. But how do you know when to intervene?

Could it be when the child develops an out-of-sorts alcohol dependency?

Perhaps. However, considering that Dahmer was raised by a woman with severe psychiatric challenges and a man who admitted to being a pyromaniac as a child, something was always going to be amiss.

The Making of a Monster

When Dahmer entered adolescence, the manifestation of his early years' upbringing and troubles would only grow into something that would not only change the course of his life, but also those he would later target, forever.

According to a close friend of Dahmer's during his time at the Revere High School in Richfield, Ohio, there was something obviously different about the troubled teenager. John Backderf was Dahmer's friend, and one of the few that he was able to keep due to his behaviours. Years after Dahmer's horrors came to light, he wrote a graphic novel, which was later adapted as the motion picture, *My Friend Dahmer.*[7] His story tells a close and personal account of what it was like to know Dahmer as a teenager, and it shows a very compassionate version of a man that others would go on to know as a monster.

He told Ohio State University: "I tried to just enjoy the moment and let it wash over me all while staying respectful to the topic, which is not something you should be flip with. Jeffrey Dahmer caused misery and pain to everyone he came in contact with. It was a contrast, and I tried to pull both off."

Allegedly, Dahmer pretended to have epileptic fits in the school hallways, which drew a group towards him in the form of the Dahmer fan club, which included Backderf as a member, and Mike Kukral. Backderf recounted that he discovered Joyce was suffering from nervous episodes at home and would have seizures. This display in the school hallways may have been a teenager simply imitating something that he believed to be funny, or even a way to imitate his sick mother. Regardless, it was disturbing for those who were close with him.

His 'crazy cerebral palsy imitation' was somewhat of his 'schtick' at the time, which was one of the more harmless behaviours he would develop during his time at school. This is because the troubled teenager would be harbouring another concerning habit – his alcohol dependency.

Backderf explained: "He's holding a Styrofoam cup in his hand, and that's what he used for his booze when he'd walk around school. Scotch, or whatever."

He said, 'he walked around with hard liquor every day, and never got caught'.

However, his drinking problem became continuously worse, leading to him to drop out of college years later, as well as being discharged from the army.

The school friend added that he was 'the loneliest kid that I'd ever met' and 'he was self-medicating' through his dependency to alcohol, and 'trying to quell these hideous urges that were taking him over.' However, it wasn't long until these dark urges would finally win, and Dahmer's first victim was claimed.

Psychology Today reported that 70 per cent of criminals who went on to become the most violent to humans in a prison system all shared a history of animal abuse, and other studies also found that 43 per cent of school shooters have at some time in their lives, abused animals. As Dahmer had quite the portfolio of maiming and disturbing carcases of animals, his trajectory may have been somewhat expected.

18 June 1978 was the date that everything changed for the life of Dahmer, and Steven Hicks. Hicks was three days away from his nineteenth birthday when he encountered a teenage Dahmer, who had graduated from high school just weeks prior. Dahmer picked up the hitchhiker in his vehicle and reportedly lured him back to his home and when Hicks attempted to leave, Dahmer bludgeoned Hicks to death with a 10-pound exercise dumbbell before physically strangling him.

Allegedly, he had lured Hicks to his home with the promise of driving him to a concert before attempting to seduce him. When he was rebuffed, he murdered him and later told investigators that he had intercourse with the dead body, which fulfilled a fantasy of his. After chopping up the teenager's body, Dahmer buried him before digging him up at a later date to dissolve his skin in acid, crush his bones to dust, and scatter his remains in the woods. He was said to have become aroused whilst dissecting dead animals; sexual arousal was also what he felt later on from dissecting his dead victims.

After becoming interested in anatomy, Dahmer had finally taken his fantasies into the physical world, and this would mark a tragic turning point in the lives of many.

According to Backderf, he wondered what happened to his old school friend, but it wasn't until 1991 that he learned of the horrors he had committed. He told The Independent: "There was always a darkness about him that was really kind of repellent. I was OK with hanging out with him, if there was other people around. I was never going to be alone with him. And I'm pretty happy I had that instinct, because that could have well been me chopped up in the trunk of his car."

He said: "I've had a few sleepless nights pondering that one. Especially because that first crime was a crime of opportunity, as opposed to his other victims, who were methodically stalked. Yeah, it could have been any of us, and that's something that took me awhile to come to terms with."

But while he understands that he could have been Dahmer's victim, he recognises that there were numerous failings which led to Dahmer traveling down the path he ultimately would. As a child and teenager, there were opportunities for intervention that had been missed.

Backderf explained: "Well, everybody did everything wrong."

He added: "Everybody, either through incompetence or indifference, just let this kid go. And it's astonishing to me that nobody noticed or said they didn't notice a thing. The drinking — this kid reeked of alcohol at school."

He said of the failures of others to intervene that 'the result was a pile of bodies'.

"I think I certainly humanize him, which is, I understand, controversial for some people. But to me, he was just a friend, he was just a kid who had committed no crime."

He added: "What would have happened if somebody helped him, or just tried?"

The author went on to say: "What you have to remember is what is at the end of the story – and that is a pile of bodies and thousands who mourn his many victims. Dahmer – at the end – there's nothing sympathetic about him. He chose to kill."

Calling him a 'pathetic parasite', who 'spread misery and heartache', Backderf's memories about his former friend is very telling.

The New Yorker categorised Dahmer as: "A beige, recessive spectre who didn't blend into his surroundings so much as he blended into himself; his occasional bouts of attention-seeking revealed either a profound misunderstanding of social cues or a trollish disregard for them."

Perhaps his attention seeking behaviour and penchant for playing pranks and consuming alcohol was the result of a tumultuous upbringing.

His home life may have played a vital role in what would eventually become his lasting legacy. As per neighbour Susan Lehr, whose sons used to play with a young Dahmer, the divorce between Joyce and Lionel wasn't the end of their toxicity. In fact, two years later, in 1980, the police would be called 'several times'.

She said: "At the time I knew him, there was something devastating going on in his life and there wasn't anybody there to help him. I feel bad about that."

His mother was also known for her prescription pill taking, and Dahmer's alcohol dependency as a young teenager could have followed in her footsteps. But could the divorce of his parents and the following altercations have created a catalyst in which Dahmer felt as though he needed a release from? Or even an escape for a short period of time?

While his drinking continued throughout high school, Dahmer was left in the family home alone after the divorce during the summer after graduation. He seized the opportunity to act on his fantasies with Hicks, and then dissected, dissolved, pounded, and scattered his body to know how it felt to kill.

Perhaps he was moving on from dissecting animals, and this was a natural progression of the feelings he had held since his toddler years. Professor of psychology Louis Schlesinger told A&E that childhood animal cruelty often comes hand in hand with making a serial killer. Carl Wahlstrom, the forensic psychiatrist who evaluated Dahmer, was told by Dahmer that he poured gasoline into the tadpole's aquarium and set it on fire.

"If somebody is harming an animal, there is a good chance they also are hurting a human," said John Thompson, deputy executive director of the National Sheriffs' Association. "If we see patterns of animal abuse, the odds are that something else is going on." Unfortunately, his entrance into harming humans was not something that he would stop.

However, Dahmer did take a nine-year extended break between his first and second victim.

Dahmer joined the army after killing Hicks, and was stationed in Baumholder, West Germany, before being discharged in 1981, according to the *Los Angeles Times.* After his brief stint in the military, he flitted between homes, moving to Florida and Ohio before settling in West Allis and residing with his grandmother.

Musician Chris Butler bought the home for $244,500 in 2005, with the man telling the Observer: "The house has a great vibe, I mean, after all, the *house* didn't kill anybody, and I don't believe in ghosts, and there's absolutely no reason to think there's anything untoward here."

Butler still owns the home and let scenes from the Backderf's movie *My Friend Dahmer* be filmed on the property.

As for his military stint, Dahmer may have taken part in crimes against his fellow soldiers. When he then enrolled in the US Army in 1979, he was continuing to drink heavily, but was able complete his training and was sent to Germany as a medical specialist in combat. During his second year, his superiors noticed his alcohol abuse and, after showing up drunk, and an unsuccessful alcohol abuse program attempt, he was discharged as 'unsuitable for military service due to alcohol abuse'. But it was there at Baumholder, West Germany, in the 2nd Battalion, 68th Armored Regiment, 8th Infantry Division that he met Preston Davis. Davis claims that he was raped by the serial killer in October 1979, while he was working in the medical unit alongside Dahmer, as per the *Daily News*. Davis was 20 years old at the time and described how after their military vehicle broke down and was towed to a train station, Dahmer assaulted him, and because of 'memory gaps', he believes that he was drugged. Another victim, Billy Capshaw, was just 17 when he first met Dahmer and the two became roommates. He described how Dahmer would tie him to the bed and torture him, as well as rape him.

Just eight years after leaving the army, Dahmer would be in serious trouble with the police. Keison Sinthasomphone, a 13-year-old boy, and the younger brother of a later victim of Dahmer's, managed to escape from his apartment in 1988 after he sexually assaulted the boy. Dahmer was formally charged with the assault and sentenced to one year in prison.

It appeared that Dahmer's life was quickly spiralling out of control, and he was beginning to taint and even destroy the lives of some of those he came into contact with. But was it his drinking that exacerbated his path to destruction? The statistics are interesting, and they provide a lot of insight as to why teenagers drink alcohol to excess.

While many may go on to experiment with alcohol at some point in their life, others will take an unhealthy liking to the feeling it provides them. Be it emotionally, physically or psychologically. Sometimes, it is the feeling that a person is chasing when they consume alcohol. As per the HSE service: "If you drink heavily over a period of time, the brain's chemistry adjusts to the effects of alcohol. You may start to rely on alcohol to relieve negative feelings or deal with problems. You might need to drink more and more to get the desired positive effect."

However, there is a difference between a person who is drinking mildly, moderately and then severely. This distinction can separate groups of people within the public into either drinkers, moderate drinkers or those who have developed an alcohol dependency.

So, what is the difference between a person with a dependency, and someone without? The American Psychological Association describes it as: "A drinking pattern that results in significant and recurrent adverse consequences. Alcohol abusers may fail to fulfill major school, work, or family obligations. They may have drinking-related legal problems, such as repeated arrests for driving while intoxicated. They may have relationship problems related to their drinking."

Similarly, Drink Aware states: "People who are becoming dependent on alcohol notice they need to drink more to get the same effect. They often give priority to drinking over other activities or obligations (such as work or family life), or continue drinking despite harmful consequences - for example, liver disease or depression caused by drinking."

According to the National Institute on Alcohol Abuse and Alcoholism (NIAAA), 6.2 per cent of adults in the United States who are aged 18 and older have an alcohol use disorder. A government survey also revealed that approximately one in five individuals aged 12 to 20 were current alcohol drinkers and around two in five young adults, aged 18 to 25, were binge alcohol drinkers, and one in 10 were heavy alcohol drinkers. This shows that alcohol misuse is prevalent in our society. However, there are several reasons as to why this could be.

For Dahmer, it may have been an escape from his childhood trauma, or his lack of social standing, or a number of other reasons. As he was noted to have been drinking extensively during his school years, he may fit the category of a person with an alcohol dependency, otherwise known as alcohol use disorder. Alcohol use disorder includes drinking more alcohol than intended, being unable to cut back on its use, spending much time drinking or recovering from drinking, craving alcohol, failing at work, school, or home, as well as your relationships and activities.

A dependency to alcohol is dangerous for a number of reasons, and the effects can impact an individual for years to come. As alcohol is a depressant, it which can disrupt the balance of neurotransmitters in your brain, which can then change your thoughts and behaviour. The substance impacts the section of your brain that controls inhibition, and it can make a person feel relaxed for a short time. It also disrupts the brain's ability to adapt and learn, with a study published in the journal *Science Advances* finding that chronic alcohol exposure alters the activity patterns of cholinergic interneurons in the brain.

Because alcohol is so widely accepted, teenagers may consider it the safest drug they can take, even though it is the leading risk that can cause premature death and disability in people aged between 15 and 49.

Drinking is so ingrained in society that even a number of debunked myths continue to spread, such as 'a glass of wine a day is good for your health'. So, it is no surprise that teenagers have taken an interest in consuming beverages which they have heard is beneficial to their health and is accessible. However, little do many people know that drinking to excess can have a negative effect on your mood as time goes on. It can also increase your risk of self-harm and suicide, and if you have a pre-existing mental health condition, you might drink alcohol to try and feel better, but it will have the opposite effect.

While there is a myriad of studies written which explain the impact of excessive and long-term alcohol use, the way in which it makes people feel after consuming it could override any warning provided. This is because the brain's reward system, which makes people feel good, allows for an escape from unpleasant feelings and emotions, and this can create a dependency on the feeling alcohol provides.

But the feel-good feeling can quickly be replaced by more troubling behaviour. As per the Mayo Clinic: "Alcohol intoxication causes behaviour problems and mental changes. These may include inappropriate behaviour, unstable moods, poor judgment, slurred speech, problems with attention or memory, and poor coordination. You can also have periods called "blackouts," where you don't remember events."

There are also risk factors which can determine who is more susceptible of drinking as a teenager and becoming addicted to it. Research suggests that teenagers who have experienced childhood trauma may already have 'disrupted growth in brain regions, and patterns of connections between brain regions', that might increase their chances of engaging in binge drinking during adolescence.

While adolescent substance abuse continues to be a problem in society, the rising case of child alcohol misuse is even more concerning. According to studies, every three days a child under ten years of age undergoes treatment at a hospital facility for alcohol-related problems. Thousands of teenagers drink alcohol underage, with 44 per cent of children between the ages of 11-15 drinking alcohol in 2018. This is approximately two-fifths of all children who may not realise the harm that alcohol can do to their mental and physical health. Shockingly, over half of children aged between 11 and 15 believed that it was acceptable to consume alcohol at that age.

For teenagers who have developed an addiction to alcohol, it can cause a variety of problems. For example, consuming alcohol whilst underage can cause issues in school. This problem can stem from engaging with alcohol or drugs, leading to permanent or temporary exclusion or expulsion from the institution.

It can also negatively affect the teenager's life, and as it is linked to over 60 medical conditions, it sets the foundation for suffering through health issues further down the line, such cancer (mouth, throat, breast, liver and stomach), as well as high blood pressure and liver problems (cirrhosis of the liver).

Abusing alcohol can also impact a teenager's mental health, causing depression as well as worsen any pre-existing symptoms of depression. This can have negative consequences and can also put a young person in situations which are dangerous or vulnerable. In England alone, approximately ten thousand underage drinkers are admitted to hospitals as a result of alcohol consumption every year. It can also increase the risk of injury, seizures and common ailments such as low blood sugar. Abusing alcohol at a young age may also go on to encourage impulsiveness and risk-taking behaviours. Developing an alcohol dependency at a younger age can also increase the risk of developing anxiety, which can then present as an adult. Alcohol, a known carcinogen, is a truly high factor for developing cancer, which is not typically something that teenagers or children think about as a consequence of their consumption. However, it is a serious risk.

For example, head and neck cancers, oesophageal cancers, liver cancers, breast cancers, and colorectal cancers can be a direct consequence of heavy alcohol consumption. While alcohol problems do present ongoing and often serious mental health issues, it is important to note just how damaging it is to the body.

Teenagers of today are increasingly worried about the term ‘brainrot’, which means, as per the Oxford Dictionary, ‘the supposed deterioration of a person’s mental or intellectual state, especially viewed as the result of overconsumption of material (now particularly online content) considered to be trivial or unchallenging. Also: something characterised as likely to lead to such deterioration’. The term was one of the most searched terms on the internet in 2024. Alcohol can affect a person’s brain functioning, causing the neurons in their brain to shrink, causing brainrot to occur. Excessive drinking can then lead to alcohol-related dementia, which can impact every aspect of the sufferer’s life. Whether the alcohol consumer is 16 or 60, abusing alcohol regularly overwhelmingly means that the risk of developing an alcohol addiction rises.

Studies at McLean Hospital have also shown that alcohol affects the brains of adolescents in profound and dangerous ways. During the teenage and early adult years, the brain is still developing, making it more vulnerable to alcohol than the adult brain. According to the study, the earlier a person begins to drink, the more likely they are to develop serious problems with alcohol or drug addiction later in their life.

According to the Centre for Disease Control's 2015 *Youth Risk Behavior Study*, when students were asked about their activities during the previous 30 days, an overwhelming 33 per cent admitted to drinking alcohol, 18 per cent reportedly binge drank and 8 per cent participated in drink driving.

Studies have also shown how this impacts teenagers, citing that 'alcohol significantly impairs learning and memory in teens' which is a severely dangerous side effect of drinking excess alcohol.

So, why is this relevant to Dahmer's case and the psychology behind his upbringing and teenage years?

Well, the psychological risks of underage drinking show that alcohol consuming teenagers have a higher risk of developing mental health problems such as depression, suicide, and psychosis as adults and that teens who drink are more likely to have poor impulse control, which present as risky sexual behaviour or violent outbursts.

If Dahmer was a habitual drinker during his high school years, as told by his friend, his psychological health could have been further negatively affected and created more risk to himself and those who were around him.

Sadly, Dahmer's mounting interest in death and sex would begin to spill over after his graduation, marking a significant change in history.

Exploring Dahmer's upbringing, alcohol dependency and future crimes, Dr Naomi Murphy, a Consultant Clinical and Forensic Psychologist, Honorary Professor, Sensorimotor, Psychotherapist and expert with more than twenty years in UK prison systems, believes that everything can be explained by unpacking his formative years.

Murphy was the UK's most senior psychologist in the UK prison service for the National Health Service (NHS). She worked 1-2-1 with men who committed acts of murder, rape and violent crimes in high-security prisons. She is a highly respected forensic clinical psychologist and was appointed Honorary Professor of Psychology at Nottingham Trent University in 2021. Murphy is a Board Member of the All-Parliamentary-Group on Restorative Justice and qualified as a clinical psychologist in 1997 and as a consultant psychologist in 2003.

Having left a 20-year career in prisons in 2023, she now runs her own private practice called Octopus Psychology, where she works with the general public as well as professional athletes.

Her career has seen her operate in some of the most challenging settings and she is highly regarded for her cutting-edge work with those in the criminal justice system where she been instrumental in introducing ground-breaking trauma focused therapy services within high-security prisons to enhance the lives of some of the UK's most challenged people.

She regularly shares her wide-ranging expertise, writing for leading psychology journals and speaking at major conferences, events and in broadcast interviews and she is often called as an expert witness in criminal and family proceedings.

Murphy has been featured on television and radio many times and has appeared as a mental health expert on BBC Radio 4 Today, BBC News, BBC World, GB News, BBC Five Live and others.

Her expertise in this topic is extensive, and her knowledge of criminal behaviour, upbringing and alcohol dependency is invaluable.

She believes that there are complex reasons for why a teenager would begin to abuse alcohol, but notes that it is not unusual for an adolescent of 14 or 15 years of age to begin to experiment with alcohol and substances.

During a sit-down-interview, she explained the link between childhood trauma, alcohol and violent crimes.

****

How is alcohol dependency defined, because you have so many different things online that you see… how it is really defined, medically?

I mean, so for that you can look to the Dm5 (criteria) for instance. Nowadays, we won't really call it alcohol dependence, we call it alcohol misuse disorder, and so that includes tolerance. You know: if you're actually needing to have more [alcohol] to get drunk and the presence of withdrawal symptoms when you get up in the morning, or your hands are shaking.

Larger amounts: You're drinking large amounts, or you're going to [drink] a lot. You're drinking for a lot more of the day than you're not. People often start off, for instance, binge drinking at weekends and it becomes a daily occurrence.

And then they're getting – because they know they're in early in the day that they're drinking – sort of a wish to cut down or kind of like, repeated efforts to cut down and not being able to do that.

Spend a lot of time engaged in alcohol use, and I suppose crucially affecting relationships. Your ability to work, you know. It has to be dysfunctional in some way, so it's affecting the quality of your life and the way that you're able to live your life. And I suppose also knowing the fact… that the fact it's impacting negatively – it's harmful, but you're still doing it despite that.

I suppose it's quite a large criterion that someone has to meet in order to be defined as dependant on it, but are there many types of psychological and environmental factors that could contribute to someone developing this in the future?

It tends to be people who aren't very good at managing the emotions. So, I suppose that's why it often stems from [the] beginning, that some of the pathway to that would be there from their childhood. Because actually, we learn how to manage our emotions from how we're parented. If you're raised in an environment where you feel safe, and loved, where your emotions are responded to, you'll be able to register that you feel sad now or feel hurt or ashamed.

If you're raised in a family [where] there's a lot of dismissiveness about your emotions or if you're punished when you cry, for instance, then obviously children have to find a way to eliminate the emotion, and alcohol can work really well.

You get factors around people who perhaps – people with low confidence – might end up finding themselves drinking more because they appreciate that they are dropping their inhibition, then find that they're able to be a bit more gregarious when they're out. So, they drink to overcome anxiety.

For instance, you've got musicians and actors who often end up with drink problems because they have to overcome their anxiety about getting out on stage. Just in terms of going to a party or even kind of like meeting their friends, they might feel like they always need alcohol on a date.

They might feel like they always need to have a drink to be able to do that. When working in the prison, taking people's histories, you can see amongst people who end up in prison that they've often started drinking much earlier than most people, and you also see, for instance, cannabis appearing much earlier in their use of substances than it otherwise would do.

People start experimenting much, much earlier, and doing that on their own. So, it can also be a bit of a 'fuck you' to the family. And to society: 'I'm gonna do this' and I suppose wallowing in a sense of victimhood sometimes.

It can be angry, it can be a total just avoidance of feelings, or it can be a bit of an angry gesture. People would say there's a genetic component to it. But to be honest with you, I've not ever met someone with any sort of substance misuse disorder where there hasn't been environmental factors from childhoods. I think maybe it makes you vulnerable, but I'd say that you need that poor environment in order to bring it out.

You know, in terms of how genes are expressed, it's the same with all sorts of mental disorders, really. The kind of people found to be prison lack of optimum functioning environments.

We've touched upon the early family, life and lack of emotional connection with parents influencing misuse. I suppose it's also the connection between mental health issues, such as depression or social isolation and the development of misuse as well. I wonder how – as you were saying that the anxiety and the lack of confidence – this also comes under maybe societal isolation, making them feel like they need something more to kind of manage that within themselves.

I suppose the thing with anxiety and depression – again, I would see the roots to that being early– when you speak with people about their histories, how they are now, whatever, their mutation of problems is whether it's anxiety, depression, substance misuse and violence. Actually, people always make sense, you can always find out if you listen to their story. You can always see how that seemed to make sense for that person in the context of their lives.

So, it might look like a crazy kind of behaviour or a nonsensical behaviour, but you can see that. The same factors that would cause somebody to experience anxiety or depression are likely to also be there in relation to drink, but it will depend on the individual.

You may have mum and dad also drinking heavily or have alcohol around the house, which then means the child, or the teenager, can access it very easily. Whereas in another family, the parents might not drink very often but might be really focused on education.

So, then you might have somebody over-focused on achievement at school and that might be their coping strategy. Alcohol, I'd say is very much a coping strategy. I tend to see anxieties are coping strategies quite often, because it's avoiding other deeper emotions. Maybe a teenager struggles with loneliness and rejection.

Does this also play into alcohol misuse? I suppose it could start out as like a 'fitting in' type of thing. It begins with binge drinking and stuff like that. But could it start as trying to be accepted or fit in, or maybe just kind of shunning away other people's rejections and like retreating further into themselves using alcohol.

Both of those are possible. Especially what I've tended to see; when alcohol has been part of the picture, it's typically being done with peers. It's not intended to be. If it starts at an early age, it's typically started with peers, people who drink, just because of a lonely person.

I've spent 25 years working in prisons. My experience is the people that drink through loneliness, that tends to be a behaviour that starts a little bit older, but that's not to say that it can't happen at a younger age. If somebody's parents are drinking, if somebody's happened upon drink in some way, but usually, you know, teenagers start drinking with their mates and as the peer pressure of that… and actually who ends up drinking more heavily might be the people who have poor ability to cope with their emotions anyway, so I'm not saying it would never happen. Patterns for problematic drinking would be for people to start with friends initially.

Is there a significance to the age in which someone starts? Misusing alcohol.

Yeah, I would say so. And I think generally, I think with all intoxicated substances, a kind of normative range of ages, use it.

And also, especially when you're applying this to Jeffrey Darmer in terms of his age, I don't know how old he was, he was in high school when he started, so I think about 14 – I was wondering about decades talking about this. It would have been the 70s and 80s.

So, I think really, you're a normal age for that period that would have been around 15 or 16 onwards. These days when you see people in prison who have started drinking at an earlier age, you're probably sort of thinking more about 13 or 14. And cannabis. Also, in fact, sometimes cannabis precedes [alcohol]. It's kind of normal experimentation with cannabis and alcohol to begin at like 15 or 16, you know? I wouldn't be too troubled by a teenager that's had alcohol to drink at 15 or 16.

I think if you kind of like, see it at 13 or even younger, then you'd be concerned about why a child of that age is seeking out alcohol. I'm a parent of a 13-year-old and yeah, I think there's some laughing and joking about alcohol, but I can't imagine for a moment they would actually like the taste of it, for instance, or push the drink out. Definitely not a nice taste, that's for sure.

If an adolescent begins drinking, certainly if they begin to misuse their drinking, does this impact their brain development or their emotional regulation?

Yeah, it does. So, it's like the three phases of life for us that are most crucial in terms of our brains. Obviously, when we're developing in the womb, it impacts on two areas. If you hit your hippocampus, which is where we really rely on learning and memory formation. If you think about what's going on for an adolescent and the expectation that they're learning and revising for exams, what you see in those teenagers who drink heavily, is kind of like a 10 per cent reduction in size of the hippocampus. That obviously could then be lasting in terms of that impact.

If they've had heavy drinking in their teenage years, it makes it difficult to make new memories and new information. So learning is going to be problematic. And if you think about the kind of behaviours that are normal for teenagers experimenting with their environment, kind of like seeing how far they can push boundaries, obviously, they're not able to really learn that effectively because they're, half pissed half the time. There's going to be some problems.

And then, the secondary is the prefrontal lobe that's involved in things like planning, decision making, inhibition of risk, and language, and so people who drink in their teenage years have smaller, prefrontal lobes and we already associate adolescents with risk taking and impulsivity, dangerous behaviours and that goes on actually into our early 20s.

Anyway, that's why young men in particular are much more likely to get into trouble and end up breaking the law through delinquent kinds of behaviours. So obviously if somebody is drinking at that point, it's going to impact on their ability to think through the consequence of actions and make sensible decisions.

Is there a relationship between this and disorders, such as antisocial personality and borderline extreme behaviours or even criminality violence?

I'm not sure. I think there's a correlation between them. I wouldn't say that alcohol use causes those sorts of disorders. So, a lot of what you're touching on there is personality disorder, which is really complex. It's post-traumatic stress in the sense of it arising as a product of what's happened early in childhood.

You get a lot of the same kind for somebody who's drinking prematurely and getting drunk. Premature in that you see a lot of the same sorts of factors around, maybe poor parental boundaries. Parents who might be role modelling drinking to excess. Parents that can't and don't help their children cope with their feelings.

An environment that a child isn't feeling safe and isn't feeling loved, isn't feeling treasured. You've got those same things happening [in] people who you can't diagnose with a personality disorder in their teens. But say the antisocial behaviour and violence is there, you get the same result.

It's the same sort of roots, but actually whether somebody ends up having a drink, obviously makes it more likely there'll be actual violence. Quite hostile aggressive, kind of like 'fuck you' at the world, kind of attitude. Then alcohol is going to increase your ability to act on that and do something that's destructive because it's such a disinhibitor.

You often see those with alcohol misuse going hand in hand with those sorts of disorders. And personality disorders are characterised by difficulties with managing your relations, so, yeah, antisocial personality disorders are about using anger as your crutch. So rather than allow yourself to feel sadness or loneliness or shame, you end up making yourself angry because that makes you feel more powerful.

And, of course, drink is great for that because then, if you feel defective and not good enough, but you can go out and pumped up with alcohol or coke [cocaine] or what have you, then that's a great way of dampening how you might actually feel inside – which might be quite kind of like small and insignificant.

Could it be a way to self-punish yourself or escape the feeling because of the nature and the environment of where they may be coming from? It's a way to further hammer in that they are what they believe themselves to be, which might not be quite worth much.

Yeah, it definitely can be. But I think what you'd be looking more at is what happens when they are drunk. Are they sleeping with people that they wouldn't want to sleep with if they were sober so then they can end up feeling really lousy about themselves?

Or are they engaging in other sort of dangerous practises or behaviours? I would look more for the self-punishment to be some of the other stuff. We even really have such a negative attitude about teenagers drinking as we would perhaps ought to have.

I'm not sure it really comes imbedded with enough emotional salience to feel like it's a self-punishment about self-worth. That's not to say it couldn't happen, but I think you'd be more likely to look at what other behaviours are there. And you're right that people feel bad about themselves.

They do quite often get into right negative cycles where they're perpetuating their beliefs about themselves. So, I suppose that maybe the causation of developing these things is how they're brought up and these dysfunctional and complex things around them.

Is there any type of mental health support or treatment during their formative years that could stop them from developing an alcohol issue?

Well actually, to be honest with you, having a single adult that they've got a good supportive relationship with, one that they feel of value to, you can see that even if the parents are rubbish, having a teacher who believes in you and values you make it clear that you have some worth. But I think part of the problem with young people these days is that so many resources have been stripped out of youth services.

So then actually, if you've got lousy relationships at home, what you end up with is youths hanging around on the street and those hanging around on the streets are not the ones that have got loving supportive homes, where their parents want to know where they are and want them to be home by a decent reasonable hour. You've got the kids who also come from troubled backgrounds hanging out outside together. This means that they are often grooming younger years, not necessarily for sex, but maybe in antisocial behaviour, or county lines.

You see all the same sort of pattern of behaviours. In terms of intervention, having decent youth services or youth workers, and counselling available in school. However, quite often these children would be people that would fall through the necks. They wouldn't go to school.

So, they wouldn't get into those services. But maybe finding a way to offer them something that they can engage with. Around puberty is the sort of key point.

Is there a broader psychological theory that links substance abuse to heightened aggression or a lack of impulse control? Or perhaps, something that has been perpetuated which may not be quite true?

I do keep an eye on the literature around substance misuse. I don't know of any particular theories to draw your attention to.

There are some specialist AA groups that specialise in young people, but it's that idea of 'alcoholism is a disease' and it somehow takes away responsibility from you and I understand the wish to remove stigma as an alcoholic. Especially, the more conscious you are of your parents' drinking patterns or whichever family member's drinking patterns, the more that you can make sense of that.

Think, 'how did that affect me?' All of us have the power to change that and have a different destiny. The more we allow ourselves to really feel our feelings then the better equipped we are to deal with them.

Part II

The Spree

A Grim Pattern

After years of alcohol misuse, which was clarified by his friend at school, Dahmer suddenly vanished into thin air and away from his former friend group.

After the murder of Hicks, Dahmer took a number of years away from his crimes, and without his military career, he began to start a life for himself. A life that would all begin when he embedded himself into the nightlife scene of Milwaukee's gay clubs. However, this would open up an opportunity to prey on unsuspecting men, who he would lure to his grandmother's home, and to then his own apartment to carry out his murderous urges.[8]

There were nine years between the murder of Hicks and Dahmer's next victim, and while individuals can only speculate as to why that was, his alcoholism and dishonourable discharge from the military could have been two things that Dahmer was struggling with for quite some time. But that would all change, and his calculated and chillingly methodical spree would begin.

But his spree was more than just the killing of 17 young boys and men; it was the total dismemberment of families, futures of dozens, and the people who were discarded by him. His rampage lasted such a short time, but the damage it inflicted is limitless. However, there are those who believe that had he murdered sporadically, as opposed to frequently, he may never have been caught. With the opportunities that police had to catch him, that may not be an unlikely scenario.

When Dahmer moved into his own place, his killings escalated in frequency. Needing a way to dispose of the bodies of his numerous victims, Dahmer employed the skills he had learned as a child in reducing human bodies to bones via caustic chemicals. Perhaps the smells from the multiple corpses he had in various stages of decay, awaiting his method of disposal, might not have attracted the attention of the police officers who knocked on his door after his last victim was able to escape.

- Steven Hicks, 18
- Steven Tuomi, 28
- Jamie Doxtator, 14
- Richard Guerrero, 25
- Anthony Sears, 24
- Ricky Beeks, 33
- Eddie Smith, 28
- Ernest Miller, 24
- David Thomas, 23
- Curtis Straughter, 18
- Errol Lindsey, 19
- Anthony Hughes, 31
- Konerak Sinthasomphone, 14
- Matt Turner, 20
- Jeremiah Weinberger, 23
- Oliver Lacy, 23
- Joseph Bradehoft, 25

The Victims

Stephen Hicks - 18 June 1978

As previously explained, Dahmer committed his first murder in the summer of 1978 at the age of 18, just weeks after his graduation. At the time, he was living in the family home alone, and with the recent divorce from Dahmer's mother, Dahmer's father moved from the home, whilst his mother left with his younger brother, David. So, as he was alone and his compulsions were increasing, on June 18, Dahmer saw an opportunity when he picked up the hitchhiker. Hicks, who was due to turn 19 in four days was lured to Dahmer's empty house to listen to music before he was bludgeoned with a 10-pound dumbbell. While Hicks was unconscious, Dahmer strangled him to death with the bar of the dumbbell, stripped him of his clothes and masturbated as he stood above his corpse. One day later, he was dissected in his basement and buried in a shallow grave in Dahmer's backyard.

Dahmer went on to say that, after putting Hick's remains in garbage bags, he was pulled over by law enforcement whilst the bags were in his car. However, he was able to convince them that the bags filled with garbage and he was issued a traffic ticket. This near-miss with the law may have been enough to stop him from killing for nearly a decade.

From there, Dahmer shared that he was obsessed over the possibility that the body would be found in his backyard, and so he exhumed Hicks, and pulverized the bones with a sledgehammer, as per The *New York Times*.[9]

Steven Tuomi - November 20 1987

Steven Walter Tuomi grew up in Ontonagon, Michigan[10] and worked as a short-order cook in a Milwaukee restaurant before his death. Remembering him as quiet but artistic by his classmates, Tuomi 'could do just about anything artistic.' Before he became the only murder victim of Dahmer's to not be part of his sentencing due to lack of evidence, he was a healthy young man with a bright future.

However, on November 20, 1987, Dahmer met him at a bar and persuaded him to return to the Ambassador Hotel where he had rented a room for the night. According to Dahmer, his intention was to drug and rape him, but when he awoke in the morning, Tuomi's chest was 'crushed in' and Dahmer's fists and forearms were covered in bruises.

According to Dahmer, the two of them had been drinking heavily at a gay bar and he believed that he must have murdered him in a drunken haze, noting blood was coming out of the side of Tuomi's mouth.

Following the killing, Dahmer purchased a large suitcase and took Toumi's body to his grandmother's basement, where he had sex with the corpse, masturbated on it, dismembered it one week after killing him and disposed of him in the trash.

Dahmer's method of disposal became somewhat of his signature, as he filleted the bones from the body before cutting the flesh into small pieces, wrapped the bones into a sheet and pounded them with a sledgehammer. He later informed investigators that he could not believe he had killed him, painting the image of a man who had no intent or recollection of the murder.

After two weeks, Dahmer boiled Tuomi's head in a mixture of Soilex (an industrial detergent) and bleach in a bid to preserve it as a tool for masturbation. However, it was too brittle, and so he disposed of it.

The death of Tuomi appeared to be a pivotal moment in Dahmer's life. While he claimed that he did not mean to kill him, this did mark the start of when he began to actively seek out victims to kill, and his trajectory steadily increased to the point where some victims were mere days from each other. Dahmer's thirst for bodies was past its tipping point, and the aftermath left victims and their families in a great deal of pain.

Jamie Doxtator - January 16 1988

James E. Doxtator was born on March 1, 1973 and lost his life on January 16, 1988 in Milwaukee, after he was murdered by Dahmer. As Dahmer's 3rd victim, and one of the youngest at just 14 years old, there has been much published about Doxtator. According to reports of the time, particularly from The Tampa Bay Times, Dahmer met the young boy while waiting at a bus stop outside of a gay club, called The 219 Club. He then lured him back to the home he shared with his grandmother and offered him cash to pose nude. However, Dahmer had an ulterior motive. Dahmer strangled the boy in his grandmother's basement before dismembering his body, using a sledgehammer to smash the remains into pieces.[11]

It was reported that the teenager ran away from home to escape an abusive stepfather on January 16, 1988, and met Dahmer just two days later. His mother reported his disappearance to the police, however, she did not know of his fate until he was named as one of Dahmer's victims.

As for what Dahmer has shared of his time with Doxtator, he did not remember his face but instead recalled him by a scar on his body, which appeared to be similar to cigarette burns above each of his nipples.

The Native American teenager was described as having a troubled life, and his death proved to be the final tragic event in his young life. The teen was half Stockbridge and part Oneida, liked to play pool and ride his bike, but his violent home life meant that he often ran away from home. Law enforcement had previous contact with him due to this, and one of the photographs of Doxtator was a mug shot from when he was in trouble with the police for stealing a car.

Despite his troubles, it was reported that he had high hopes for his future, but a $50 reward in return for a nude photoshoot would change everything. It was after taking the teen back to his grandmother's house that Dahmer strangled him, dismembered him and ensured that his body could not be found.

Debbie Vega, his mother, explained to police that she had left Milwaukee out of fear of her ex-husband (after Doxtator was reported as missing).

"For our own safety, we left," she said. "The only times we've been back was to search the streets of Milwaukee (for Jamie)."

The teenager's mother went on to describe him as lively and cheerful, outgoing and that he also loved making new friends. While Dahmer never knew of his victim's name, he shared that he was '75 per cent sure' he recognised the boy's face. But when talking to West Allis detectives, he discussed the burn marks on Doxtator's chest, which was enough evidence to charge him with first-degree murder in that case. Because Dahmer lived in the same house as his grandmother, disposing of the body was no easy task. So, he left Doxtator's body in the basement for two weeks, and used his grandmother's absence to dissolve the pieces in acid before crushing his bones, as he did with his previous two victims.

Doxtator was murdered just two months after the murder of Tuomi, and while it has been reported that the teenager was a prostitute, there has been no conclusive evidence to state that this was fact. At just 14 years old, the teen had a lot that he was going through when he encountered a budding serial killer, and running away from home may have felt like his escape from a place that should have been safe for him. Despite all that he had been through during his short life, many publications have described him as brave, and how resilient he was in the face of his abusive home life. After his death, many came to realise just how tragic his life and death truly was, and Dahmer's preying on a teenage castaway was evident.

Richard Guerrero – 24 March 1988

Having officially begun his killing spree, Dahmer yet again went out on the hunt for another victim to pick up and take home with him. That's where he met 22-year-old Richard Guerrero – Dahmer's only Hispanic victim. It was on March 24, 1988, that he encountered the bisexual man outside a gay bar called The Phoenix and lured him to his grandmother's residence. The way in which he was able to bribe the man to his lair, was via offering $50 with the pretext of spending the night with him. However, once he was able to get Guerrero alone, Dahmer drugged him with sleeping pills and strangled him to death with a leather strap before performing oral sex on his corpse. Just 24-hours after murdering him, Dahmer dismembered his body, dissolved the flesh in acid and disposed of the remains in the trash. However, he did bleach and retain the skull before pulverizing it several months later.

Guerrero was born in 1967 and was of Mexican descent, according to police reports, he had only $3 in his pocket and no proof of identification when he was last seen by his family in Madison, Wisconsin. At the time, it was claimed that he was going to visit a friend in Milwaukee, but when he didn't make it to their home, nor did he arrive at his own, the alarm was raised.

His family swiftly declared him as missing, with his sister, Janie Hagan, believing that something had been done to him. She told the *Sentinel Journal* years after his disappearance: "If he had wanted to leave, he would have at least called my mother and let her know that everything was fine, instead of leaving us in the dark, with my mother praying to God every day to send her son home."

The family went on to hire a private investigator to look into his disappearance as they felt as though police were not taking the case seriously – likely due to their ethnicity- however, the private investigators scammed the family and ran away with a large amount of their money. This left the family without answers until Dahmer was apprehended years later.

Hagen would go on to address Dahmer in Spanish at Dahmer's trial where she called him 'diablo, el puro diablo' (the devil, the pure devil).

Weeks later, Dahmer would go on to fail at his next murder attempt, having been hindered by his grandmother. On April 23, Dahmer lured Ronald Flowers Jr. to the home he shared with this grandmother, as he had done with many others.[12] However, after plying Flowers with drugged coffee, Dahmer's grandmother called down to the pair and signalled that she knew her grandson was not alone in the basement. With that interruption and understanding that his grandmother could present as a problem for his plans to murder, Dahmer instead transported Flowers to a nearby hospital once he became unconscious due to the drugs.

Flowers had been living in Lake County, Illinois and met Dahmer by chance after visiting the night club 219 in Milwaukee with friends. It was after he attempted to drive his car home that he realized that it was not working and Dahmer showed up as a good Samaritan and claimed that he could come back with him to his grandmother's home and Dahmer would jump start his car.

Flowers has only ever given one interview about his experience, in which he explained the 'sheer terror' he felt after being drugged. He also shared that he woke up in the hospital with a ligature mark around his neck and his underwear was inside out.

While he did make a police report, it was alleged that nothing came of it, even though Dahmer had been brought in for questioning regarding the altercation. Flowers has long regarded his grandmother as being the sole reason he survived that day.

He also went on to accidentally meet Dahmer again after the ordeal, one year later at the same club, and when he confronted Dahmer, apparently, the killer pretended not to know him. With that, Flowers warned an unnamed black man from getting into Dahmer's car, calling the killer 'crazy'.

In September 1988, Dahmer's grandmother, Catherine Hughes asked him to move out because of his drinking and because she struggled with his sexuality. However, it could have also been due to the awful smells that she complained about coming from the lower levels of the house. Whilst her doting grandson convinced her that it was a dead racoon and his love of taxidermy, it was in fact the bodies of his piling victims. With her kicking out her grandson, she ended their nine years of living together, but little did she know that this would open up new opportunities for Dahmer to kill in peace.

Shortly after his initial meeting with Flowers, Dahmer met the brother of one of his eventual victims, Somsack Sinthasomphone, and persuaded the 13-year-old Laotian to go to his apartment after being offered money in exchange for nude photos. Dahmer then drugged Somsack and sexually abused him. However, Somsack managed to escape and reported the incident to the police, leading to Dahmer being arrested on a second-degree sexual assault and enticing a minor charge on September 27. He was then given a sentence of five years' probation, with one year being at a work release camp, and was also required to register as a sex offender. He was released two months early from his work program and went on to move into a Milwaukee apartment in May 1990.

On his release, Dahmer was put on probation and although he showed up at the probation office every month, his caseworker didn't visit Dahmer in his home, which is a requirement according to a state department of corrections spokesman. His agent was overworked and therefore the visitation was waived and Dahmer moved back in with his grandmother.

Just two months after his conviction of second-degree sexual assault and two months prior to his conviction, Dahmer struck again.

Anthony Sears - 25 March 1989

Anthony Lee Sears, 24, was the last victim that Dahmer drugged and strangled at his grandmother's home; he was also the first victim from which Dahmer permanently retained any body parts, choosing to preserve his skull and genitals in a filing cabinet when he moved to his new apartment at 924 North 25th Street weeks later. Sears worked at a Baker's Square in Milwaukee and had been promoted to manager before his death. His mother, Marilyn, revealed that his family had planned a dinner in celebration of his promotion, but Sears never made it to the event. His mother said: "He never showed up, so I figured he just went out to celebrate with his friends." Even though he had not shown to his celebratory dinner, he was not reported missing until four weeks had passed, leaving his family and girlfriend to worry about his whereabouts until his remains were later found in 1991.

The aspiring model met Dahmer at a gay bar on March 25, and according to Dahmer, he was not looking to victimise anyone – but Sears 'just started talking to me', presenting the killer an opportunity to lure him to his grandmother's home, engage in oral sex before drugging and strangling him. It has been claimed by *Men's Health* that Dahmer was only able to murder Sears after the judge presiding over Dahmer's sexual assault cause handed him work release instead of prison time, allowing him to be free at the time his paths crossed with the young man.

The following morning after murdering Sears, Dahmer molested the corpse before dismembering the body, stripping the flesh from it in his grandmother's bathtub and continuing with his usual process when disposing of bodies. However, it was reported by Tru TV that Dahmer boiled the head, removed the flesh from it, painted it grey so that it would resemble a medical test skull in case it was discovered and stored it to masturbate in front of. He also preserved Sears' head and genitalia in jars filled with acetone and stored them in his work locker before transporting them to his new apartment. According to Dahmer, the mummified head and penis of Sears were kept in a black cabinet when he was serving his one-year sentence for second degree sexual assault on Somsack.

Whilst he was living with his grandmother, Sears' remains were very nearly discovered by his father, Lionel. Dahmer had been storing them in a wooden box at the time, and during one of his father's visits to Dahmer's grandmother's home, he asked his son to open the box. Dahmer angrily told his father that the box held his pornography collection and said to him: "Can't I have just one square foot of privacy?". To this, his father accepted his lie as the truth. What would have happened if Sears had been discovered in the box? Perhaps his fifth victim would have been his last.

On May 14, 1990, Dahmer moved out of his grandmother's house and into 924 North 25th Street, Apartment 213, where he killed his sixth victim within just one week of moving in.

Raymond Smith (Ricky Beeks) - May 20 1990

There is not a lot of media coverage on Smith's murder, but from what has been reported, it is known that Smith was Dahmer's first murder after leaving prison. He met the 32-year-old sex worker and proceeded to offer him the same $50 that he did to his other victims. After drugging, dismembering and disposing of his corpse, he took polaroids of it. He then preserved his skull and kept it close to Sears remains in the filing cabinet at his apartment.

Eddie Smith – 14 June 1990

On the evening of June 14, Edward Watten Smith was last seen leaving The Phoenix Bar in Milwaukee and it is believed that he met Dahmer at the bar before going back to his apartment. Unlike most other victims, it appeared as though Smith and Dahmer were well acquainted for at least one year prior to his murder as the aspiring model's friends told the police that they had seen the two men together at different clubs in Milwaukee before Dahmer murdered him.

Friends of Smith told police that they had seen the two men together at a birthday party on June 22, 1990, one week after it is believed he was murdered, which blurs his timeline tremendously. However, no other sightings were since seen, and he is believed to have been murdered that evening, if not one week prior. The 28-year-old's body was never found, however authorities confirmed Dahmer had murdered him after finding photographs of Smith in the apartment. Dahmer also confessed to murdering him, citing that he felt 'terrible' as he could not retain any part of his body. Smith was Dahmer's seventh victim, and allegedly, the killer also took pleasure in calling his family to announce that he was dead.

"He just said, 'Don't even bother looking for your brother anymore'," Caroline Smith, Eddie's sister said of a call she received at her house. Smith said the caller she spoke to told her, 'He's dead.' When Smith said asked, 'How do you know that?' the man told her, 'Because I killed him.'

"A chill went through me," Smith told the Milwaukee Sentinel. "I hung up the phone and called police." According to the Charley Project, a website that runs missing person advertisements, Smith was an 'African-American male' with black hair and brown eyes, who was known as 'Sheik' in his neighbourhood because of 'the turban-like head covering he habitually wore'.

Ernest Miller - 3 September 1990

Born in 1968, Ernest Miller was known as a talented dance student who also worked as a busboy at a hotel in downtown Chicago at the time he met Dahmer. Miller was incredibly close with his family and attended every family gathering planned. Considered a caring and loving person, his family reported that he was last seen in September. However, this sweet man would unfortunately go on to meet Dahmer by chance, just like the others. It was on the corner of North 27th Street where the killer approached him with a $50 bribe to accompany Dahmer to his apartment so he could allow him to listen to his heart and stomach. But things took a sinister turn when Dahmer attempted to perform oral sex upon Miller, laced his drink with two sleeping pills and slashed his carotid artery with the same knife he used to dissect his victims' bodies. After murdering him, Dahmer then photographed the 22-year-old as he was bleeding out, before he placed his body in his bathtub, dismembered him, dissolved Miller's flesh with acid, bleached his skeleton and stored it within a wardrobe in his apartment. The killer also preserved Miller's biceps in his freezer for later consumption. Dahmer reportedly kissed and talked to the severed head while he dismembered the body, wrapped Miller's heart, biceps, and portions of flesh in plastic bags and placed them in the fridge before he boiled the remaining flesh and organs into a 'jelly-like substance' using Soilex. He also painted and coated Miller's skull with enamel.

David Thomas – 24 September 1990

David Courtney Thomas was just 23 when he encountered Dahmer near the Grand Avenue Mall after he was lured to Dahmer's apartment, like others who were promised money for posing nude. However, Dahmer once again laced his victims' drink which rendered Thomas unconscious. Shockingly, Dahmer decided he 'wasn't my type' and feared that Thomas would be angry upon waking, finding that he had been drugged. So, Dahmer strangled Thomas and took polaroid photos of the dismemberment process without retaining any remains.

Thomas was last seen on September 24 and it is believed that he met Dahmer sometime during the day and returned to his residence. Sadly, Thomas left behind a 3-year-old daughter and although it is reported that he had left home for weeks at a time, he always returned to visit her, even after being put on probation for retail theft. At the time of his disappearance, Thomas' family had reported that they had not heard from him in over month. When he failed to return home, his probation officer suggested his ex-girlfriend file a missing person report in October as he was in and out of her home for 12 years.

Curtis Straughter - 18 February 1991

Curtis Durrell Straughter was just 17 years old when he died by the hands of Dahmer. Born on 6 April 1973, the African American teenager was approached by Dahmer as he waited at a bus stop near the Marquette University and was subsequently lured to his apartment of horrors, where he was drugged, handcuffed and strangled with a leather strap before being dismembered in the bathtub. Like many others, Straughter's skull, hands, and genitals were retained as trophies.

According to Dahmer, he lured Straughter just as he had with the others, with an offer of money for posing for nude photos, but this time there was an added incentive of sexual intercourse. Also, such as the case with the other murders, he had photographed each stage of the dismemberment process.

Friends who knew the young teen fondly remembered his nicknames of Demetra and Curta, describing him as a young, vivacious person who had the whole world in front of him. Straughter lived with his grandmother at the time of his death, and after losing his nursing job, he had dreams of becoming a model and finishing his college degree. Dreams which were never fulfilled due to him meeting a serial killer that day. Straughter is buried at the Holy Cross Cemetery and Mausoleum in Milwaukee, Wisconsin.

Errol Lindsey - 7 April 1991

Errol Lindsey, 19, was the first victim that Dahmer practiced his 'drilling technique' on. This was a procedure where he would drill holes into the victim's skull and then injected hydrochloric acid into the brain to create a living zombie. According to Dahmer, Lindsey woke up after the procedure and was murdered afterward.

After meeting Lindsey whilst he was running a key cutting errand, Dahmer bribed him to come back to his apartment, where he was drugged before the holes were drilled. But once Lindsey woke up and complained of a headache, Dahmer drugged him again, strangled him and decapitated him. Like many others, Dahmer retained his skull and attempted to keep his skin, but it became too brittle to keep.

Those who knew the young man described him as an upstanding and generous person who loved to make new friends. He was also quite popular and was particularly close to his mother and sister. As the youngest of six children the plaster figure worker was surrounded by love in his life, but his family cannot understand how his death occurred.

"I can't understand how it happened, how he met Errol," Lindsey's mother, Mildred, told reporters: "Errol wasn't the type to talk to just anybody. He went to work and then he came home. He was a mama's boy. He wouldn't even go out with his friends without calling me to see what I was doing."

Sadly, Lindsey left behind an unborn daughter when he died, who is now also a mother herself.

Tony Anthony Hughes - 24 May 1991

Whilst frequenting the local gay clubs, this is where he met his alleged partner, Terry Hughes. There are many conflicting reports about the exact nature of Dahmer and Hughes' relationship, however, the depiction of the character in Ryan Murphey's *Monster*, a Netflix 10-part series, shows that that the pair were lovers, and for quite some time. Titled *Monster: The Jeffrey Dahmer Story*, it tells the tale of Dahmer's life after he becomes an adult and his descent into his horrific crimes. Through the use of documentaries, podcasts, and media reports, Murphy was able to put forward a dramatised account of the crimes, which also explores his murders through the victims' points of view. In episode six of the 10-part series, the audience is introduced to Hughes's, who is played by the actor Rodney Burford. While his time on the screen was short-lived, Hughes was allegedly well acquainted with Dahmer for some time before his death. In fact, he was apparently friends with Dahmer for around a year, up until he became the 12th of his 17 known victims.

Born on 26 August 1959, according to FBI files, Hughes was mute and deaf after permanently losing his hearing ability due to side effects of medications he had taken as a child, as per *The Scottish Sun*. It was after graduating from the Wisconsin School for the Deaf that Hughes moved to Madison, Wisconsin, and he met Dahmer afterwards. His mother, Shirley, described him as 'outgoing, jolly, happy' and he 'could easily make friends' during her 1991 interview with *The Associated Press*, which could point as to why he may have felt that loner Dahmer needed a friend. But were they in a romantic relationship? Well, while 'Monster' implies that the pair were in a romantic relationship prior to his murder, the real-life Dahmer denied knowing Hughes before killing him. However, according to Hughes's friend, Dahmer and Hughes were acquainted with each other for over a year, and another claimed their friendship extended two years before the murder of Hughes, according to the *Milwaukee Journal Sentinel*. Hughes's mother also told AP that her son was visiting a friend named Jeffrey at the time of his disappearance. Brian Masters, in his book 'The Shrine of Jeffrey Dahmer,' claimed that Dahmer and Hughes met at The 219 Club where Hughes asked three friends to give him a ride to Dahmer's apartment as the pair wrote notes to each other at the table.

While a lot of this is speculation, what is known is that on 24 May the 31-year-old was last seen at a bar before Dahmer wrote him a bribing note and took him back to his apartment to capture nude photographs. He then drilled holes into his skull and killed him upon the fatal injection of hydrochloric acid into his brain. His body was then left on Dahmer's bedroom floor for three days before being dismembered, dissolving his body in acid and retaining his skull as a keepsake.

Konerak Sinthasomphone - 27 May 1991

Konerak Sinthasomphone was the youngest of Dahmer's victims, and at just 14 years old, he could never know the danger that awaited him as Dahmer took him back to his apartment for a few drinks and the offer of money in exchange for photographs. According to the Chicago Tribune, the teenager was drugged, and a hole was drilled into his skull before the naked, bruised, bleeding and heavily drugged teenager escaped from Dahmer's apartment. But he didn't escape for long.

Netflix's documentary, *Monster: The Jeffrey Dahmer Story*, detailed how the serial killer filled Sinthasomphone's head with hydrochloric acid via the drilled hole and showed the sinister way in which he methodically murdered his victims. Not only did it show a dramatisation of the killing, but also the near-escape of Sinthasomphone just thirty minutes before his eventual death... and the police failings that led to it. It was when Dahmer made the mistake of leaving his drugged victim alone in his apartment while he left to go to the grocery store, that the teenager awoke. Confused, bloodied and in a strange place, Sinthasomphone immediately bolted for the door and ran into the street. There, he encountered three passers by – Sandra Smith, Tina Spivey and Nicole Childress. The women called the police, believing that he was in dire need of assistance, and that is when the unthinkable occurred.

John Balcerzak and Joseph Gabrish responded to the call that evening, witnessing the three ladies surrounding the incoherent boy and noting his state of undress and injury. But ultimately, they chose to hand him back to Dahmer after being convinced that he was his 19-year-old lover.

"At the time, with the information we had – to this day, I think we did the appropriate thing, the best that we could," Balcerzak said in an interview after Dahmer was arrested according to *AP News*. Allegedly, the police officers believed Dahmer when he told them that the teenager was his lover, and that the pair had simply engaged in a lovers' spat that night. Sadly, when the police escorted him back to Dahmer's apartment of horrors, within half an hour, Sinthasomphone would be murdered with a lethal injection to his skull. Because of this, critics accused the police of insensitivity and discrimination toward homosexuals and minority groups, leading to the two officers being fired.

Konerak Sinthasomphone was born on 1 December 1976. He died on 27 May 1991 in Milwaukee, Wisconsin, USA.

According to reports, when the police officers arrived, Dahmer had returned from the grocery store and was holding Sinthasomphone up, which didn't seem suspicious to the cops because Sinthasomphone was not trying to break away from his captor. So, when the officers questioned Dahmer, and he politely answered their concerns and gave Balcerzak his personal information, they believed him. Dahmer alleged that Sinthasomphone was a man named John Mung who had drunk too much alcohol as per the *Monster*'s true crime portrayal of the event. Balcerzak is said to have repeated his questions to Dahmer to test whether or not he was telling the truth, and according to the officer, his answers were the same each time, which led him to falsely believe that he was being sincere. However, Dahmer was just a skilled liar, and Sinthasomphone successfully became his next victim.

Sinthasomphone grew up in Wisconsin with his family and older brother, Somsack – the boy who was previously molested by Dahmer. The Sinthasomphone family experienced financial challenges as their sons grew up, which led to the sons attempting to help earn money, which allegedly also included prostitution. While it is not verified whether Sinthasomphone was really prostituting himself, the claim must have been a hard detail for the family to come to terms with during the exposing of the crimes Dahmer had committed.

Matt Turner - 30 June 1991

Matt Cleveland Turner, a 20-year-old was waiting at a bus stop near the Chicago Pride Parade on June 30 when Dahmer, who had attended the parade, noticed him. Just as he had with his other victims, the killer persuaded him to go back to his apartment to post for photographs. But, as usual, that wasn't all he was interested in. Sadly, once Matt arrived at the apartment, he was drugged, strangled with a strap, and then dismembered in the bathtub. Later, Dahmer put his head and internal organs in the freezer and his torso was kept in a 57-gallon drum when Dahmer purchased it on 12 July.

Born on 15 October, Turner was allegedly known by another name, Donald Montrell, and there is not a lot of information readily available on who he was as a person. But what is known is that he had left his family home to stay at a Chicago halfway house just a year prior to meeting Dahmer and that he had high aspirations of becoming a model. What is also known is that after being murdered by Dahmer, his torso was dissolved in acid.

Such as the case of the other victims, Turner was not known as a victim until remains were being found, one by one. When the complaint was filed against Dahmer regarding Turner's murder, even his own father condemned him for taking the life of the young man. Lionel is reported as having claimed: "There's no doubt he's insane. I feel like I should wake up any moment. I don't think I knew him at all."

Jeremiah Weinberger - 5 July 1991

Jeremiah Benjamin Weinberger was just 23 when Dahmer met him at a gay bar in Chicago and persuaded him to travel to Milwaukee for the weekend. Of course, there would be no weekend getaway for the pair, and the killer had much more sinister plans. Namely, he wanted to drill a hole through Weinberger's skull and inject boiling water into the cavity- something he eventually succeeded in doing the day after the man arrived at his apartment after voicing his intention to leave. The murderer would go on to call Weinberger's death exceptional, as he was the only victim who died with his eyes open.

The Puerto Rican man believed that they would have nothing more than a good time together, as the pair had engaged in oral sex on the first day of his stay. But when it became clear that Weinberger wanted to leave, Dahmer gave him a drugged drink, 'strangled him manually' and dismembered the body, while taking photos of the process and keeping his body next to Turner's in the 57-gallon acid-filled drum.

While Weinberger was just another kill on his long list, to those who knew and loved him, this was a tragedy like no other. Before meeting Dahmer, Weinberger was working as a customer service representative for a video store, according to *USA Today.*

"He loved art and was very meticulous," his roommate, Tim Gideon, shared. "His desk was always straight, and he knew where everything was. He always dressed nice and always worried about what he wore and how he looked."

Oliver Lacy - 15 July 1991

Oliver Joseph Lacy was a 24-year-old bodybuilding enthusiast who had the misfortune of running into Dahmer just ten days after Weinberger.

Born on 23 June, 1968 in Chicago, he was a track racer at River Forest High School and was described as outspoken, according to *USA Today*. As the youngest of three sons, Lacy was said to have been a family man and wore his father's cross after his passing. Shortly after his father's death, he moved from Chicago to Milwaukee. According to *The Cinemaholic*, Dahmer introduced himself as a professional photographer. Sadly, Lacy was also the father of a two-year-old child and was engaged to be married before he was enticed by Dahmer to his apartment, with the promise of money in return for posing for photographs.

Once he was within the killer's lair, Lacy was drugged and strangled with a leather strap before being decapitated, and his head and heart were placed in the refrigerator for later use. Dahmer also retained his skeleton to adorn one side of a shrine of skulls and skeletons Dahmer was attempting to create.

Joseph Bradehoft – 19 July 1991

Joseph Arthur Bradehoft was Dahmer's last successful victim before he was apprehended by the police just days later. Aged 25, Bradehoft was the eldest of his siblings and he grew up in Illinois where he married his wife Cheryl and produced three young children ranging between the ages of two and seven. The hard worker had moved to Milwaukee shortly before meeting Dahmer and was living in an apartment rented by his brother as he searched for a job to help financially support his family back home in Minnesota. On the day of his murder, Bradehoft had left for a job interview, and was never heard from again. His family later shared that he loved sports and fishing and was also a devoted father to his children.

According to reports, Dahmer received word that he was fired from his chocolate factory job after his work-release prison-ordered time was finished on the day that he murdered his last victim, giving him an opportunity to strike his next victim without being restrained by his work. Unfortunately, the father would meet Dahmer at a bus stop in Milwaukee that day, where he was offered $50 to pose nude. Once at his apartment, Bradehoft was drugged and strangled to death and left to lie on Dahmer's bed for two days before Dahmer removed the sheet to allegedly find the head covered in maggots. So, he dismembered the body and kept his skull after cleaning the head and torso, which were then retained and frozen.

Tracy Edwards (survivor)

On July 22, just one day after dismembering his last victim, Dahmer attempted to kill again. He met a man by the name of Tracy Edwards, 32, at a bar and offered him $100 to come back to his apartment. Once there, Edwards was handcuffed, although he managed to manoeuvre himself so that only one wrist was restrained before Dahmer began to watch the *Exorcist 3* movie. Whilst Dahmer was preoccupied with his film, he began to display strange behaviour, and he allegedly told Tracy he would 'eat' his heart while holding him at knifepoint. Once Dahmer had settled back into his movie, Edwards later revealed how he began to speak in 'tongues', rocking back and forth and becoming unstable. So, he pretended to befriend the killer, and later asked to use the bathroom. Once he was walking past Dahmer in the bedroom, he attacked him, and bolted for the door, which was locked with multiple devices.

Thankfully, he was able to unlock the door and ran into patrolling officers who believed his story and arrived at Dahmer's apartment to investigate the kidnapping claims. From there, by chance, an officer saw polaroid images of Dahmer's dismemberment process and later found remains of bodies, leading to his arrest.

Finally, Dahmer had been caught.

The Apartment of Horrors

When police officers were approached by Edwards with handcuffs dangling from one of his wrists and told of a dubious story of him being held captive for hours, of course the officers were intrigued. However, when they appeared at the apartment in question, in search of the handcuff key, they found a lot more than they bargained for. Upon entering Dahmer's bedroom in search of the key, a drawer of Polaroids caught their eyes, and soon, the full horrors of his home would be revealed. According to reports, and testimonies from the officers who attended the scene that day, the apartment was littered with human remains. This included several human heads in the refrigerator and freezer; two skulls on top of the computer; a 57-gallon drum containing several torsos decomposing in chemicals in a corner of the bedroom, evidence to suggest that Dahmer had been eating some of his victims and more.

Dahmer's apartment was a 'killing factory,' as per *The New York Times*, and police quickly realised the methods the killer was using to murder his victims were inhumane and startling. For example, they found ether and chloroform, which is believed to have been used to drug his victims, and a barrel of hydrochloric acid which he used to dissolve the men's bodies and also preserve skeletons. There were also gruesome souvenirs, bones, and the corpses of 11 people, according to FBI records. Alongside remains and chemicals, there were knives and sawblades, a hypodermic needle and an electric drill.

Michael Dubis, who worked for the Milwaukee Police Department for 34 years, was horrified when he discovered the remains in the apartment, telling the Fox Nation documentary *My Son Jeffrey: The Dahmer Family Tapes*: "I was a 31-year-old young man with two years of experience on homicides. To see something like that, just understanding what it would take to do that to another person, was a shock."

He found a tray of blood drippings, two human hearts, part of an arm, a torso and a bag of human organs and flesh in several places within the property. The officers also discovered two skeletons, a pair of severed hands, two severed penises, a mummified scalp, and 74 Polaroid pictures detailing the dismemberment of each victim, including necrophilia with the deceased.

There was barely an area in Dahmer's home which did not contain some form of paraphernalia involved in his killing, as body parts and severed heads were in his fridge, freezer, filing cabinet, and even in a kettle. *TIME* reported that the kettle 'contained what are thought to be decomposing hands and a male genital organ'. Of course, having been caught with so much evidence against him, Dahmer was arrested without a struggle.

According to homicide detective Patrick Kennedy in an interview with radio show *Rover's Morning Glory*, as he looked into the refrigerator the 'freshly severed, bloodless, human head' of a 'black male with his eyes and mouth open with an expression of almost excitement or surprise' was positioned inside. The sight of the head led to his mind telling him: 'Man you need to get the hell out of here.'

But of course, this wasn't the first time officers had been inside of Dahmer's apartment, as in May, they returned a partially naked and drugged 14-year-old boy they found wandering the street. Dahmer even said after being arrested that 'if officers had looked in the next room they would have found skulls, frozen body parts, severed heads, torsos in an acid-filled vat and preserved genitals,' according to *The New York Times.*

Rolf Mueller, one of the first officers to enter Dahmer's home, said of the apartment and its condition as per the *Washington Post*: "You think you've seen it all out here, and then something like this happens."

Mueller said Dahmer gave him the 'creeps' and was thankful they were able to stop him from killing another man. FBI photos from the time of Dahmer's arrest revealed that Netflix's series depicting the murder is scarily accurate, according to *Esquire.* Many images show that Dahmer had decorated his apartment of torture with a beige couch, a vintage fish tank, carpet on the floor, an analog television, and a barrel for acid and dissolving bosies. There were also blood stains in his bedroom that were almost impossible to remove.

So, what happened to the apartment after his arrest? According to Newsweek, Dahmer's apartment was torn down in November 1992, just 15 months after his arrest at the request of the victim's families. Most tenants moved out of the building after Dahmer's arrest, and the complex was purchased for $325,000 by the Campus Circle Project three years later, which also helped all remaining tenants to find new homes. The empty lot was almost converted into a playground, but those ideas were quickly scrapped. As for now, the land is deserted, and plans to plant grass and flowers were put on hold, as per *The Tab.* The president of the project, Patrick LeSage, called Dahmer's apartment a 'symbol of anger, pain, violence, and death' when talking to *The Bulletin* in 1992. He added: «It needs to be replaced with a sign of our commitment to support the healing process and to work together as a community of people who care."

Part III

Psychological Analysis

Inside the mind of a monster

Dahmer had officially been classed as a serial killer, who had taken the lives of many boys and men to satisfy some dark need inside of him. But why did he have such a need, and were his compulsions enough to prove that he was sick? Sick enough to successfully campaign that he was insane during his trial?

Dr Park Dietz, a forensic psychiatrist who interviewed and testified at the trial of Dahmer appeared on the documentary, *Conversations with Killers,* in which he recalled his intimate encounter with one of the most infamous criminals.

Describing the origins of Dahmer's paraphilia (the act incorporating dead animals into sexual fantasies), Dietz talked about his conversation with Dahmer whilst he was incarcerated.

Dietz was approached by the Milwaukee DA's office to evaluate Dahmer, and he met with him for several days before later testifying. The expert, who has seen 20 serial killers across his career said that it was extraordinary how open and honest he was about his crimes.

"What's frightening to the public about criminals like Jeffrey Dahmer is that he seems so normal," Dietz previously said about the killer. "He was so able to explain what he'd done and why he did it."

Dietz said that Dahmer was 'trying to come to terms with what he's done' and 'he's as perplexed as anyone as to how this began'.

"He was the most honest criminal I can remember evaluating. And I'm used to being lied to hour after hour after hour. People fake mental illnesses, they fake retardation, they fake being mute, they tell all kinds of lies about their crimes. He didn't."

"We talked about every crime he committed in exquisite detail," he said, explaining that he asked Dahmer questions such as: "How did you make sure the knife didn't glint in the moonlight? What did the blood taste like when you ate that?".

They even watched movies together and gay porn.

Dahmer had eaten some of his victims' muscle tissue, had tried to dig up a corpse to have sex with it, attempted to create zombies via injecting mild acid or boiling water into their skulls which indicates that Dahmer is a paraphilic (a sexual deviant or a pervert) and not psychotic.

The pair spent so much time together that Dahmer opened up about a shrine he had intended to erect which would be fashioned out of his victims' skulls. The killer, who had been diagnosed with BPD (borderline personality disorder), Schizotypal personality disorder, and a Psychotic disorder after his arrest, was ultimately declared sane to stand trial.

The reason? Dietz found that he was aware of his intent to harm. According to the *LA Times*, Dietz explained that Dahmer did not want to kill and had to force himself by consuming alcohol.

He said: "I found him responsible for a number of things, but there were two points that had the greatest impact for public perception or at least a jury, and they were that he used a condom, and that he had no particular desire or interest to kill them and had to get himself drunk to overcome the revulsion of the killing."

"If Dahmer had had the delusion that he'd have companions for life if he killed them and ate them, and that that was somehow a good thing and not criminal, that would make him insane. But those weren't the facts at all. Even the defence experts agreed that Dahmer knew it was wrong."

Dietz said Dahmer thought about finding one man to keep permanently via freeze-drying them but when he found out that the apparatus would cost tens of thousands of dollars, he reconsidered. His preference was allegedly to have sex with a consenting adult, and that had his victims chosen to stay with him, he may never have killed.

His testimony on the stand put forth the idea that Dahmer could have chosen not to kill, and this was a turning point in successfully dismissing the insanity defense plea.

When Dahmer was convicted, his defence attorney, Gerald P. Boyle, said he warned him that they would have lost the insanity defence plea, and after it was dismissed and the verdict was given, Dahmer told him, 'Thanks for trying'. He shared that he knew he was sick, but not sick enough for his defence.

For Dietz, his role was to prove that Dahmer was 'sick' and not 'evil.'

Paraphilia, necrophilia, partialism, and other features were involved in the trail, and Dahmer was also diagnosed as suffering from alcoholism, a personality disorder not otherwise specified, and an antisocial personality disorder with obsessive-compulsive and sadistic components. He was also diagnosed as having a sexual disorder not otherwise specified.

"My duty and my goal were to prove that he was insane during the commission of these offenses," Boyle told the producers of *Conversations with a Killer.* "That when he killed somebody he was suffering from mental illness."

Years after Dahmer was incarcerated for his crimes, Dietz was asked why he was not afraid to be in a room with the killer. To this he said that he was safe with Dahmer, as he was not his type. However, that cannot be said for other killers, and so the famed psychologist suggested to avoid criminals as much as possible to negate the risk.

Perhaps one of the most strange things that Dahmer had claimed, was that he did not want to actually kill his victims. He simply wanted to keep them with him. Dahmer once shared: "Killing wasn't the objective. I just wanted to have the person under my complete control to do with as I wanted."

In a separate interview with Stone Phillips on Dateline NBC, he added: "The killing was a means to an end. That was the least satisfactory part. I didn't enjoy doing that. That's why I tried to create living zombies with uric acid in the drill [to the head], but it never worked."

While Dahmer was pegged as being mentally disturbed by some, and sane by others, his psychopathic traits have been long debated. According to Dr Joel, Psy.D., a Licensed Clinical Psychologist and Neuropsychologist at Duality Psychological Services, the psychopathy diagnostic criteria is extensive.

Dr Joel took information regarding Dahmer and his hidden past and compared media coverage of his childhood, personality and murder of the young men to compile a theory as to how he may have either lived with psychopathy all along or developed it. Dr Joel's interview shared his findings as he attempted not to directly diagnose Dahmer, but to draw comparisons between his actions and behaviours to those who meet the psychopathy criteria. Dr Joel Frank also explored Dahmer's criminal trajectory and his similarities to psychopathy.

Psychopathy, commonly associated with the clinically recognised diagnosis of Antisocial Personality Disorder (ASPD), [a behavioral disorder which can cause a person to lack empathy, find it hard to make connections, lie, and be more likely to commit crime) is part of a broader spectrum of personality profiles characterised by a pattern of disregard for and violation of others' rights.

It's a complex condition often misunderstood in clinical settings and popular culture. At its core, psychopathy involves a profound lack of empathy, manifesting in manipulative, deceitful, and often criminal behaviour.

Contrary to media portrayals, not all individuals with psychopathy are violent; some channel their traits into socially acceptable or even successful ventures, harnessing the lessened empathy and manipulative tactics for professional gain.

Research has consistently highlighted the significant role that adverse childhood experiences (ACEs) play in the development of psychopathic traits, with a strong correlation between early exposure to violence, neglect, and emotional abuse and the severity of psychopathic traits in adulthood.

The aetiology of psychopathy is multifaceted, involving genetic, neurological, and environmental factors. Twin studies highlight a strong genetic component, suggesting heritability.

At the same time, neuroscientific findings point to abnormalities in brain areas related to empathy, impulse control, and emotional processing, such as the amygdala and prefrontal cortex. Environmental factors like childhood trauma, neglect, and exposure to violent behaviour significantly contribute to the development of psychopathic traits.

Family dynamics, especially parental behaviour, can profoundly impact the development of psychopathy. The absence of parental warmth and inconsistent disciplinary practices are linked to a greater likelihood of developing antisocial behaviours. Furthermore, children from families characterised by high conflict and low cohesion are more prone to exhibit pronounced psychopathic characteristics.

Cultural norms and societal values can also influence both the manifestation and perception of psychopathic traits. Cultures that prioritise individual success and competitiveness may, inadvertently, encourage traits associated with psychopathy, such as manipulativeness, callousness, and an interpersonal style that views relationships more as tools for personal advancement rather than for social connectivity.

On the behavioural front, aggression and impulsivity are vital factors that exacerbate psychopathic tendencies, often leading to negative social consequences, including legal troubles and the reinforcement of antisocial patterns.

Moreover, engagement in criminal activities acts both as a symptom and a contributing factor to psychopathy, with the thrill-seeking behaviour and disregard for societal norms leading individuals down a path of escalating criminal behaviour, which further entrenches psychopathic tendencies.

From a biological and genetic standpoint, neurobiological research has pinpointed abnormalities in brain regions associated with emotion regulation, moral reasoning, and decision-making in individuals with psychopathy.

Notably, structural and functional deficits in the amygdala and prefrontal cortex have been implicated in the disorder. Psychologically, deficits in emotional regulation are a hallmark of psychopathy, with affected individuals often exhibiting an inability to recognize and appropriately respond to emotional cues, leading to inappropriate affective responses.

A defining characteristic of psychopathy is a lack of empathy, which fundamentally undermines the ability to understand and value others' feelings, contributing to the interpersonal and behavioural problems associated with the disorder. This limited capacity for empathy can hinder the development of interpersonal relationships, leading to a cycle of poor social skills and increased isolation.

Diagnosing psychopathy requires a comprehensive clinical assessment, including interviews, self-reports, and psychometric testing, such as the Hare Psychopathy Checklist-Revised (PCL-R), which assesses traits and behaviours across interpersonal, affective, lifestyle, and antisocial dimensions.

Some key characteristics associated with psychopathy include glibness or superficial charm, pathological lying, a grandiose sense of self-worth, shallow affect, lack of remorse or guilt, and impulsivity. These traits often lead to significant challenges in interpersonal relationships. Individuals with psychopathy struggle to form genuine emotional connections, resulting in superficial relationships.

Their manipulative and deceitful behaviour can distress family members, friends, and coworkers, leading to isolated or strained relationships. The impact on interpersonal relationships can be profound, with familial bonds often strained or broken due to manipulative and abusive behaviour.

Romantic relationships can suffer from a lack of genuine intimacy and trust, and in professional settings, individuals with psychopathy may exploit relationships for personal gain, undermining teamwork and organizational cohesion.

Treatment for psychopathy presents unique challenges due to the individual's often limited insight and sometimes reluctance to seek help. Despite these obstacles, specific approaches have shown promise in addressing this condition.

Cognitive Behavioural Therapy (CBT) focuses on specific problematic behaviours and thought patterns, offering a structured way to tackle issues directly. Therapeutic communities provide structured environments that promote healthy social interactions and personal responsibility, which can be beneficial.

Although there is no specific medication for treating psychopathy itself, certain drugs can help manage associated symptoms like aggression or impulsivity. Role-playing and social situation simulations encourage individuals to understand different perspectives by acting out scenarios from another person's point of view, which can enhance empathy.

Reflective listening exercises, where individuals practice attentive listening and mirror back what another person says, help validate others' feelings and perspectives, aiding in trust-building and developing a compassionate approach.

Narrative exposure involves sharing personal stories and listening to others, fostering an understanding of diverse life experiences, and emphasising the common humanity among individuals.

Mindfulness and emotional regulation training focus on present-moment awareness and non-judgmental observation of one's thoughts and feelings, leading to better impulse control and empathy.

Empathy-building workshops offer a variety of techniques and discussions aimed at improving empathetic skills, including analysing emotional expressions and engaging in cooperative tasks that require mutual understanding.

Early intervention, especially during childhood and adolescence, can offer a better prognosis by addressing risk factors and enhancing pro-social behaviours. Although there is no "cure" for psychopathy, ongoing research into treatment efficacy and its neurological underpinnings holds hope for future management strategies.

Supporting individuals with psychopathy and their families requires a comprehensive approach, including mental health support, education about the condition, and techniques for managing challenging behaviours. Building a supportive network and accessing specialised therapeutic services help mitigate the impact of psychopathy on interpersonal relationships.

Jeffrey Dahmer is one of the most infamous serial killers in American history, notorious for his crimes from the late 1970s to the early 1990s. His case is a complex example of environmental, behavioural, and psychological factors converging to contribute to the development of psychopathy, resulting in severe antisocial behaviours.

Per information contained in the available media, it has been previously theorised that Dahmer's neglected childhood and lack of emotional support from his parents, who were often entangled in their relationship, deprived him of necessary emotional nurturing, possibly fostering feelings of isolation and inadequacy. The family's frequent moves might have exacerbated his sense of instability and alienation.

Per previous professionals who examined Mr. Dahmer, during his school years he was an introvert struggling with social interactions and failing to form meaningful connections, further possibly contributing to his internal distress and development of harmful fantasies.

Previous analysts identified that from an early age, Dahmer exhibited an interest in dead animals, collecting carcasses and dismembering them, indicating an early sign of his fascination with death and possible lack of empathy, precursors to his possible antisocial behaviour.

Per previously published media, his first murder occurred shortly after high school, marking the beginning of an escalating spiral into increasingly violent behaviours characterised by a pattern of luring, drugging, killing, and then dismembering his victims. Individuals who exhibit these behaviours tend to harbour deep-seated needs for control and dominance, traits common in psychopathic behaviour.

Previous analysts postulated that throughout his life, Dahmer displayed a significant emotional disconnect, showing little to no remorse for his actions, a lack of empathy that can be a hallmark of psychopathy. Theorists have proposed links between his sexual identity and preferences and psychopathy, suggesting he sought to create submissive, compliant partners through murder, driven by fears of abandonment and rejection. The emotional neglect Dahmer experienced during his formative years, according to previous theorists, likely contributed to his inability to form healthy emotional attachments and fostered a sense of detachment from society.

His isolation during adolescence may have intensified his psychopathic tendencies, providing fertile ground for the development of harmful fantasies. The escalation of his behaviours following his first murder suggests that each act of violence possibly desensitised him to suffering and reinforced his pathological behaviours.

Dahmer's lack of remorse and detachment from his actions are indicative of the callousness and lack of empathy that characterize psychopathy. The possible intersection between Dahmer's sexual identity, fear of abandonment, and violence highlights the complex psychological issues that can combine to result in violent behaviours.

Jeffrey Dahmer's childhood could be characterised by isolation and neglect, showing an early interest in dead animals, which is often linked to psychopathic traits. Similarly, Ian Huntley, a man from the UK who murdered two little girls in 2002, grew up in a turbulent home environment lacking stability and emotional warmth, potentially contributing to psychopathic tendencies.

Dahmer's criminal acts included murder, dismemberment, and necrophilia, possibly driven by fantasies and a desire for control over his victims. In contrast, [other renowned killers such as Ian Huntley in the UK who] murdered two young girls in what appeared to be an opportunistic act without documented post-mortem interactions characteristic of Dahmer's crimes.

Both Dahmer and Huntley exhibited traits consistent with possible psychopathy, such as a lack of remorse and manipulativeness, but, per previously published media and professional analyses, Dahmer showed a higher level of interpersonal and affective deficits.

Previous analysts conveyed his pattern of behaviour, possibly suggesting a deep-seated need for control and possession, escalating his crimes to fulfil his fantasies and exploiting his victims' trust. Huntley's actions, lacking Dahmer's ritualistic and prolonged nature, seemed more opportunistic, focusing on maintaining a facade and avoiding detection.

Based on the available media and previous analyst descriptions, both individuals exhibited traits and behaviours consistent with other individuals who harboured psychopathic characteristics.

Still, Dahmer's previously documented extensive dehumanising behaviour and possibly complex psychopathic needs indicate a deeper psychopathic pathology. Huntley, though also exhibiting traits consistent with psychopathy, might have been driven by a need for power and control in moments of opportunity, showing a possibly different manifestation of psychopathic traits.

Jeffrey Dahmer and Ian Huntley's cases illustrate diverse manifestations of possible psychopathy, with Dahmer presenting a more traditionally media-portrayed psychopathic profile driven by complex psychological needs and Huntley's behaviour suggesting a different, opportunistic profile with less intricate motives behind his crimes.

When exploring the inner mind of Dahmer, the argument of Nature versus Nurture is inevitably called into question. This theory states that a person may be shaped, either by their own fated path, or the world around them. Simply put, does a person become who they are as an adult because they were always going to be this way, or were there external factors?

Caitlin Weese, Founder and Psychotherapist at Intuitive Healing and Wellness, shared how Dahmer's childhood plays a significant role in how he became a mass killer. During our conversation, she revealed the key themes that create negative outcomes as an adult, particularly Adverse Childhood Experiences.

****

How do childhood experiences, such as emotional neglect or a lack of physical affection, typically impact psychological development in children?

These childhood experiences can have a significant impact on the psychological development of children and lead to the development of an insecure attachment style (such as anxious, avoidant, or anxious/avoidant), difficulties with emotional regulation (increased emotional reactivity, problems coping with stress in adaptive ways) as well as lead to low self-esteem, increased likelihood of mental health struggles and struggles forming or maintaining healthy and fulfilling relationships with others.

From a psychological perspective, what are the potential long-term effects on a child who grows up with a parent struggling with mental health issues, such as suicidal thoughts or depression?

Studies such as the Adverse Childhood Experiences Study have shown that childhood exposure to a parent with mental health struggles can lead to increased mental health difficulties. We know that mental health struggles such as depression and bipolar disorder are highly genetic, and the risk of suicide is significantly increased for family members of those who have died by suicide. Because children are naturally egocentric, they naturally internalise a person's behaviour, leading children to feel that their parent's depression is "their fault."

How might having a "germaphobic" mother who avoids physical contact influence a child's attachment style and emotional regulation?

Lack of physical contact or adequate mirroring of a child's experience results in an insecure attachment style. Insecure attachment styles can result in heightened or numbed emotions, making maintaining or achieving emotional regulation very difficult. Furthermore, from an evolutionary perspective, our drive for attachment is rooted in the need for survival; without our parents, we cannot survive independently. Therefore, seeming rejection of or disinterest in this attachment would be highly anxiety-provoking for a child, leading to either high anxiety and dependence or low anxiety and hyper-independence or a mix of both.

What role do early childhood trauma and attachment issues play in shaping the future behaviour of individuals, particularly when they experience emotional neglect or lack of nurturing?

These issues would have a large impact on behaviour. Beyond difficulties in relationships, these individuals would likely develop maladaptive beliefs about themselves and others such as "I can't trust anyone" or "if you don't take advantage of someone they will take advantage of you" and likely struggle with identifying emotions in themselves and others.

Do you believe that adverse childhood environments, such as Jeffrey Dahmer's, can contribute to violent tendencies later in life? If so, how?

Yes, the presence of continual and pervasive childhood trauma during the formative years of one's life can lead to a lack of empathy for others, sensation or thrill-seeking, high emotional reactivity and a lack of alternative coping skills.

Are there common psychological traits shared by people who come from dysfunctional homes, particularly those who go on to commit extreme acts of violence?

A lack of empathy or a lower level of empathy for others, pervasive feelings of boredom, impulsivity, substance use and narcissistic tendencies are all characteristics these individuals might display.

In your opinion, what is the relationship between early childhood trauma and the likelihood of someone becoming a serial killer or engaging in violent behaviour?

Many people experience childhood trauma and even pervasive childhood trauma and do not engage in violent behaviour. However, it is my opinion that when childhood trauma occurs, the child either internalises or externalises their experience, choosing to either turn their anger inwards towards themselves or outwards onto others. This shift to externalising one's anger often leads to aggressive behaviour and violence towards others.

Is there evidence to support the idea that all serial killers experienced abusive or neglectful childhoods, or are there other factors at play that we should consider?

Research has suggested that the 'profile' of a serial murderer typically includes abuse during childhood, like neglect, but also physical, sexual, or emotional abuse (Ressler, Burgess, Douglas, & Depue, 1985). However, there are also cases of serial killers who appear to have no discernible traumatic experiences in childhood. Continued research into the brains of serial killers has begun to reveal there is also a genetic component to the formation of these types of behaviours.

How might a child's emotional and psychological needs be influenced when they grow up with parents who are not emotionally available or who have severe psychological difficulties?

This would greatly impact a child's emotional and psychological development. Because we learn about what emotions look like, feel like, and how to express them from our parents, having a parent who is unable to mirror our emotional state or is suffering from their psychological issues would significantly impact the development of these skills. This would likely result in an insecure attachment style, trouble developing and maintaining healthy relationships (such as a history of chaotic or one-sided relationships), a lack of emotional intelligence or possibly a lack of empathy, struggles regulating their emotions, and a higher likelihood of developing a substance use disorder.

What are the critical psychological factors in early childhood that could potentially prevent someone from developing violent tendencies despite experiencing an adverse home environment?

Protective factors such as nurturing, safe and stable "enough" relationships with peers or adults, or adults who worked to attempt to meet a child's needs were both seen as protective factors that decreased the negative impact of adverse childhood experiences on future outcomes (Crouch et al. 2018).

****

With those protective factors, Dahmer may have been able to curb his compulsions to commit harm and potentially steer himself in a different trajectory and life's path. However, his obsession with death may have been too much for him to quell.

An Obsession with Death

Obsessions with death are something that has been seen throughout history. Whether it is a fascination with the morbid, such as True Crime TV shows, reading up on gory details from real-life murder cases or even partaking in collecting items that were used during a murder or were recovered from the scene of a crime. For some, this is a hobby like no other. But the line between fascination and putting yourself in the way of inflicting or receiving potential harm can become stretched for a select group of people in the community.

For Dahmer, his obsession with bones and flaying carcasses stemmed from childlike wonder, but decades later, he would go on to become one of the world's most known serial killers, leaving devastation in his wake. For others, the allure of such a man that could go on to commit such crimes become their obsession.

Throughout the history of serial killers, we have seen women write love letters to men that are incarcerated for the most violent crimes, often against women and children. Whether they begin a relationship via a pen pal system, or they go on to marry the criminal, such women do exist in society.[13]

Hybristophilia is the word which encapsulates a person's attraction to those who commit crimes, and it is also known as the Bonnie and Clyde syndrome – inspired by the real-life robbers and killers of the 1930s.

Katherine Ramsland Ph.D. once wrote: "Some mental health experts have compared infatuation with killers to extreme forms of fanaticism. They view such individuals as insecure people who cannot find love in normal ways or as 'love-avoidant' females who seek romantic relationships that cannot be consummated."

An example of hybristophilia would be Ted Bundy's courtroom girlfriend-turned-wife Carole Ann Boone. Boone was a single mother, who became romantically involved with Bundy in 1974 whilst he was sitting trial in Florida for the murder of two women at the Chi Omega sorority house at FSU. They then wed during the trial as per Florida Law, which allows two people to marry if they state it in a court room in front of a judge. Then, Boone became pregnant with Bundy's child after engaging in conjugal visits. The relationship lasted nine years before she filed for divorce in 1984, and Bundy was put to death in 1989.

But how were they able to wed, particularly during a high-profile murder trial? Well, according to Anne Rule's book *The Stranger Beside Me*, an arcane Florida law meant that 'a public declaration, properly phrased, in an open courtroom in the presence of court officers would make the [marriage] ceremony legal.'

This was a shocking moment for many who watched the televised occurrence, but for Boone, it may have been a dream come true to marry her criminal lover. Louis Schlesinger, PhD, and professor of forensic psychology at the John Jay College of Criminal Justice shared her opinion on the phenomenon.

She stated: "In nearly every penitentiary across the country you'll find female employees, like lawyers, therapists, and guards, getting involved with inmates."

But why do people, and more so women, find Dahmer fascinating, or specifically, sexually appealing despite his marinade of murders?

Kelly Keller, an expert at Whitecap Counselling explained that there are a couple of reasons as to why this might occur – and it is based in the psyche of those who actively seek out convicted criminals or privately obsess over them.

She shared a framework that clarifies the phenomenon and gave a simple explanation as to why this may be something that happens when a killer receives notoriety.

"One explanation for why some individuals become infatuated with or defend serial killers can be understood through Dr. Gad Saad's concept of "suicidal empathy." This concept suggests that excessive, unchecked empathy—when directed toward harmful figures—can cloud rational decision-making and lead to self-destructive outcomes. In this context, some individuals adopt this form of empathy to relate to the world, making them vulnerable to romanticising or defending dangerous figures like serial killers, even to the point of contacting or trying to date them.

"This tendency is often rooted in early attachment trauma. Childhood abuse or neglect can cause individuals to form unhealthy attachments, sometimes even to their abusers. This dynamic of seeking validation from harmful figures can continue into adulthood, resulting in people-pleasing behaviours that cause individuals to sacrifice their well-being to gain approval. These tendencies can make someone more likely to empathise with a serial killer, as they seek acceptance, even in unhealthy or dangerous relationships.

"The cultural shift toward extreme empathy reinforces these tendencies. Historically, empathy was balanced with rationality and protective boundaries. Today, empathy often overshadows these boundaries, particularly when directed at harmful figures. Media portrayals of individuals like Dahmer humanise them and distort their true nature, creating a false sense of connection and encouraging attachment.

"Ultimately, it's a combination of early personal vulnerabilities and cultural influences that drive some individuals to romanticise or defend dangerous people, even serial killers."

According to David Wilson, Emeritus Professor of Criminology at BCU, there are two types of hybristophilliac characteristics; there is the passive hybristophilliac and the aggressive hybristophilliac. A passive hybristophilliac will fall in love with a criminal, whilst an aggressive hybristophilliac will want to actively work with them to commit crimes. We can see this from cases such as Myra Hindley and Ian Brady, the Moors killers. Brady and Hindley were convicted of the1960s abduction and murders of two, and three [respectively] of four young children. Hindley was thought of as an accomplice to her lover, Brady for years, while Brady would say that she was as much a part of it as he.

Rose and Fred West are another example of a hybristophilliac or equally sadistic relationship. Between the pair, they committed at least twelve murders between 1967 and 1987 in England, with it believed that Fred committed the first two prior to knowing Rose.

Time and time again, there have been cases where members of the public will seek out a friendship or romantic relationship with a violent criminal, which is a shocking factor.

Fotoulla Menikou, The Friendly Family Lawyer dove into this phenomenon and expressed how childhood trauma could be the cause of why specifically women choose to have relationships with violent prisoners.

****

What psychological factors may contribute to a woman developing an obsession with a prisoner, particularly one who has committed violent crimes such as murder? Could childhood trauma play a significant role in this behaviour?

Over the years, many women have been attracted to men behind bars, sometimes to the point of obsession. Several serial killers have received marriage proposals in prison, despite their heinous crimes.

At the heart of this are women who are psychologically damaged. Women who have undoubtedly experienced childhood trauma, which has shaped their behaviour in adult life. In their formative years, these women will have experienced ACEs (Adverse Childhood Experiences). These are potentially traumatic events which occur during childhood, such as abuse, neglect or household dysfunction. ACEs can disrupt brain development and lead to long term health problems, behavioural issues and mental health challenges. The toxic stress caused by ACEs can play a significant role in our adult behaviour and our relationships throughout our life.

How do early childhood experiences, such as neglect or abuse, influence a person's attachment patterns and potentially lead to an attraction to incarcerated individuals, particularly those who have committed severe crimes?

Early childhood experiences, particularly the quality of a child's relationships with their primary caregiver, can profoundly shape their attachment style, impacting their ability to form and maintain healthy relationships later on in life. Children who experience inconsistent, abusive or neglectful caregiving, may develop insecure attachment styles. This can influence an individual's relationships, self-esteem, emotional regulation, and mental health in adult life. Exposure to traumatic events or adverse experiences during childhood can also lead to deep seated trust issues. As my answer to the question below shows, this can make entering a relationship with an incarcerated individual seem attractive.

Are there specific types of childhood trauma or dysfunctional family dynamics that are more commonly associated with women who develop romantic relationships with prisoners? If so, what patterns do you observe?

Women who have been abused (emotionally, psychologically, sexually) usually by their parents or prominent male figures in their lives, such as their fathers, uncles, boyfriends, husbands, enter adulthood psychologically wounded. These are women who have been deeply hurt and traumatised. As difficult as it may be for others to understand, when you're in a relationship with a man in prison, he cannot physically hurt you. In fact, it is often the woman here who is in a state of control. They are the ones on the outside. They are free. They decide when to go in and visit their prisoner partners or write letters to them. It is up to the woman to decide how far she wants to take the relationship. Knowing she cannot be hurt is key here. Childhood neglect and abuse often leads to difficulties with trust in relationships but when a woman enters into a relationship with a prisoner, she knows where he is at all times. Those trust issues are not present.

Can childhood trauma, such as abandonment or emotional neglect, create an unconscious desire for 'rescue' or a need to fix others, which might manifest in relationships with prisoners or individuals who are perceived as needing help or redemption?

Yes, childhood trauma can lead to a desire to 'fix' others in adult life. This often stems from an unconscious need to repeat or control situations that mirror their childhood trauma, or a belief that others need their help to survive. When these women enter relationships with prisoners, there is often this view that the whole world is against them and only they can 'rescue' that individual. The idea that "it is us against the world".

When I trained in trauma I was astounded at the impact adverse childhood experiences have on us. In my experience, these woman have ALWAYS experienced trauma as a child. The need to seek redemption because they couldn't fix a parent itself implies that there was trauma in their childhood.

****

Similarly, Holly Keller of Whitecap Counselling, a therapist with extensive experience in breaking dysfunctional cycles shared that there is a phenomenon called 'suicidal empathy' which can lead them to gravitate to people who are harmful.

One explanation for why some individuals become infatuated with or defend serial killers can be understood through Dr. Gad Saad's concept of "suicidal empathy." This concept suggests that excessive, unchecked empathy—when directed toward harmful figures—can cloud rational decision-making and lead to self-destructive outcomes. In this context, some individuals adopt this form of empathy to relate to the world, making them vulnerable to romanticising or defending dangerous figures like serial killers, even to the point of contacting or trying to date them.

This tendency is often rooted in early attachment trauma. Childhood abuse or neglect can cause individuals to form unhealthy attachments, sometimes even to their abusers. This dynamic of seeking validation from harmful figures can continue into adulthood, resulting in people-pleasing behaviours that cause individuals to sacrifice their well-being to gain approval. These tendencies can make someone more likely to empathise with a serial killer, as they seek acceptance, even in unhealthy or dangerous relationships.

The cultural shift toward extreme empathy reinforces these tendencies. Historically, empathy was balanced with rationality and protective boundaries. Today, empathy often overshadows these boundaries, particularly when directed at harmful figures. Media portrayals of individuals like Dahmer humanise them and distort their true nature, creating a false sense of connection and encouraging attachment.

Ultimately, it's a combination of early personal vulnerabilities and cultural influences that drive some individuals to romanticize or defend dangerous people, even serial killers.

****

Does the media depiction and sensationalism turn [criminals] into idols for people to look up to [and] covet? I wonder if a person who 'falls in love' with an incarcerated killer like Dahmer would go on to have similar tastes in their personal relationships. Would they be drawn to abusive people [or] criminals, or is it the fantasy of being with someone who is in prison and ultimately cannot harm them?

I agree that media depictions and sensationalism can elevate criminals like Dahmer into larger-than-life figures, almost like idols.

In response to your question, I think someone who falls in love with an incarcerated killer could develop similar patterns in their relationships. One concept that helps explain this is trauma bonding, where repeated abuse, mixed with moments of being "saved," creates an attachment. This can develop in adulthood as a result of childhood trauma, where the brain links love with abuse or neglect. In the case of a serial killer, it could be an extreme version of this bond. It's not about being drawn to hardened criminals, but rather an unconscious pull toward abusive dynamics that feel familiar.

Additionally, it's important to note that individuals who are abusive are more likely to engage in criminal behaviour. So, someone attracted to abusive relationships may be unconsciously drawn to others with antisocial tendencies.

As for the attraction being about the fantasy of being with someone who can't harm them, I think it's more about an unconscious draw to abusive dynamics. People who've been in relationships with narcissists, for example, may find themselves attracted to similar manipulative patterns, even if they don't recognise it. In narcissistic relationships, victims often idealise the abuser due to their charm and love-bombing tactics, which can feel familiar despite the harm.

An overly empathetic person, especially one with a history of trauma, may feel an urge to "fix" or "save" someone like Dahmer. If they hear he felt misunderstood or lonely, they might identify with his pain, even though his actions were horrific. This emotional manipulation—portraying oneself as a victim—can trigger a strong empathetic response and create an attachment, despite the person being harmful. It's a distorted attachment driven by empathy, where the individual fails to recognise the danger involved.

****

Dr. Manpreet Dhuffar-Pottiwal, a Chartered Psychologist explored Dahmer's paraphilic compulsions and how they may have come about, stemming from his early childhood.

Jeffrey Dahmer's crimes remain a grim testament to the interplay of childhood trauma, psychological pathology, and institutional neglect. Decades later, advances in forensic psychology illuminate how adverse childhood experiences (ACEs) and paraphilic disorders converged in his case, raising fraught questions about culpability, intervention, and whether his atrocities might have been preventable.

Adverse Childhood Experiences (ACEs)

Dahmer's early life was marked by profound neglect and instability, factors now recognised as critical ACEs linked to violent behaviour. His mother struggled with borderline personality disorder and attempted suicide when Dahmer was 18, while his father prioritised work over emotional connection. Isolated and bullied for his effeminate demeanour, Dahmer retreated into macabre fantasies, dissecting roadkill and hoarding animal bones by his early teens – a known precursor to necrophiliac behaviour. Modern ACEs research highlights how such trauma disrupts emotional regulation and fosters detachment, yet in the 1970s, these red flags were dismissed as eccentricities. Dahmer's middle-class whiteness likely shielded him from scrutiny, underscoring systemic biases in identifying at-risk youth.

Contemporary psychology classifies Dahmer's urges as paraphilic disorders, defined by the DSM-5 as intense, persistent sexual interests

Anthony Hughes was supposedly Dahmer's friend before he was murdered (FazeEma/ Wikimedia Commons)

Steve Tuomi was a young man with high hopes (Ontonagon High School 1979 Yearbook/ Wikimedia Commons)

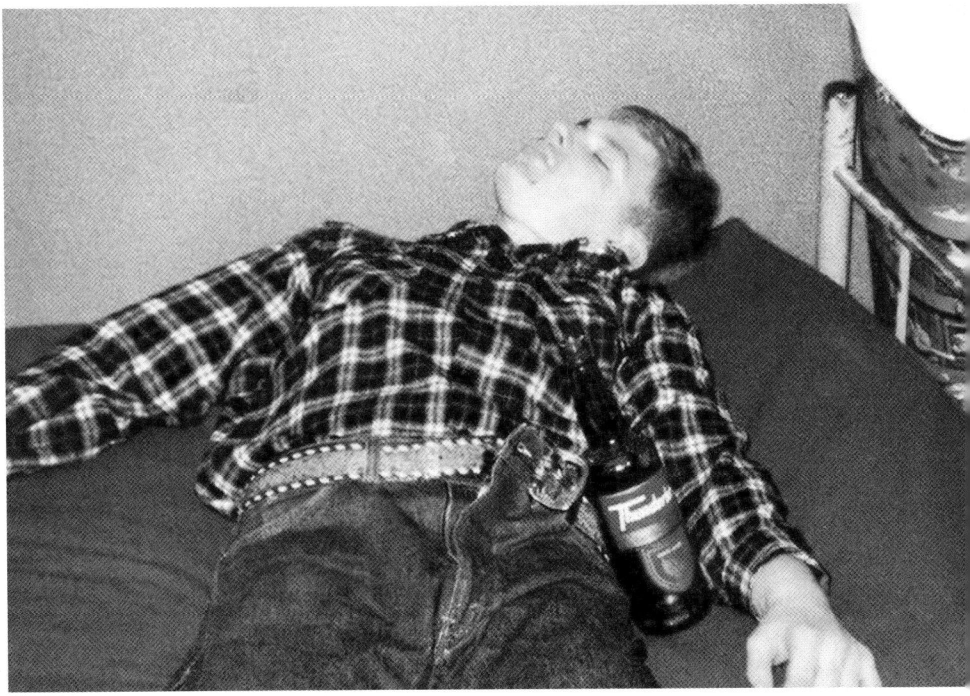

The killer murdered 17 young men and boys: Dahmer on the sofa. (David Rodriguez/ Wikimedi
Commons)

Dahmer had fantasies of killing long befor
he began his spree. (Revere Senior Hig
School/ Wikimedia Commons)

Anthony Hughes was deaf and mute. (Wisconsin School For The Deaf High School 1977 Yearbook/ Wikimedia Commons)

This bar is said to have been a frequent spot of Dahmer's. (Stephen Hogan/ Wikimedi Commons)

ahmer would frequent gay bars to pick his victims. (Stephen Hogan/ Wikimedia Commons)

A doodle from Revere Senior High School's yearbook in 1978 (Revere Senior High School Wikimedia Commons)

Dahmer was caught with a gruesome amount of evidence in his apartment (Adobe, file numb 468840612)

The killer used to dismember bodies in his bath tub (302820816)

Police found human remains in his refrigerator (410182758)

Police at the scene believed Dahmer's story (103931606)

Dahmer was dishonorably discharged from the military (334050717)

The teenager developed an alcohol problem (267227788)

He was known to be a strange, but isolated teenager at school (121097965)

Dahmer regularly attended Pride events and bars (122716309)

Many believe that the police were biased towards the victims (357956463)

Dahmer would dismember his victims (133686185)

The killer kept skulls in his home (115946044)

Dahmer was eventually caught after Tracy Edwards escaped (339509530)

Dahmer was once arrested for molesting a young boy (313531246)

Dahmer was handed 15 life sentences (233651206)

Investigators were horrified at what they found in Dahmer's apartment (243455589)

Dahmer grew isolated as a teenager (342835264)

As a young boy, Dahmer was neglected (243455589)

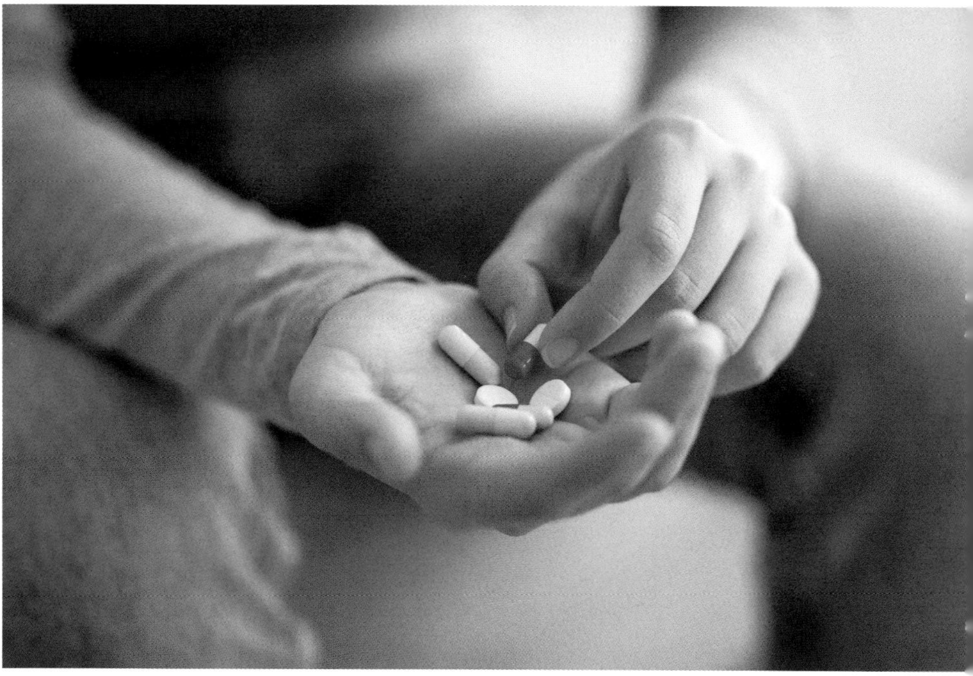

His mother took numerous pills when pregnant with him (470531824)

in non-consenting targets or acts causing harm. His necrophilia and attraction to adolescents (hebephilia) fit this framework, but modern research complicates the notion of "irresistible impulse". Kafka's work (2010) posits that paraphilias involve dysregulated dopamine pathways, akin to behavioural addictions. (Dahmer's rituals – e.g., preserving organs, constructing a shrine of skulls reflect this compulsivity). Yet his capacity to meticulously plan crimes (sourcing acid, evading police) suggests retained agency. Unlike psychosis, where reality-testing fails, Dahmer's awareness of his acts' illegality undermined legal claims of insanity.

Modern interventions

Today, paraphilic disorders might be managed with selective serotonin reuptake inhibitors (SSRIs) to reduce obsessive thoughts or anti-androgens to lower libido. In Dahmer's era, such treatments were stigmatised or reserved for extreme cases. His 1981 arrest for sexually assaulting a 13-year-old boy (a glaring missed opportunity) could have triggered court-mandated chemical castration, a practice used in the UK since the 1960s. Instead, he received probation, reflecting a systemic failure to link paraphilias to future violence.

The insanity dilemma

Dahmer's trial hinged on whether his mental state absolved him of responsibility. His defence argued that schizophrenia and necrophiliac disorder rendered him unable to control his impulses, but the jury rejected this. Under the M'Naghten Rule – insanity requires proof the defendant could not comprehend their acts' wrongfulness. Dahmer's calculated efforts to hide evidence (e.g., posing body parts as "medical specimens") demonstrated awareness, rendering his compulsions legally irrelevant. Even today, courts remain sceptical of volitional defences, fearing they excuse heinous acts. Recent proposals to expand insanity criteria to include "substantially impaired control" might reframe such cases, but ethical concerns persist.

Missed Interventions

Dahmer's escalation was punctuated by institutional failures, for example:

- 1978: After his first murder, he enlisted in the army but was discharged for alcoholism. No mental health evaluation addressed his paraphilic fixations.
- 1981: His conviction for sexually assaulting a minor led only to probation. Modern safeguarding frameworks, like the UK's Multi-Agency Public Protection Arrangements (MAPPA), would mandate risk assessments and treatment.
- 1986: Hospitalised for alcohol poisoning, Dahmer confessed to fantasies about "zombies". Staff dismissed this as drunken rambling, not a psychiatric crisis.

Had trauma-informed care existed, interventions might have included cognitive-behavioural therapy (CBT) for childhood cruelty or dialectical behaviour therapy (DBT) to manage compulsions. Medication, alongside monitoring, could have curbed his urges. Instead, indifference and stigma allowed his pathology to flourish.

Final notes:

Dahmer's case defies simple categorisation. His paraphilic disorders and ACEs explain his motivations but do not absolve his moral agency. Modern psychiatry offers tools to mitigate such compulsions, yet ethical tensions endure: pathologising "deviant" desires risks undermining autonomy, while ignoring them imperils public safety. For criminologists, Dahmer's story is a cautionary tale, a reminder that societies must intervene earlier in traumatised individuals, not to excuse future harm, but to prevent it. His atrocities were not inevitable, but the product of systemic failures as much as individual evil.

The Trial

Dahmer's trial was something that the whole nation was keen to follow, and the slew of horrid details that came to light proved to be too much for many to comprehend. After all, it proved a horrible thought: That even those who appear to be an everyday man, could be a killer lying in wait.

Dahmer's three-week trial was plagued by grim facts and evidence given by psychologists, criminologists, forensics and officers who attended the scene, but it was also a moment many had waited for. A moment where they could see the man who murdered their family member and tell him how they felt.

While the public watched with a detached and morbid curiosity, the families of the victims were listening to details about the torture their loved ones had suffered through in their final moments. For them, this was more than a crime of the century – it was their lives, their loss, and their pain.

While the prosecutors attempted to prove that Dahmer was sane, and the defence was unsuccessfully trying to prove that he was insane, the victims' families sat through horror after horror until it was their moment to speak to Dahmer face-to-face for the first time. Looking the man who had stolen the lives of their kin, their words were filled with anguish and grief – an enormous anger for some.

Carolyn Smith, a sister of Eddie Smith, said before the hearing that relatives hoped to 'let America know about Eddie and what we've been feeling all these months we have been going through this.'

"Don't let this man ever walk our streets and see daylight again," Janie Hagen, sister of Guerrero, said to the judge.

"Did you ever stop to think that this was someone's son? Did you ever stop to think that this is someone's brother, nephew, uncle, cousin, grandson, or just someone's friend," one family member asked. While the grief-stricken family members remained calm as they addressed

Dahmer one by one, the sister of Errol Lindsey screamed: "Jeffrey, I hate you!" numerous times. Even though nobody can know for sure just how they would react if they were forced to encounter their brother's, son's, cousin's murderer, they can very well understand why some family members reacted the way in which they did.

On February 15, 1992, Dahmer was convicted of the murder and dismemberment of 15 victims which led to him being handed a life imprisonment for each killing. Dahmer pleaded not guilty by reason of insanity. However, to find him insane, 10 of the jurors agreed that he did not suffer from a mental disease that prevented him either from knowing right from wrong or from being able to control his actions, echoing Isreal Reyes' description of an insanity plea in a court of law – something that will be explored in the next chapter.

The ruling was incredibly important to the prosecution, the families of the victims and to the nation, who had been watching and waiting for the news to break. It meant that legal justice would be served, and that this man, who had been unassuming in his looks, was not a madman who had begun a terrifying killing spree. In fact, he was merely a man with dark thoughts which he acted upon. Now, this is terrifying for a number of reasons. This is terrifying for a number of reasons: it meant that Dahmer was not a fluke or a person who had been struck down with a debilitating mental condition which made him act out beyond his control; he was a man who inflicted this pain knowingly, and even willingly, regardless of the consequences. Therefore, any person could go on to replicate the crimes, given the right circumstances and life experiences.

In 2026, a child could be born right now, with one parent who is emotionally neglectful, and another that is mentally struggling for a number of reasons. With little emotional bonding or attention, this child could go on to isolate themselves, even pick up a morbid hobby to satisfy themselves. Then, in an age of online presence, they may join groups and forums with other people who are interested in the grotesque, and it would be increasingly easy to find more and more deprived content. From there, those fantasies could spiral and coupled with alcohol consumption and the need to be close to somebody, by any means necessary – a killer is born. The Netflix show, *Adolescence* addresses this birth of a murderer perfectly.

Without intervention and with community services facing the chopping block when it comes to budgeting by local authorities and the governments, it is very easy to see how this could happen- even fifty years after Dahmer was sentenced to life in prison.

Part IV

Public Reaction

Elreacy Dock, a certified therapist on grief used her expertise to explore the overwhelming grief that Dahmer left in his wake. This included many different communities, families and the nation as a whole.

A City in Shock

The impact of Dahmer's crimes tore through Milwaukee, but also through the nation and even the world. From the victims' families to the local law enforcement, nobody made it out unscathed. However, those who felt it the most were those who were the closest to the crimes. Now, there were many groups that were directly affected by Dahmer's killings. The relatives, who lost loved ones to a senseless crime, the LGBTQ+ community, who had been preyed upon, at a time where tensions were high and discrimination and anti-LGBTQ+ crimes were not uncommon, and the community, who felt shocked, confused and devastated by the depravity seen in the case.

There also would have been profound guilt, confusion, grief and shock in the Dahmer homes, as their eldest son had been found to be a man capable of murder, sexual assault and even cannibalism. Elreacy Dock, a Thanatologist, Certified Grief Educator, Death Educator, Author, and Behavioral Health Consultant who has featured in publications such as *Vogue* and *BAZAAR* sat down with me and explained the many layers of grief that may have been felt at the time of the Dahmer exposure.

Grief Among Families of Dahmer's Victims

Decades after the initial loss of their loved ones, the victims' families continue to carry long-lasting grief and trauma. Media portrayals often provoke painful memories of the loss with explicit details of victim deaths or reenactments of events. Such exposure can lead to re-traumatisation among victims' families and cause intense grief responses. For example, following the release of the Netflix series *Dahmer – Monster: The Jeffrey Dahmer Story*, many of the affected families spoke out against the dramatization of their lived experiences.

These families stated that they weren't notified about the production of the series, emphasising that its release was deeply upsetting to those who are actively grieving and others who have navigated an extended path toward recovery from the trauma associated with the violent losses of their loved ones. Since information about the victims' murders is considered public record, their families typically aren't notified or compensated when documentaries are produced. These families are continually exposed to images and scenes that reactivate the trauma associated with the initial loss, often unexpectedly. Concerns surrounding the lack of consent from families and the dramatization of tragedy for mass consumption continue to emphasize the importance of questioning the ethics of true crime as a genre.

Grief Within Affected Communities

Since the majority of Dahmer's victims were boys and men of color within the LGBTQ community, their deaths highlighted the vulnerability experienced by individuals who belong to multiple marginalised groups. The collective grief that emerged among these communities was not only representative of mourning the individual lives who were lost to Dahmer's crimes but also the loss of safety within venues that were once considered safe spaces before Dahmer meeting victims in gay bars and other LGBTQ-friendly settings.

As the Dahmer case revealed multiple instances of systemic inequality, racism, and discrimination in law enforcement's handling of the crimes committed against LGBTQ individuals and minorities, collective grief shared in these communities was also reflective of a loss of security from the larger systems that had failed to protect them adequately.

The Grief and Guilt of Dahmer's Parents

Although often dismissed by society, Dahmer's parents faced a unique and complex grief experience that was frequently compounded by guilt and blame. While deeply impacted by the deaths of their son's victims, the Dahmers' also experienced many secondary losses resulting from his crimes. Most parents maintain hopes and dreams for their children's lives and the Dahmers weren't any different in this regard. However, their hopes and dreams for their son's future were lost amidst the violence of his crimes.

In learning about the severity of his actions and the deaths of his victims, the Dahmers' lost the sense of security they once had. Their perception and image of the son they had raised now differed significantly from who he had become, and these differences were difficult to reconcile. They experienced an ongoing internal conflict that was frequently misunderstood and disenfranchised in the eye of the public: two parents' love for their child in stark contrast with the gruesome reality of his deadly choices.

Amidst the scrutiny and hostility of public opinion, they would also scrutinize themselves with blame for Dahmer's actions. This ranged from concerns surrounding poor parenting and progressed to concerns regarding the potential lack of appropriate mental health support. Still, regardless of what rationale influenced the reasons for blame, the resulting guilt continued to exacerbate their grief for years.

The stigma surrounding their identities as parents of a serial killer ultimately led to social isolation, dismissal, and frequent misunderstandings, often to the extent that the Dahmers' relied on using aliases to avoid drawing any further attention to themselves. During Dahmer's imprisonment, the presence of ambiguous loss would also be a prominent reminder for his parents, emphasised by his absence in their lives and the impact of his actions in the context of their underlying family dynamics. When Dahmer was later murdered in 1994 while serving his sentence in prison, his parents faced backlash as they grieved.

As the Dahmers' mourned the loss of their son, much of the public response to the news of his death was supportive. Victims' families also had mixed responses, some of which were celebratory. These reactions undoubtedly contributed to an intensely emotional experience as the Dahmers' continued grieving throughout the remainder of their lives.

Dock's analysis of the crime's effect on those around Dahmer shows the magnitude of his criminal activities, but also with how it didn't pull the community together in its shared grief – it divided it. The ostracised Dahmer's' faced what parents of killers typically have to survive, and the fallout in this instance was immense and lasted until their deaths.

Of course, the Dahmers' were not the only people to receive such backlash, as the police department were also slated for what the public and victims' families believed to be failings in the department and also the judicial system.

To this, Alex Alvarez, an attorney and partner of Integrity for Justice spoke about his time on the force in the 80s and beyond.

Alvarez is no stranger to judicial scandals, as he played a key role in The Miami River Cop Scandal in 1984.

At this time, there were a group of 19 police officers who were eventually convicted of various state and federal crimes including murder, racketeering, robbery, drug possession, civil rights violations and even conspiracy charges.

The group of corrupt officers began to steal money and drugs from motorists stopped for traffic violations to sell for a profit in an organized criminal operation. They then started to go after bigger operations through tip-offs from police informants, but this was their undoing. On July 13, 1985, the officers seized hundreds of kilograms of cocaine which were hidden in the *Mitzi Ann*, a boat docked at the Tamiami Marina. On this day, ten people dressed as officers forced their way into the Jones Boat Yard and raided a pleasure boat named the *Mary C*, which saw them seize $10 million worth of drugs. However, during the raid, three of the seven crewmembers who were unloading the cocaine drowned whilst attempting to escape. When the bodies were found by police at a later date, it was believed that it was a drug bust gone wrong, until witnesses revealed that police were responsible for attempting to steal the goods, with some revealing that officers screamed 'kill them'.

The corruption was uncovered during the investigation into the deaths of the crew when officers were apprehended attempting to sell the cocaine to undercover agents. Alvarez headed a covert recording sting operation, blowing the case wide open.

With so much expertise in investigations, policy, courtrooms as an attorney and more, Alvarez's insights into the failings of the Dahmer case were an eye-opening conversation.

****

I know that you were on the Miami River Cop Scandal, what I was interested in was: Because you've been on such a large scale investigation before – I was wondering whether you could talk me through your role in the Miami River Cop Scandal, and then also how you would tackle an investigation such as Dahmer's; something so big and so scandalous.

Right. So, you know, the trick to working big cases is the way you should work a normal case. The moment you start straying from what you would normally do in a case is to try to come up with something different. That's when things usually go wrong. I always say, rationalisation is the enemy of objectivity. Right? Because people tend to rationalise other people's action. That's called confirmation bias.

So, you just got to follow the evidence, and I think when these big cases- what ends up happening with a lot of investigators is they get they get consumed by the fact that they're working on such a big case and that they don't follow the rules, and they don't follow the procedures like they should, and you just got to tune everything out and just focus on what's in front of you. And that's what we did. We did do some unique stuff in the Miami River Cops case because typically homicides are a reactive investigation, right? It's like something happens and then you react, and then you work backwards.

There's an aspect of that in every homicide case, and the river cops' case we did that. But we also did what we called a proactive investigation. In that case, what we did is we found out who these crooked cops were working with on the street, we got them to roll over, we got them to wear wired wires on these people and sent them in to talk to [the corrupt cops]. So that was very helpful. That's not typically what ends up happening in a homicide investigation, because I would say that probably 99 of all homicide investigations are reactive.

You work your way backwards, right. We had to do both, and so that's what I think made this case unique and we were working to find guys who were cops. So, we knew that that was going to be (obviously) a problem.

It would just seem to me that [in the Dahmer case] the lights never went off on the investigators' screen, you know. So, I don't know how much of that was because they just weren't paying attention. I think the way they finally caught the guy is that some guy got away, right? Some guy got away that he was trying to kill, and that guy kind of led them, and they went back and the whole thing kind of, you know. But I'm sure that there should have been warning signals, the guy killed like 20. At some point somebody had to connect the dots and that's the problem with serial murders, isn't it?

Sometimes it takes a long time to really connect the dots, and, unless you're really paying attention, it's very, very difficult. I'm not critical of what they did because I don't know enough about it to be critical one way or another. But I could tell you that, being a homicide investigator – to be an effective homicide investigator, you've got to cancel out all the noise and all the politics, and all the influences that that come with a big case. I mean I was 26 years old, when I had that case. So, to be honest with you, I was too young to realise that there was pressure. There's a reason that they send kids who are 18 or 19 to war, right? Because they don't question it. I think a lot of it was that probably at 40, I probably would have been more influenced by the pressure of what exactly we were doing. I felt no pressure. To be honest, I felt zero pressure. To me it was just 'okay, there's bodies here, these cops are involved. How are we going to catch them? Let's go. Let's do this.' We just worked our way through it and I didn't realise the magnitude and the scope of how much media attention it was getting, and when it finally got there, it was like 'no big deal', I don't really care. It's not changing me. It's not changing the way I'm going to do things but, the bottom line is, for people that do this work – you've just got to tune things out and just do the same thing that you would normally do and the moment you start deviating from that is when things can fall through the cracks because you're not following the procedures there. The rules are there for a reason.

With the Jeffrey Dahmer case – so a little bit of background on his trajectory: so as a child, he had a neglectful childhood, he had a hernia operation in his groin which made him quite obsessive about his genitalia, and then he started to become obsessed with animal bones and dead bodies and the anatomy. From there, he wanted to control people. specifically, men because he was struggling with his sexuality. Some reports say that he was molested at age eight, and he did go on to molest another boy, as an adult.

The brother of that boy he molested was his victim and that boy was 14 at the time. He escaped from Dahmer's apartment, and he had rectal bleeding, and he was disorientated and drugged, and he ran into two cops. Dahmer was then able to convince the cops that he was his boyfriend, and they released him back into his care before he murdered him. So, it was a little bit of an 'opportunities were missed' situation. But this was in a time and an area that was quite known for poverty, crime and the gay scene as well. So, I suppose maybe if you're not looking for a murderer, you're not going to find a murderer?

Right, yeah. That's confirmation bias right there. So, what you have there is some officers being confronted with facts: A disoriented kid rectal bleeding, dishevelled, saying he was molested and some guy said, 'this is my boyfriend'. People want to take the path of least resistance, the path of least resistance to do nothing and say, 'this is just a dispute of the disturbance between two people who have a relationship', you know? No report [to be filed by the cops]. Obviously, that was an opportunity to address this issue, and they didn't do it. I'm sure that happens a lot in low-income areas. If this is a rich kid, that's not going to happen. The parents are going to come and this is going to be a bigger issue. That unfortunately is the war, [and] that's the world we live in. There's a culture in law enforcement.

Every profession has a culture and the longer you're in that profession, that culture becomes more ingrained. I imagine these guys were uniform Patrol officers who are trained to clear calls and go to the next call – go to the next call and go to the next call and put out fires. Their jobs aren't to be social workers or [their] jobs aren't to be investigators, although if they see something, they're supposed to call an investigator.

[The boy Dahmer murdered] was still part of a minority group, there's an issue with minority groups and law enforcement, right? I think we've come a little further, but we haven't come nearly as far as probably people who want it to. That's why you're going to miss things. This is a systemic problem; it's not a one-off problem. That's how [the cops] were trained. They're trying to move on. When you're given two competing stories, the story that typically the cop on the street's going to go with is the one that confirms that this is probably the disturbance between two lovers. "I'm done with this. I'm not getting involved in this. I'm moving on." That's the easiest way to get out of it, right? So, that's what happened. It's unfortunate. In training, they don't train to de-escalate, and they don't train to investigate. They train to protect you from everything, and you think that every traffic stop, someone's going to try to kill you. It's probably less than point zero, zero of one percent that on a traffic stop an officer is going to get hurt. But yet we train that every stop is a potential [cop death]. We're training the wrong way.

You see, you're training the wrong way. It's a systemic problem in our criminal justice system, all the way through. Do I blame these officers? No, I just think they're just a victim of the culture.

I wanted to ask you about systemic failures, because of the two cops who let him go, but also because there were 17 victims, and a lot of people came out to say that the Milwaukee police had failed to stop him sooner.

They let the boy go and that was failure. However, would there really have been many more opportunities to catch him if he was targeting men in gay clubs and taking them home, making them believe that they were going to have sex? And if these were people that are underage and in clubs, they probably weren't closely monitored by their families. They probably had a lot of freedom, so was it a systemic issue that he wasn't caught sooner or was it more that the people he chose just happened to be people that wouldn't be found [by police] so easily?

So, he's a predator who's a pro. Just think, the predators prey on the weak. Just like for example if you're in Africa in the Savannah and you look at the lion, who's he chasing? He's chasing the weakest one right he can catch. That's the same thing here. Predators are trained instinctively to pray on the weak. They're not going to pray on somebody who's surrounded by his family, and his friends, he's in a group, and he looks like he's well liked and they're having a good time, and he tries to pull somebody away from that. That's not what's going to happen. The thing happened with Wayne Williams, the Atlanta murders. The same thing happened there. If you look at all these serial murderers, they're all obviously disturbed, but they always pick on the on the weak link. Whether they're prostitutes like the ones in LA: the hillside murders. When you look at all those things, there's a similarity in preying on easy victims, and those are the people that are discarded the quickest by law enforcement.

Those are the ones that are the quickest to [be discarded] because they there's victim blaming. This is your problem. [They say]: "Why are we wasting our time on this?", "Do you believe this person? Look at the background that goes on." I don't know if there's a solution for that.

That's how these guys get away with doing, 15, 20, or something murders, before they get caught. The only reason this guy got caught was by accident. Some guy got away, and he probably still would be doing this. Of course.

Who had so many? Was it BLK?

Yeah, Kansas City. This guy went for almost 20 something years before he got caught. I think he did a Manifesto, and I think that's finally how they were able to trace some of it back to this guy and he lived a normal life, right? He was married wife and kids, and he had a stable job. But look who we prayed on. You know the FBI has a group that does a lot of profiling and all that is data mining. It's just looking at looking at the science and looking at similarities and being able to piece it together. It's: "How are you going to catch these serial murderers?" I think the way to catch them is the is the go upstream and try to find these find these kids before they become problems. These kids are going to be poor, so they're going to be problematic kids, they're going to be mostly poor kids or middle-class kids in the school system. That's failing. Nobody wants to say, 'hey, this kid's got problems, he's going to be a serial murderer'. I don't think these teachers are trained that way, and do you want to really stigmatise these kids at a young age and put a label on them? It's going to carry them through life. There's obviously a problem with that. I don't know if there's an easy solution to that problem. I think we're gonna have to just live with serial killers for a while, and [we] just have to find a better way of trying to catch them earlier.

When you look at these kids who are doing these mass shootings – there was another one in in FSU in Tallahassee – if you look at them, they're always young, white, middle class, kids, in their early 20s. Why? In the UK, you don't have easy access to firearms, it's very difficult. It's one of the things I fought for a while: is to have more gun control here but it's not happening. It's in the culture. It may be a long time before we see any change in that but, I think it's a two-prong problem. It's mental health. You see these kids are all sick, and then it looks like it's something that develops and then they have access to guns and then something sets them off, and they go on a shooting spree. I think social science has got to study that for a while and figure out what's going on. I mean, again, the short answer is we're living in a screwed-up society with a lot of bad people. But I don't know what the answer is, to be honest with you.

It's a complex issue; there's too many nuances and layers to prevention. What we're doing now isn't working, but I can't personally see a way that we can prevent everything from happening and someone will slip through the cracks.

Of course. The idea is that to get some sort of sealer and try to seal the big holes and obviously some seepage [will occur] but if you try to cover these big holes… I don't think gun control is the answer altogether because you could just ban, but people are gonna get guns, right. People are gonna keep too many guns out there. These guys aren't going to turn in their guns. This is not going to happen, right? So, there's enough guns in there to kill the world, a hundred times over again. I think 'it's an upstream issue' [is correct]. You've got to catch these kids upstream [and] if you don't catch them upstream, it's just too late. You're just gonna have to live with the consequences downstream.

Alverez to me: *What is your interest in Dahmer on this? Why Dahmer versus someone else?*

For Dahmer, it's really the fact that I like to know how people turn into killers. In this case, he looked unsuspecting, and also because there's so many conflicting reports from his parents on his childhood. However, witness statements say that he was neglected, his mum was very mentally ill, his dad was very emotionally neglectful, and he had this trajectory of just so many instances where you could have picked up that something was wrong. So, he was a teenage alcoholic, he was a toddler obsessed with murder and obsessed with skinning animals and preserving them in jars. He was also a loner who was very awkward with social interaction, he was very smart, but academically – not at all. He was dishonourably discharged from the military because of his mental health and then he just went on this crusade and in a very strange way.

I mean, he injected acid into someone's head to make them stay with him forever, like a controllable zombie. He wanted – I feel like – at the root of it all, he was just a very deeply disturbed and lonely person.

I really wanted to find out the areas of where you can pinpoint where he could have been helped or stopped before the murders began.

I wanted to approach it more as like a criminologist's point of view, rather than a sensational, True Crime entertainment book. I think he was the biggest one that I'm quite interested in as opposed to Bundy and the Green Bay killer and people like that.

Back to Alvarez, who talks about the issues within the law enforcement industry, who he states do not collaborate with one another.

The other systemic problem that we have is that when you say government, what does that mean? You look at South Florida, Miami-Dade County, there's 30 municipalities, there's 30 police departments, do they share? No. Each one of them has their own little precinct. You can't assume that you go a mile, you're in another place, and you do a crime there. Is there coordination? No, I mean we saw that after 9/11.

The CIA doesn't talk to the to the FBI, the FBI doesn't talk to the NYPD. There's just not that [collaboration]. Some of that has changed after 9/11, but when you look at law enforcement, you look at these people who are or were the problems, there's not an organised way that I imagine [to be created].

Now with AI, you can probably throw all that data into AI, maybe not their medical records because they are protected by something called HIPAA, but their student records and their criminal records and things like that – you could probably get a good idea of who your problem people are and prevent it with counselling or, I don't call it surveillance, but more follow-up. That's a good use of AI. No one's thought about that yet. If I could wave a magic wand and I was King for the day in the United States, maybe I would do something like that. But it would take legislation to make sure that everybody talks to each other, and bureaucracy doesn't like sharing. Those are the systemic problems that I see, but using AI for positive… [could be a solution].

That's really eye-opening and especially with the prevention issues and how complex that is. I thought maybe it was a little simpler, but obviously, of course, there's the problem that you don't want to stigmatise these kids. It will follow them, and they're probably already being bullied, or they have a bad home life. It's a little bit more nuanced and there's more things going on in their lives that are probably contributing to this, and you can't really pinpoint who's at risk to actually cause harm, and who's just at risk of thinking of negative things or being depressed.

Whilst people may have heavily focused on Dahmer, his home life, the ways in which his crimes could have been prevented – there was also another issue that was at the forefront of his case. People were angry at what they perceived as police negligence. Many who followed the case were particularly struck by the failing of two police officers who had released a victim back to Dahmer, allowing him to be murdered not thirty minutes later. This question, and the question of Dahmer's trial considerations, which focused heavily on whether there should have been a specific way the trial was carried out due to his extensive history of psychological issues and childhood infatuations with the dead, led to a special interview with Israel Reyes. Reyes is a former US investigative detective, judge, and now works at his own law firm in Miami.*

Reyes is the founder and Managing Partner of The Reyes Law Firm, P.A., in Coral Gables, Florida. He is a former Circuit Court Judge of the Eleventh Judicial Circuit of Florida appointed by former Governor Jeb Bush on August 14, 2003, and he retired on May 22, 2011, after approximately thirty years of public service as a judge, assistant state attorney, and police detective. Currently, he works on civil and criminal litigation cases, representing attorneys, receivers, commercial entities, and individuals. While a member of the judiciary, he served as the Associate Administrative Judge of the Circuit Civil Division in both the Criminal and Juvenile Divisions. While serving as the Associate Administrative Judge, he began the eCourtesy

Submission Service. This is an online delivery method for providing served documents and proposed orders to judges. Prior to this, he was a County Court Judge in the Criminal Division.

Before taking the bench, Reyes was an Assistant State Attorney in the Racketeering and Organized Crime Unit, Civil Forfeiture Section. He handled the litigation of civil forfeitures concentrating on illegal drug money laundering cases, and he was one of the principal drafters of the revised state money laundering bill signed into law by Governor Bush on July 1, 2000. He authored 'Florida's Anti-Money Laundering Statutes' in 1999 and was the attorney of record in several Florida Appellate Court cases dealing with civil forfeiture actions.

His knowledge on police handlings, training, detective work and judge considerations is extensive, bringing forth important insights into just how it would have been for the police officers to work on the Dahmer case through the 90s.

Israel Reyes

I'm writing a book about Jeffrey Dahmer, but I'm writing a book that's more from a criminologist perspective. So, his upbringing, the judicial system, and the trial, and then also maybe how he became a murderer and if there were any failings along the way to prevent it or to stop him earlier. Really, what I like to focus on is – because of his mental health conditions, he was psychopathic, and he was necrophiliac and all of these types of things – how this would impact maybe a courtroom, or a court system, and then also because of how high profile it was: How would this also impact a fair and a just trial?

I was a homicide detective and then I eventually became a lawyer, then I became a judge dealing with criminal cases in addition to murder cases. So, I presided over murder cases as a judge in addition to other types of criminal cases and I was a homicide detective. So maybe that's a way we can talk about it, from those two perspectives.

From your experience on the bench, how would you evaluate the overall handling of the trial from arraignment to sentencing?

As far as mental issues involving a case like this, there are crimes that are made up of elements- every crime has elements which I always call the recipe. That's the recipe for the crime. But overall, generically the elements of a burglary or entering and remaining. In Florida, entering and remaining in a structure or conveyance with the intent to commit a crime. That's the elements of a burglary. But the elements of a crime, a generic crime, is 'mens rea' which is the mental intent to do something; plus, actus reus: which is doing the act; plus, concurrence: as they both have to be happening at the same time; plus causation: It has to cause the crime and then minus any defences.

So that's the crime equation – mens rea plus actus reus, plus concurrence, plus causation, minus defences equal a crime. Let's talk about the insanity. Really, insanity is not a medical condition, and insanity is not a legal defence. It's a defence that that has developed over the years with the M'Naghten test and a few other things, that is basically the best way to remember it. Insanity is a mens rea eraser. It says: 'you did not have the mental capacity to know right from wrong so there's no mens rea, therefore you're guilty of the crime but you have a defence'. Because remember, I told you, you've got to have all these things to have a crime.

So, it's a mens rea eraser and it has to be occurring at the time you commit the crime. That Insanity, that defect of the mind, of the brain, has to be occurring at the time you come into crime because if it happens after, well, it doesn't matter because it's not a mens rea eraser – that ship has sailed so to speak. So that's Insanity.

Now incompetency – which is different – is something that arises during the course of the trial, another trial of the litigation of the

Court proceedings. That basically says that, because you have some mental defect, you cannot assist in your defence. You don't understand the implication of the charges, the ramifications or you cannot assist in your defence. When the defence attorney raises incompetency, the court procedure [Florida in this instance], the court will appoint psychologists that will examine the defendant and say he's competent or he's incompetent.

If a court finds that he's competent, we continue with the litigation, but if a court finds that he's incompetent, then you suspend the proceedings, you don't drop the charges, you end the proceedings, you get them psychiatric help that they need to restore them to competency and once they're restored to competency, then it's 'let's bring him back'. Some people cannot be restored to competency, but most of the time, they can. There's a lot of malingering that goes on by the way, as we all know. So those are the main differences between those two criminal aspects and of course, there's mental retardation.

Mental retardation means that you have a defect of the brain, you have something you can't adapt, but that has to occur before you're age 17. With mental retardation an adult can't come in and say, 'by the way, I've never been diagnosed with this but I'm mentally retarded'. It could be something else but it's not mental retardation. Mental retardation does not shield you from crime, as it's not competency and it's not mitigating and it's not dissenting. You could still be charged and sentenced.

It's interesting. With the Jeffrey Dahmer case they probably raised insanity because they're saying, 'hey listen, he had a defect, such that he didn't realise what he was doing, therefore, he couldn't form the intent'. So that's a no for mens rea or no crime because of that missing part of the equation.

Now, from a perspective of a homicide detective, we understand all that. We just go ahead and investigate the case as if the person is competent and not insane, that's not for us to make that call. Except if we, as detectives, are reading somebody their Maranda rights and we can say 'listen, he cannot knowingly intelligently and voluntarily waive his rights because this person doesn't know, you know, anything, he doesn't understand what's going on'. Whatever the reason is, we're not doctors, we're not doctors and especially we're not mental health professionals. So, we plough ahead and let the courts decide. If the person gives a confession, we document what they wrote and that's it. In all my years as a detective, there was only one time that I did not go forward with a statement.

It was an older woman; I think she had dementia. You know, actually, she was senile and whatever I was putting in front of her, she was signing, she wasn't even reading, she was signing. I didn't take a confession, I said, 'listen, I'm not gonna do this and whatever happens, happens. Sure enough, she had all these things, and she was never convicted and she eventually died in a mental health facility. That's the only time I've ever done that because it was so overt, you know, so clear. She just didn't understand anything else going on and she had stabbed her longtime friend. She was washing dishes and her longtime friend – who's another elderly woman who said something to her -- and she was washing, she turned around and with the knife and just stabbed her and killed her. So that coupled with what I saw when I had her in the interview room, I said, 'listen, I'm not even gonna try to get her to waiver rights'. So, anyway, people – sometimes murderers – they'll try to fake it. We just plough ahead, and we let the court decide. That's from my perspective as a homicide detective and as a judge.

I would have competency issues arise and insanity issues – but I'd have competency issues arise, not just within the homicide context – within any other crime because it could be used for other crimes. [As a judge] I'm going to appoint doctors; I ask the state, who do you want as a doctor and then I ask the defence; who do you want?

They would examine the defendant individually. Sometimes the doctors agree, sometimes the doctors didn't agree [but] when they agreed the lawyers would stipulate that either he was competent or not competent. When they disagreed, I'd appoint a4e3 third doctor and then I have a hearing and after the hearing I determine whether they're competent or not to go forward. It's a very simple process in that sense.

Then I put it on a status report every month or so to see how he's doing. Now, in Florida, if a judge declares someone incompetent and sends them to a hospital, we suspend the proceedings [and the person] goes to the hospital. If that person remains [in the hospital] and it remains in that status that he's incompetent for five years or more and a judge doesn't declare that person competent…

Even if a doctor finds that he's competent, the charges against them have to be dismissed. I remember a case that I had where I had someone who committed a very, very serious crime and the prosecutor screwed up, they forgot to put it in front of a judge, even though doctors have found him competent. They forgot to put it in front of a judge, so the judge could hold the hearing and make that determination. Because the rule in the statute says it has to be a judge who finds [him] incompetent, not that a doctor has just found incompetent. If he remains incompetent for five years or more, the charges against him must be dismissed.

I have no choice but to dismiss the charges. So, it's a very interesting. An order I wrote on a murder case I had as a as a judge where someone, a man, committed a crime – shot and killed a probation officer. He's on probation and during the time that he was on death row and all the countless appeals that they that they can file. The Supreme Court said that if you're mentally retarded, you cannot be executed. You cannot be executed. So, of course, he says, 'hey mentally retarded', you know?

They file a motion. I appointed doctors. I wrote around a 45-page order and I found out he wasn't mentally retarded because no time before he was age 17, had that ever come up. It might have been something else. In other words, you could have the same symptoms and the same disease as someone who's been diagnosed [as] mentally retarded, but it's not a mental retardation. It's something else if it didn't manifest before you were 17.

With intense media coverage and like public outrage, how does this impact having a neutral courtroom proceeding as well as like a neutral and fair investigation?

That's a very good question. So, because of the First Amendment and the freedom of the press [Act], you can't do a press blackout. You can't do that. The press is free to write whatever they want to write. I think that's a great thing, honestly. My last three years on the police department, when I was going through law school, I was assigned to the media relations office. We have laws about that, and I followed the statute, whether I agreed with it or not, and it is what it is. But one thing that the law does mandate is that all the police records that are turned over to the defendant are automatically public records. The media can get him, anyone can get them, right? It's a very open process, except a confession. The public and the media do not have the right to public records. That outline, the confession of a defendant, they'll hear it whenever there's a court proceeding eventually, [and] they will hear that in court. When the circumstances of whether or not there was a confession and what the defendant said, then it's fair game.

But before that, the media is not allowed and it's not permitted, and the police department does not have to turn over [nor does] the prosecutor. The fact that the defendant confessed and why he said that, because that will highly prejudice the potential jurors because the potential jurors come from the community. What the court can do, is the court can order the media not to reveal the jurors' names [and] not to film the jurors. Of course, the court cannot close the courtroom [just] to close the courtroom. It's a long process and it just never happens; it never happens in those murder cases.

It'll happen in a child molestation case – you can do that – and a child can testify via close circuit TV. But as far as a murder case, it's got to be an open process, because there have been people that have been wrongly convicted. I have no problem as a public official. When I was a public official, as long as the law permitted of everybody to see whatever we were doing, I welcomed that. So that's how you try to protect the percentage for the due process to protect everyone's due process rights.

I was working another big case, it was called the San Pedro case. That was the name of the main defendant. It was a corruption. Fraud, murder-for-fire, huge case. His girlfriend became an informant, [and] she put a microphone in his office. We had one of our one of our detectives working undercover as himself, but as if he was corrupt. He was playing a part of himself, [and] every meeting he had, we recorded, we were all there listening because he wasn't corrupt. That was his thing.

And then we have a police Union. So, we had the president of the Union, who was a police officer – he went undercover for us as the president of the Union who was willing to be 'bribed'. Of course, we had his girlfriend who was living with him and she was very upset with him and so she put a microphone in his office for us. We were listening to conversations that were going on when he was meeting all these people. It was a very, very interesting case. It was a two-year case, his name is Alberto San Pedro, and it was a very interesting case. But during that time, I was working at Alex [Alvarez], who was working the River Cop case.

He's been on the Cocaine Cowboys series, [and] he's a lawyer now too. He has a law firm now.

Regards to Dahmer, there was an instance of where he could have been stopped. Well, there were two. In his early days, he was arrested for molesting a young boy, and then he was given a very light sentencing because he hadn't been in trouble before. Then a couple years later, after he was beginning to murder people, it was the brother of the boy he molested that had escaped his apartment and ran into two cops. Dahmer convinced the two cops that he was his boyfriend or friend, and he was allegedly inebriated, and he should come back home with him. However, the boy who was 14 is said to have exhibited displays of being heavily under the influence of a drug or alcohol, scared and also having injuries on him. But the police gave him back to Dahmer. So, I'm wondering from an investigator's point of view: is this just individual failing, or is there a process here, that maybe they should have followed?

No, I'll give you an opinion by the way of not knowing everything. I'll tell you of course it was a failing, right? Because and eventually that kid was murdered, right? Of course it was a failing, when there are times when police interact and someone dies, something failed – whether it was on the police's end or on the social aspects. Before even the police got involved, it's a failure where that failing comes from.

I don't know, [it] could have been improper training, could have been the policy of the department at the time. Could it be the incompetence of the officers, could have been the laziness of the officers? Who knows? But clearly there's a failing because someone died, right? And whether that failing arises to the level of negligence or not, you know, that's for someone else [to determine].

But you know the society or that society (the police and the government), I think their number one thing is to protect life in property, right? And so when something happens to one or both of those things, there is a failing somewhere along the line. Whether it was police or something that led to the police being involved that happened before, that was out of the hands of the police, there's nothing they could have done something.

In regards to the criminal justice system, how is it equipped to deal with defendants who have severe psychological disorders, someone that has such a long history of psychological issues and petty crimes, and that trajectory… at the time of sentencing?

If it's in that sense, the Florida statutes have very clear mitigating factors a court has to consider when the jury recommends this. I can tell you the statute number and then at the same on the other side of the equation, there are aggravating factors that the state can rely on to try to convince the court to impose it. But it comes from a jury recommendation.

There's so much jurisprudence out there, in fact mostly from the US Supreme Court, and then of course, from the Florida courts. There's a lot of case law that's recently changed. Florida changed the framework after the Marjorie Spellman Douglas shooter. I think two jurors didn't vote for death and even though the majority of the jury wanted death, the judge was handcuffed and couldn't impose death.

If you Google him and the death penalty and what the governor said, they passed the new statute that changed that procedure. So, that's taken into account. Of course, if you were mentally retarded, if you were diagnosed with mental retardation, unless that's changed, you can't be put to death.

There's always what's known out there as jury nullification, although the jury never sentences in death cases – the jury recommends – but sentencing is always a purview of the judge, a judge could take into account.

If he or she wants to take into account that he's legally permissible to do. So, depending on the circumstances of the case – it depends on what the law was at that time. Because the death penalty jurisprudence is always evolving. There's always something going on and somebody making some kind of appeal, for example, there are there are two appellate courts in Florida. There's a district courts of appeal and six of them are on the state depending on where you are geographically, and then there is the Florida Supreme Court, which is the ultimate Court for state law.

When you're sentenced to death, whether the defendant wants an appeal or not, the defendant gets an automatic appeal to the Florida Supreme Court. They skip over the first appellate level, and it automatically goes to the Supreme Court. Even if the defendant says, 'I'm ready to die.' It's an automatic appeal. And then, of course, if they want to keep going, then they can go through the federal system and have appeals. Then when the governor signs the death warrant, automatically they have judges on standby because the automatic appeals start again, all the way to the USA Freeport. It's a very, very long process. For the judge's State, the law allows him to take into consideration in determining sense.

I know the police got a lot of backlashes after the Dahmer case was released, and mainly they said that police turned a blind eye to Dahmer because his victims were black, gay and poor. I'm wondering how, as an investigator, would you handle this if you were working in a marginalised community and a big serial killing crime had happened there? How would you feel that people were saying this but then also, how would you mitigate it as well?

What people's opinions are about me and about the police, I don't listen to. Because honestly, I do everything the same. I go out there – I'm talking about when I was a homicide detective. It doesn't matter to me. If it was the richest neighbourhood in town or the poorest neighbourhood, I spent the majority of my time working murders and, in the hood, in the worst areas of Dane County. Life is a life; it didn't matter to me. So, all those all those peripheral things never played a part in my investigations. I did everything the same way. You know, it doesn't matter to me who was killed, whether they were a good person, whether they're a bad person; it doesn't matter that. That never played a part in in my analysis. In my investigation, I went out there, I vacuumed the facts. I put everything in my report, I didn't see anything one way or another, I presented to the court system and whatever the court system did with it – I wasn't there to make any type of social [or] take any type of social position or anything like that. It doesn't matter. Those are not factors for me, honestly. So, I suppose it would be stressful though. I suppose it would be really stressful with the scrutiny that police would have been under, and the judge would have been under. We call them media cases, it's a media case.

So of course you're going to be second guessed, and things like that. The thing is just to handle the case the way you would handle any other case, [and] don't let that encroach or seep into your investigation.

Follow the established investigative steps, and techniques and law and just go out and do what you got to do. So again, to me, a murder was a murder. I worked the same way. There would have been more resources at my disposal, of course, because you have multiple victims. It's like, it's extensive and that case is going to be heavily defended, but it doesn't matter. Even if the case is not going to be heavily defended, we always went in, and I have to pride the training I got. I have to pride myself on the training I received and pride myself in the fact that I worked for the Miami-Dade Police Department, which is now called the sheriff's office. Now, we had the best training and our mandate was getting to the truth. If the truth honours someone, great. If it doesn't, great. Just get to the truth. That's it. That's all we want you to do.

There's always pressure when you're investigating a murder because somebody's dead and you want to make sure that [you are] following all the constitutional and statutory, and investigative steps [and] that you don't railroad someone. You protect your rights because, look, even from a self-serving standpoint, if you don't protect the defendant's constitutional rights, he's going to walk. So for the integrity [of the] investigation, you want to do that, right?

You always want to make sure you investigate that case to the extent that you can with the resources you have. Because you don't want that person… if they're gonna kill, you want to prevent that person from killing again.

It's all about constitutional rights, you know, of the of the defendant and of course, the Constitutional rights of the victims and the kins have constitutional rights too.

But if you follow the law, I have to tell you, you're gonna be fine as a law enforcement officer if you follow the laws. In a way, it's very easy. Those jobs are very easy. If you don't have an agenda, right? And [if] you don't have an outcome. But when you have political agendas and you're trying to change the facts or you're trying to not apply the law, because you don't like the law and that's not the job of the executive, and it's not the job of the Judiciary either. You're not supposed to ignore the law, just because you don't like it. A judge cannot do that, a judge, whether he or she agrees with the law or not, you have to apply that law.

So as long as you do those two things, you're fine, whatever the outcome is. You can't change the facts, and you can't change the law.

Authors Note: **Mental retardation is an outdated and often offensive term, and is now known as 'intellectual disability'.**

Media Frenzy

As with any high-profile case, those who were present throughout the trial and aftermath will know just how much people wanted to know about Dahmer, his life, his family, his crimes and so much more. However, when does it take it too far?

While most of us read and hear about monstrous crimes from the safety of our homes, there are those out there who are reporting on it, and while a lot of the reports are done so with care and respect, there are other forms of media which appear to take little to no consideration for the families, nor the victims.

For example, television has created a popular trend of True Crime dramas, which delves into the lives and crimes of murderers for years on However, it has very much so gained traction within the past decade – ramping up even more after the Coronavirus pandemic which saw viewers forced to confine at home, with simple means of entertainment for company.

Unfortunately, this presented an issue: criminals and their murders were becoming dramatized to the point where it almost romanticised the perpetrators and gave very little respect for those who were killed. While other production companies were reflective in their portrayal of Dahmer, asking questions such as whether he could have been apprehended sooner, or even if avenues of intervention had been missed, some projects instead focused on the gore.

Of course, in a world dominated by social media, Dahmer soon became a trending topic when Murphy released his Dahmer series on Netflix, and it even led to a fad of people dressing up as Dahmer, sporting similar glasses, hairstyles and fashion items as they danced to Psycho Killer by American rock band, Talking Heads.

Where do we draw the line?

The TV show was allegedly also made without the consent of any of the victims' families, and since its release, several of them have publicly expressed their upset at the show's existence. When the show was released, *The Guardian* asked, "Is Ryan Murphy's Jeffrey Dahmer show the most exploitative TV of 2022?" while Anna Leszkiewicz at the New Statesman, suggested that the series was 'morally indefensible' in her article titled: Abolish True Crime.

Many critics came to the conclusion that the series, and similar series, were profiting off pain and misfortune, with reviewer Jack King writing for GQ that 'it feels as though Murphy is aping the likes of *The Texas Chainsaw Massacre* and *The Hills Have Eyes*, Peters' performance not so distant from a socially-stunted Hannibal Lecter'. There has been an increasing feeling that from books to documentaries and series, that they have all refocused the narratives away from notorious murderers and onto their targets. However, are serial killer-centred narratives a better option? If the Dahmer-related

Tik Toks have proved anything, it is that if not created with the correct narrative, viewers may even express sorrow or sympathy for Dahmer. They might even create 'romantic' edits of him and express their infatuation with a man who murdered many.

Jarryd Bartle, a criminology and justice studies lecturer at Melbourne's RMIT University wrote of the way in which shows profit from talking about murder. He shared that the show has more of a focus on the victims than many other true-crime dramas, the second half of the series does indeed refocus away from Dahmer and towards the victims, with the focus being on Hughes for a particular episode. But if this is the case, surely the victim's families must consent to such content?

Vox culture reporter Aja Romano wrote of this: "Make your true crime dramas if you must but make them with the assistance of and respect for the victims. Model your true crime dramas after Ava DuVernay's *When They See Us* [the Netflix drama about the Central Park Five] made with the full support of its subjects, rather than at their expense".

Murphy initially remained quiet around the show, but stepped up to defend himself once the backlash began to turn into a storm. He said: "We weren't so much interested in Jeffrey Dahmer, the person, but what made him the monster that he became".

He added that 'it's really about white privilege. It's about systemic racism. It's about homophobia'.

However, as Leszkiewicz pointed out: "His portrait is coloured with a warm lustre, set between metallic gold panels."

"Dahmer has, quite literally, been exalted: raised high over the city in a gilded frame like a god."

As the Netflix series premiered, a family member of one of Dahmer's victims spoke out – Rita Isbell – the older sister of Lindsey, who was 19 when he was murdered broke down in court, and Rita's cousin Eric condemned the show for its retelling of her breakdown.

He said: "I'm not telling anyone what to watch, I know true crime media is huge rn [right now], but if you're actually curious about the victims, my family (the Isbell's) are pissed about this show.

"It's retraumatizing over and over again, and for what? How many movies/shows/documentaries do we need?"

Isbell on the other hand shared: "If I didn't know any better, I would've thought it was me. Her hair was like mine, she had on the same clothes. That's why it felt like reliving it all over again," she continued. "It brought back all the emotions I was feeling back then."

After leaving the courtroom, AP News reported the sister said in 1992: "They all had to just sit there and hold it in."

"What he saw out of me ... is what Errol would have done. The only difference is, Errol would have leaped over that table."

His victims left behind loving family. Some, like Lindsey, never got to meet his daughter, who was born six months after his murder. His sister has since shared that through her grief, there were unlikely people who were willing to enact revenge on her behalf, as for the two years leading up to Dahmer's death, she would hear from men that claimed to be prison inmates, offering condolences and promises to her that Dahmer would be 'taken care of,' according to The Baltimore Sun.

She added that she expected the killer to die, when talking about how he was eventually murdered in prison.

As for Lindsey's daughter, Tatiana Banks, she has been deeply affected since the Netflix show was released. She told *Insider* that she's had trouble sleeping ever since it came out. "Honestly ever since that show's been on I haven't been able to sleep. I see Jeffrey Dahmer in my sleep," she said.

Banks shared that she only watched one episode of the series, which showed her aunt's emotional statement during Dahmer's trial. Like others, she also claimed to have not been contacted about the making of the series, explaining: "I feel like they should have reached out because it's people who are actually still grieving from that situation."

With so many people unhappy with the new drama, it begs the question of whether this has happened before, and if so, what were the ramifications? According to the BBC, Netflix was forced to settle a lawsuit with Georgian chess master Nona Gaprindashvili over what she believed to be an inaccurate portrayal of herself in their hit 2020 miniseries *The Queen's Gambit*. Rachel DeLoache Williams, who was the former friend of Anna Sorokin, a woman who was imprisoned for fraud, claimed to be suing the production company for defamation and false light invasion of privacy after a character portrayed her in *Inventing Anna*.

In another instance of a person being very unhappy with the company, Michael Peterson suggested he was going to consult lawyers about the making of the HBO drama *The Staircase*, which dived into the true-crime case of his wife's mysterious death. He said the series contained 'egregious fabrications'. As for Dahmer's show, it was reported that Dahmer's father Lionel was seeking legal advice against Netflix for its two shows about his son. One, which was Murphy's, and another called *Conversations with a Killer: The Jeffrey Dahmer Tapes*.

It is clear that a lot of people have been unhappy with the portrayal of Dahmer and his victims, but are we, as the public, to blame for the rise in True Crime popularity?

According to sociology teacher Trever Zahn who spoke to Spartanshield: "I would definitely say society tends to romanticize or obsess with these types of people. You can simply look at the top Netflix shows and the Dahmer, Ted Bundy, John Wayne Gacy and Laurie Vallo documentaries are right towards the top in terms of popularity."

Of course, morbid curiosity has long been part of human nature, but for the victims' families, it brought that pain back to the forefront.

Rita Isbell, the brother of victim Lindsey said she was not informed her courtroom breakdown would be recreated as she told Insider: "When I saw some of the show, it bothered me, especially when I saw myself – when I saw my name come across the screen and this lady saying verbatim exactly what I said."

She said Netflix should have given some of the profits to the victims' children and grandchildren, adding: "If the show benefited them in some way, it wouldn't feel so harsh and careless. It's sad that they're just making money off of this tragedy. That's just greed."

Eric Perry, Lindsey's cousin again slammed the hit series in a tweet, sharing that the recreation of her public anguish was 'wild'. He wrote: "Recreating my cousin having an emotional breakdown in court in the face of the man who tortured and murdered her brother is WILD. WIIIIIILD".

Anne E Schwartz, the journalist who broke the story of Dahmer's crimes just hours after he was arrested, told the *Independent* external that Netflix had 'sacrificed accuracy for the sake of drama', and that Murphy had had taken 'artistic licence' with many core details of the case, explaining that the show 'does not bear a great deal of resemblance to the facts of the case'. She also said the 'depiction of city police officers as racist and homophobic was incorrect'.

Since its release, reviews have been mixed by viewers and professional reviewers alike, with the *Guardian*'s Stuart Heritage, writing: "Worst of all, by some degree, is the show's choice of focus... The one good thing a show like this can do is steal the spotlight from the murderer and show who these people actually were. But Dahmer, for the most part, is unfortunately too infatuated with its star attraction for that."

The Hollywood Reporter's Daniel Fienberg, also called the series an 'infuriating hodgepodge', and claimed 'reducing most of the victims and their families to their pain is closer to exploiting that pain than honouring any memories'.

However, Paul Tassi at *Forbes*, said: "I don't know if 'liking' the series is the right word, as it's pretty unsettling to watch, but I do think it's well-acted by everyone involved, and the show does do a lot of work to maintain the focus is on the victims, the ineptitude of the police and the damage that Dahmer left in his wake."

According to Douglas Klutz, an instructor in the UA Department of Criminology and Criminal Justice, crime shows have been capitalised by the media to feed its audience's fascination with crime.

He told *The Crimson White*: "These true crime specials lead to a skewed conception of the types of crime being committed and their usual frequency of occurrence, and, in turn, how those crimes feature in these popular media portrayals actually work their way through the criminal justice system."

But it seems as though the production of Dahmer's series did at least attempt to mitigate some of the focus on the killer, even if some may think it missed the mark. Evan Peters, who portrayed Dahmer, reportedly told Murphy that he would only work on the film if it did not focus on the point of view of the killer. "As an audience, you're not really sympathising with him [...] You're more sort of watching it, you know, from the outside," Peters said before the show was released. But with mounting fans claiming to feel sorry for Dahmer after watching the show, there could be a deeper issue of having traditionally handsome men playing the role of killers. This was seen after viewers lusted over Zac Efron as Ted Bundy in the *Extremely Wicked, Shockingly Evil and Vile* show, and David Tennant when he played Dennis Nilsen in *Des*. Research has even shown that people instinctively trust people who are deemed attractive. So it might present problems for viewers as they are watching a person that they want to find attractive, but the subject matter is telling them otherwise.

"By depicting serial killers as complex, intelligent and interesting, and choosing attractive actors to play them gives them a sense of appeal," said Dr Melanie Haughton to Dazed. She is a senior lecturer in psychology at the University of Derby. But according to Melissa Hamilton, professor of law and criminal justice at Surrey University, casting handsome men to play murderers can be a 'lesson' in associating 'beauty and handsomeness with honesty, friendliness, safety'.

Of course, this is something which happened in real-life to unsuspecting victims of Bundy, who was known to be a handsome and charismatic man, in an affluent school, ran in political social circles and was interested in law. For him, preying on young women by pretending to be injured or in need of help, worked in his favour. His charm allowed him to seem friendly, attractive and a safe person. However, this would not be the case. In fact, he was a prolific killer, who murdered thirty known women and young girls in the 70s. Bundy, like Dahmer, experienced adverse childhood experiences, particularly when it was revealed to him that his sister was actually his mother and his parents were actually his grandparents. The Floridian took this news rather hard, and his relationship between himself and women appeared to be forever skewed. That is, of course, if you are to believe the words that he said after being imprisoned and stationed on Death Row. A master manipulator, Bundy's truth can only be taken at face value.

However, while Bundy's story ended with his execution, Dahmer faced a more violent end.

Prison and Death

After Dahmer was sentenced to fifteen consecutive life sentences for the killing and dismemberment of all but two of his victims on February 17, 1992, Dahmer was sent to Columbia Correctional Institute in Wisconsin.

At his sentencing, Dahmer told the judge: "I take all the blame for what I did... Your honour, it is over now. This has never been a case of trying to get free. I never wanted freedom."

His lawyer, Boyde, told the press that no appeal was planned to contest the sentence he was handed, thus allowing justice to remain with his current life imprisonment. But things were not easy for a man convicted of slaughtering numerous people. In fact, it was hostile.

"I always asked if he was safe," Dahmer's mother, Joyce told *People Magazine* in an interview. "He'd say, 'It doesn't matter, Mom. I don't care if something happens to me."

He would regularly speak to his parents via phone calls, but while he seemingly had little thought for his own life, his parents were left to worry for his safety. After the convicted killer was imprisoned, it was reported that he was originally placed in solitary confinement for his own protection but later moved by his own consent to a less secure unit after a year of solitude. He became a born-again Christian, and was baptised in May 1994, attending weekly meetings with a minister. But his crimes would catch up with him on July 3, just two months later when fellow inmate, Osvaldo Durruthy tried to slash Dahmer's throat using a razor blade that was embedded in a toothbrush during a chapel service. While his wounds were superficial, the next attack on him would be fatal. On November 28, Dahmer carried out his two-hour daily task of cleaning the toilet block alongside inmates Jesse Anderson and Christopher Scarver. While all three were unsupervised in the shower block of the prison gymnasium, Scarver beat Dahmer, and Anderson, to death with a metal bar in the prison bathroom.

Even though Dahmer was taken to hospital, he was pronounced dead an hour later. Anderson died from his injuries two days later.

In 2015, almost 20 years after he murdered Dahmer, Scarver told the *New York Post*, he kept a newspaper article of Dahmer's heinous crimes and was 'fiercely disgusted'. So, he confronted him. He also claimed Dahmer turned prison food into fake limbs covered with ketchup to mimic blood and would leave them around the prison for others to find, that he was not repentant and had 'crossed' many people. This included prison officers, who he alluded to helping him to be unsupervised to murder the two inmates.

Of course, it might be clear to understand why Dahmer was a wanted man, but according to Scarver, Dahmer accepted his fate just before his death. Joyce, however, could not.

"I still love my son. I've never stopped loving my son. He was a beautiful baby. He was a wonderful child. He has always been loved," she said at the time of his death.

Dahmer's father wrote in his memoir of his pain, and his son's legacy as a killer: "It is a portrayal of parental dread … the terrible sense that your child has slipped beyond your grasp, that your little boy is spinning in the void, swirling in the maelstrom, lost, lost, lost."

But while Dahmer spoke to his parents, he also taunted his father. "Remember when you visited grandma? Remember that small, one-by-one square foot box?", Dahmer asked his father from prison, as shown in the *My Son Jeffrey: The Dahmer Family Tapes* documentary. "You know what was in it, don't you?" he said. "The mummified head and genitals of the last victim at the West Allis location".

The parents, who grieved in their own ways, would go on to wage a war against one another after Joyce wanted her son's brain studied for science purposes, hoping that there could be something there that might stop the development of serial killers in the future. Lionel was set against this path, and ultimately, Dahmer's brain was cremated along with his body. Joyce spoke to her son at least once a week from prison according to the *Milwaukee Journal Sentinel.*

"I said to him, I asked him, 'Do you still have these urges?'" Dahmer said, 'Yes, Mom, I'm so glad I'm locked up. I'd be afraid what I'd do if I weren't locked up.'"

"I want something useful to come from this nightmare," she said, according to the *Milwaukee Journal Sentinel.* "I haven't seen one speck of light with all the horror that happened to everyone. It's the last and only thing I can do for Jeff. I want to make some small usefulness for my own nightmare. I've located experts who feel research on Jeff's brain could be useful."

While Joyce was wracked with guilt over her son's crimes, her son did not blame her for turning him into a monster. He instead had nothing but good things to share about her, as per Carl Wahlstrom, a forensic psychiatrist who interviewed and evaluated Dahmer and also served as an expert witness in his trial.

"He said he had very loving parents," he said. "[And] that blaming [his] parents for these issues was completely off the mark."

Whether it was Dahmer's parents or not, Joyce attempted suicide months before her son was killed in prison, via carbon monoxide poisoning.

"It's been a lonely life, especially today. Please cremate me … I love my sons, Jeff and David," read her suicide note. However, she was saved by strong winds blowing carbon monoxide out of her garage during her attempt.

David, Dahmer's younger brother, went on to change his name and move far from his family to escape the legacy his brother left behind for him to carry.

Part V

Social and Cultural Impact

Policing and Prejudice

After Dahmer was sentenced and then killed, his crimes and path of pain lived on, particularly in the victim's families, witnesses and social causes. For a lot of people, Dahmer's case exposed systemic issues, including police negligence and how society apathies towards marginalised communities. Especially the LGBTQ+ and BIPOC communities.

One instance which caused a lot of disruption for the police force was when Dahmer drugged Sinthasomphone with sleeping pills that rendered him unconscious, performed oral sex and other acts upon the boy, drilled a hole in his skull and injected hydrochloric acid into the frontal lobe of his brain.

These twisted actions led to the 14-year-old to be rendered into such a state of disorientation, that when regained consciousness, he didn't react to the sight of a decomposing body in Dahmer's room. When Dahmer left his apartment, and the boy escaped, running into three women who called the police for support, this is when the mistakes were made on the force's side.

When Dahmer returned and found Sinthasomphone in the middle of Sandra Smith and Nicole Childress, things escalated to a scenario where he could have been caught. But he was not.

While the boy was fluent in English, he could only speak in broken Laotian in his state of intoxication, which caused the girls to call the police as they were concerned about his wellbeing.

When police arrived, Dahmer told the police that Sinthasomphone was his consensual 19-year-old lover and that the blood on him came from a skinned knee. He told the witnesses, and the police, that the teen became drunk during an argument, and that he often acted this way when he was upset.

While the women did not believe his story, the police believed him and later described the incident as a 'domestic squabble between homosexuals'. The officers, John Balcerzak and Joseph Gabrish, did not check Dahmer's criminal history, where they would have been made aware that he was a registered child molester who was recently freed from jail. They also did not examine Sinthasomphone's injuries, which would reveal a drilled hole in the middle of his head. They also ignored the women's pleas.

When the girls insisted Sinthasomphone was in danger, they ignored them, and many believe that racism possibly played a factor in their refusal to listen to three black women's insistence.

The police returned the boy to Dahmer's apartment and even helped to forcefully take the boy back inside, even though Sinthasomphone tried to protest.

Even at 17, Childress, the cousin of Smith, knew something was wrong. She said as per the *New York Times*: "He was struggling; he was reaching out to me for help."

After Dahmer's crimes were exposed, Grabish and Balcerzak were suspended and investigated for returning the 14-year-old victim to Dahmer, and eventually terminated for their lack of action. An audio log of their conversation after attending the scene that night also was revealed, which heard the pair making homophobic remarks. It can be heard: "The intoxicated Asian naked male (laughter in background) was returned to his sober boyfriend (more laughter)." When the officers are dispatched to another scene, one comments that, first, "my partner is going to get deloused at the station."

The officers were not brought up on charges, despite the audio recording and their failings, but the Sinthasomphone family was able to reach a $850,000 settlement from the police department after suing.

As for Cola Styles, she said she saw a 'streak of evil' in Dahmer at the scene as she attempted to rescue the boy, and that all three women were outraged by the lack of police action that night. Since then, she has changed her name to distance herself from the case and also has been plagued with guilt ever since.

She said: "I was wondering if I could get hypnotised so I could block that part of my life out. I really did not want to think about it."

She said it had taken almost 20 years to forgive herself for not being able to save him.

The death of the young boy rocked the nation, as did the officers' misconduct. Anna M. Moncada Storti wrote for Reappropriate in a 30th anniversary tribute to him: "More than half of his victims were Black and all but 3 were not white, casting Sinthasomphone in a scene of racialized and homoerotic violence that police are simply too unfit to notice, and too in service of to not be complicit in."

To help with understanding unconscious bias, Dr Manpreet poured her insights into the topic, which is her specialty.[14]

Unconscious Racial Bias, Intersectionality, and Systemic Complicity

The case of Jeffrey Dahmer can be viewed through a systemic lens through which to examine the interplay of unconscious racial bias, intersectional marginalisation, and institutional neglect. While Dahmer claimed his victim selection was pragmatic (i.e., opportunistic in a predominantly minority area), his reported admission to a street priest that he "hated black people and homosexuals" complicates this narrative. This contradiction invites analysis of how unconscious biases, systemic inequalities, and intersecting identities potentially formed Dahmer's predation alongside the systemic failures that enabled his crimes. Drawing on Keon West's research into implicit racial bias and Kimberlé Crenshaw's intersectionality theory, this commentary argues that Dahmer's actions were facilitated by a sociohistorical context that devalued Black, Brown, and queer lives, rendering them vulnerable to predation and institutional erasure.

Keon West's (2025) work on the science of racism elucidates how unconscious biases, rather than overt bigotry, often underpin discriminatory behaviours. West's studies demonstrate that individuals may perpetuate racialised harm without conscious intent, internalising societal stereotypes that frame certain groups as less human or deserving of protection. Dahmer's assertion that his choices were not racially motivated, that were framed as mere opportunism, aligns with this model of implicit bias. However, his explicit hatred of black and homosexual individuals, as reported, suggests a deeper internalisation of societal prejudices. West's findings on dehumanisation are pertinent here - when marginalised groups are systematically stereotyped as hypersexual, criminal, or disposable, as Black and LGBTQA+ communities were during the 1980s AIDS crisis, perpetrators may subconsciously perceive them as "easy targets." This aligns with Dahmer's modus operandi; he exploited the social invisibility of his victims, many of whom were sex workers or individuals estranged from their families due to homophobia. The unconscious bias framework thus challenges Dahmer's deflection of racism, revealing how societal narratives of Black and queer expendability may have tacitly informed his calculus.

To fully contextualise this, Crenshaw's intersectionality theory is indispensable. The victim's compounded identities – Black or Hispanic, working-class, and queer – placed them at the intersection of multiple systems of oppression, exacerbating their vulnerability. During the 1980s and 1990s, these communities faced overlapping stigmatisation. That is, racism in predominantly white Milwaukee, homophobia within cultural and religious institutions, and economic marginalisation due to deindustrialisation. Crenshaw's framework clarifies how these intersecting forces created a "hierarchy of victimhood," wherein crimes against marginalised individuals were dismissed as less urgent or credible. For example, the repeated failure of Milwaukee police to investigate Dahmer who famously returned 14-year-old Konerak Sinthasomphone to his apartment despite visible injuries, reflects institutional biases that de-prioritised Black and Asian victims. Intersectionality thus reveals how systemic indifference was not merely a product of racism or homophobia in isolation, but of their convergence, which rendered victims' suffering illegible to authorities.

The sociohistorical context further accentuates this analysis. The 1980s and 1990s were marked by heightened racialised rhetoric around crime (e.g., the "superpredator" myth) and virulent homophobia, exemplified by government inaction during the AIDS crisis. Black and Hispanic queer men occupied a uniquely precarious position; rejected by mainstream society and often their own communities, they were pushed into transient, high-risk environments. Dahmer's apartment, located in a racially segregated neighbourhood, became a hunting ground precisely because these structural inequities normalised the disappearance of marginalised individuals. Law enforcement's negligence, as research on institutional discrimination highlights, stemmed from unconscious biases that associated minority communities with criminality rather than victimhood. Officers' dismissiveness toward victims' families (frequently attributing disappearances to "gay lifestyles") illustrates how stereotypes distorted institutional responses, privileging dominant narratives over empirical evidence.

Dahmer's case cannot be separated from the systemic architecture that enabled it. His crimes thrived in a culture that tacitly sanctioned the dehumanisation of intersectionally marginalised groups, a reality compounded by institutional apathy. To dismiss his actions as non-racialised or apolitical risks perpetuating the same erasure that allowed his violence to persist. The theories outlined collectively affirm that unconscious biases and intersecting oppressions are not incidental but foundational to such atrocities. Dahmer's legacy, therefore, is not merely one of individual psychopathy but of a society that rendered certain lives inconsequential; a reckoning that remains urgently relevant in contemporary discourses on racial justice and LGBTQA+ rights.

Balcerzak and Gabrish were suspended, but in a twist, they were each awarded $55,000 in back pay and reinstated with Balcerzak later being elected president of Milwaukee Police Association in 2005 until 2009. He retired from the police force in 2017 whilst Gabrish also retired from the force in the 2010s.

Guerroros's brother, Janie Hagen has also spoken out about how it appears that there are those who profit from his brother's murder, particularly in the form of a walking tour. Walking tours typically occur when a group is gathered on the promise of touring historical or entertaining sights around the world. There are tours across England for art lovers, fans of William Shakespeare, but there are also tours of famous serial killer, Jack the Ripper's crime sites. Just as the case with the Victorian true time pit stop, one has been created by Bam Media and Marketing, who Hagen calls heartless. He said as per CBS News: "This whole thing opens up a lot of old wounds, a lot of painful memories. It's that same hurt all over again."

The marketing group offers a tour of Dahmer's old neighbourhood, including the areas where he met his victims, according to CBS Minnesota. At the time of Hagen's complaint, the company was selling 44 dates between March 3 and June 30. As per Amanda Morden, the company's spokesperson, the first two trips nearly reached the

20-person capacity. But victims' families and others have called out the tour as an attempt to exploit the deaths of many.

While the company had offered to donate some proceeds to a charity that supports the parents of murder victims, Nancy Ruhe, executive director of the National Organization of Parents of Murdered Children, told *The Associated Press* that the organisation would never accept money from a group that profits from murder.

"I cannot believe we can't let these people rest in peace," she said. "It's unbelievable that someone has come up with a moneymaker off those who have been murdered."

Pop Culture and A Legacy of Horror

Dahmer's legacy lived on decades after his death, in the form on numerous documentaries, docuseries, TV shows, books and more. But Murphy's Monster series was possibly something that reignited Dahmer's notoriety, in the sense that many younger generations were not exposed to the news of his crimes.

The Netflix show was released in September 2022, starring the actor Evan Peters as Dahmer, which was heavily praised.

However, did his portrayal of the convicted killer do the real-life story justice?

Upon watching the show, it was clear within the first frame that this would be a story which would show Dahmer in a dramatized light. Presenting the character of Dahmer as a disturbingly quiet and emotionally detached person, it was noticeable that Murphy had constructed Dahmer by using his childhood trauma, neglect and adolescence internalised rage as inspiration.

Peters delivered a nuanced performance, which presented Dahmer as a man with eerie restraint rather than over-the-top theatrics that one might expect from a killer, and the series heavily leaned into

Dahmer's isolation, psychological troubles, social struggles and his obsession with control.

While Peters' portrayal of Dahmer somewhat humanised him to an extent by exploring his mental health issues, the early warning signs in his behaviour and his upbringing, it carefully tiptoed around the line between explaining how he came to be a killer, and excusing his actions. Throughout the series, viewers were able to see Dahmer's relationships, his psychological spiral, and his struggle with his compulsion to kill.

However, some critics believe that with such an intense focus on Dahmer and not his victims, could over-humanize him, which could then lead to viewers empathising with a serial killer, rather than diving into the lives of those who he murdered and the impact their deaths had on their families. Of course, as it is a show about murder, graphic scenes were always going to be shown, however the dramatization of such murders focused on the tension and horror leading up to the crimes, saving viewers from having to watch gory scenes and disturbing sequences.

A lot can be said of the show, which also explored the failings of the police, marginalisation of Dahmer's victims (who were mostly of African American ethnicity), as well as systemic racism in the United States during the time of his crimes. The inclusion of these topics added important context into just how Dahmer was able to evade detection for so long, but with the storytelling so heavily focused on his spiral into becoming a killer, many have since come out to slate the show for its lack of depth into the lives of those murdered.

Instead, it structured scenes which saw the victims as perhaps being props for Dahmer's acts, and whether this was an intentional filming request as to show how Dahmer felt about his victims, it has also been hailed as somewhat distasteful, and also disrespectful to the families, who are continuing to grieve such a significant and senseless crime.

For example, scenes in the show depict Dahmer attempting to create 'zombies' by drilling holes into his victims' heads and then injecting acid into their skulls. His rituals with the bodies, dismemberment, posing and photo-taking were all aspects which were included. While this could be important to the plot and showing just how depraved Dahmer's acts were, consideration for the family members of those who died may have slipped through the cracks in the creation of the series.

One question remains at the forefront of the show: Is it accurate or is it sensationalised for a true crime obsessed audience?

While the show sticks closely to real events, the timeline, and even transcripts from the courtroom at Dahmer's real-life trial, it does have aspects of dramatization that could have been cut.

Of course, it highlights police negligence, however it also showed deep and meaningful one-on-one interactions between Dahmer and his victims before he murdered them, something that is unable to be authenticated as true or false. There are also unrealistic elements, such as dreamlike sequences, and slow-motion horror cliches, which could be playing into the true crime entertainment genre, as opposed to a factual depiction of events. Inaccuracies have also been found within the show, such as the portrayal of Glenda Cleveland as being Dahmer's neighbour, when she in fact lived in a nearby building. While the show attempted to criticise the judicial system for its racial bias and failings to capture Dahmer sooner, the show arguably did not escape from slipping into the classic trap of attempting to draw in viewers with macabre fascinations instead of an earnest interpretation of a real-life horror.

The more significant criticism of the show would come from the victims' families, with many stating that they were not consulted before the show aired, and that some scenes retraumatised them, bringing back memories of losing their loved ones. Although some have argued that the show used real trauma to inspire the content and that these scenes were necessary to examine the killer and the judicial system, there is perhaps a fine line between exploiting a tragedy and educating the public on Dahmer and his crimes.

In the end, The Jeffrey Dahmer Story achieved its goal of being a compelling dramatization of the real-life murderer, which also studied his character, critiqued society and largely kept to the truth about the timeline of the killings and its impact in the courtroom without overtly glorifying Dahmer. However, by centring his story as the main focus, it risked overshadowing the lives lost and the failures that allowed Dahmer's crimes to go unchecked for years.

The show renewed interest in a decades-old case, allowing new generations to learn about Dahmer, his victims (to an extent) and the way in which police mishandled elements that could have seen Dahmer behind bars sooner. Compared to Ross Lynch's *My Friend Dahmer*, the sensationalism is noticeable.

The 2017 film directed by Marc Meyers and based on Backderf's writings, offered a fresh perspective on Dahmer, without exploiting the victims or excusing his behavior. The film adaptation offered an unsettling portrait of the killer during his high school years, long before he became a notorious murderer. Unlike many other adaptations that typically focus on the violence, the film focuses on Dahmer's growing detachment from the world, his internal collapse and the culmination in external factors which contributed to his spiral. However, it is important to note that the way in which the filmmakers portrayed this was not sensationalised, nor was it rationalised into an excuse for his later crimes.

In fact, Lynch played Dahmer as an emotionally repressed teenager who was awkward, socially shunned, curious about the morbid and also deeply disturbed by his growing compulsions. Essentially, it unfolded the story of Dahmer with great detail on his psychological issues, and also systemic failings which led to him not receiving help before his dangerous thoughts became a reality. The film was able to tell the story of Dahmer without dramatizing it, and allowed the story to unfold as a slow-burn depiction of a teenager slipping through the cracks of supportive institutions. In the story, which is told through the lens of a former school friend, Dahmer is a loner who is fascinated by death, roadkill, and also struggling to come to terms with his sexuality, alongside misusing substances and a spiralling mental health issue – all during a time where he is largely ignored by the adults around him.

It is a tricky feat to be able to humanise a serial killer without excusing his behaviour, empathizing with him or forgetting the man he would become. However, *My Friend Dahmer* appeared to do this and more; unlike Murphy's Monster story which focuses on his crimes and the aftermath, the film acts more as a psychological study rather than a true crime entertainment drama. The story it tells is filtered through the perspective of Backderf, and it explores topics such as the neglect and social isolation that Dahmer experiences which is portrayed as a preventable tragedy which could have been avoided had an adult paid more attention to his behaviours. Dahmer's performative nature was also under the microscope, as his 'spasms' he would enact in school was seen as humour, when in fact it could have been something he did to mask his deeper issues. Then there were themes of repression, where his struggle with his sexuality and his self-identity was shown without it being dramatized or lop siding into specific judgements about his character.

As for how accurate the portrayal of Dahmer and this time in his life were, the film is based on a first-hand account of what the killer was like during his schooling years, and so the accuracy can only be theorised to be very close to the truth. Not only did the film deliberately avoid showing murder or violent scenes, it chose to focus almost exclusively on his teenage alcoholism, his obsession with a male jogger who he planned to be his first victim, and his hobby of preserving animals.

Of course, there is a clear sense of foreboding in the film, but no scene turns Dahmer into a spectacle, or explain his crimes in a way that we, the audience, can understand. Instead, it shows how a killer can be shaped during adolescence, and how warning signs can be ignored, or even misunderstood, leading to catastrophic consequences. Because of this, *My Friend Dahmer* has received a lot of praise for its ethical sensitivity when handling the story, as it does not dwell in his crimes or glorify his actions. It opts to raise a vital question: Could his trajectory have been changed, and should some of the responsibility lie with those who ignored those signs he exhibited for so long?

Now, comparing Monster to *My Friend Dahmer* and examining the differences in the storylines, artistic choices and the way in which they portray Dahmer is interesting. It is clear to see that both projects are speaking to two different audience groups. While *My Friend Dahmer* focuses on who he was before the crimes, without graphic violence, murder or sensationalism, Monster dramatizes the killings in a highly stylized way. It solely focuses on the murders, Dahmer's killing methods, his victims (albeit, briefly), and the judicial failures in comparison to the external factors which may have contributed to his descent into his crimes. Because of the regular references to murder and dismemberment, it leans more toward a true crime horror, whilst My Friend Dahmer could be categorized as a crime fiction drama film. The portrayal in the two projects are different also. While *My Friend Dahmer* sympathetically leans into Dahmer's story without excusing his crimes, painting him as a troubled teenager in need of help, Monster shows the killer as a cold and calculated murderer who was shaped by systemic and personal failures during his life. The film is centred on prevention and missed intervention opportunities, as well as asking the vital question: How could someone like Dahmer go unnoticed in society? The TV show on the other hand looks through the lens of accountability and the failure of institutions to protect the marginalized community that Dahmer inevitably targeted, be it the African American group, or the LGBTQ+ and poor community members.

Of course, one is dawn directly from a memoir of someone who was close to Dahmer, making it a grounded and also factual account of the events of his adolescence, as opposed to romanticising it or making it a spectacle. The other is largely based on true events, real victims and content that any person can verify online, but it also dramatizes the interactions between Dahmer and his victims, muddles facts such as Cleveland being his neighbour. This could be why it has been criticised online, as well as by the victims' families for not seeking consent before filming began.

Ethically, it raises more concerns than its thoughtful pondering of its counterpart. While it tries to tell untold stories and also bring to light the failures of the police force, it is very much produced in a way that invites the 'binge-watching' spectacle, dampening the fact that it is based on very real tragedies, which makes its intent feel somewhat conflicted.

When does entertainment and a quest for telling the truth meet in the middle to create something that is factual without being distasteful? The line may be more blurred than we know.

According to Amy Bentley, a solicitor in the UK, the show is nuanced and may not be as sensationalised or sexualised as others think.

****

How do you think Monster: The Jeffrey Dahmer Story handles the balance between dramatizing Dahmer's life for entertainment and respecting the victims' families and their stories?

I struggled to see any balance. The show feels very pro Dahmer, with what feels like very little consideration for the victims' families or their stories.

One criticism of the show has been that it sensationalises Dahmer's actions. Do you believe the show crosses a line in terms of making his crimes more appealing or marketable for viewers?

I wouldn't go so far as to say that the show crosses a moral line, but I do believe it tends to sensationalise Dahmer's actions. This portrayal in the show creates an impression that the audience is being encouraged to sympathise with him

In many portrayals, Dahmer is depicted with a level of charm or even a certain degree of sexualization. How does this portrayal affect public perception of Dahmer and his crimes? Do you think it unintentionally glamorises his actions?

I did not perceive his portrayal as creepy or sexualised; rather, I found it distinctly unsettling.

What is the impact of focusing on Dahmer's personality and psychological complexity in the series, rather than concentrating more on the victims and the aftermath of his crimes? Does this shift in focus contribute to a dangerous romanticisation of the killer?

The show emphasises Dahmer's troubled childhood, mental health issues, and it risks overshadowing the narratives of his victims. The show creates an environment where viewers may inadvertently sympathise with or become fascinated by Dahmer rather than recognise the profound suffering experienced by those he harmed. The psychological exploration might be seen as an attempt to understand Dahmer's mind; however, it detracts from acknowledging the humanity of the victims and their families.

This shift could be seen to contribute towards a dangerous romanticisation of Dahmer. By presenting him as a complex character with intricate motivations, may inadvertently glamorise his actions or suggest that there is something compelling about his story that deserves exploration beyond its horrific nature.

Some viewers have been critical of the way the show presents Dahmer as a 'tragic' or misunderstood character, especially in the context of his relationship with his parents and his isolation. Does this narrative shift run the risk of humanizing him in ways that downplay the horror of his actions?

In my opinion the shift occurs when viewers begin to view Dahmer not just as a perpetrator but as a tragic figure shaped by circumstances, and whilst we are told that this is true such narratives could lead to a form of cultural fascination that diminishes the severity of his crimes and reduces empathy for his victims. Creating an allure around violence and criminality could be seen to be harmful, especially if it leads to desensitisation towards real-life violence.

What do you think about the portrayal of Dahmer as a sexually charged figure in the show? How does this contribute to the broader cultural fascination with him as a 'bad boy' or 'antihero'?

I didn't see Dahmer as being portrayed as a sexually charged figure.

There has been public concern about the sexualisation of Dahmer, particularly through media portrayals that focus on his physical attractiveness and charm. Is there a danger in presenting serial killers in a way that could foster unhealthy fantasies or even fan bases?

Yes, as mentioned above I believe it could be dangerous to present Dahmer in this way.

How do you think the portrayal of Dahmer in Monster compares to other true crime shows or films, in terms of the risks of making the killer a 'sex symbol' or figure of morbid allure?

I think the show portrays Dahmer as more of a sympathetic character than others, but I don't see him as being portrayed as a sex symbol.

What kind of impact do you think shows like Monster have on viewers' perceptions of true crime, particularly in blurring the line between victimization and victimization's entertainment value? Do you see this trend as problematic?

I think it gives the viewers an understanding of the background of the type of people that commit that type of offence, as most have truly horrific backgrounds. I think that giving attention to any serious offence can always be problematic, but it can also be seen as important.

How can media creators like Ryan Murphy handle the story of someone like Dahmer responsibly, avoiding romanticising or over-sensationalising his crimes while still telling a compelling story?

I think that media creators need to understand the complexities surrounding figures like Dahmer and acknowledge the profound impact their actions have on the victims, their families, and society at large.

Do you think that Dahmer's portrayal in Monster appeals more to a fascination with serial killers as a form of 'forbidden attraction,' and what are the potential psychological implications of that?

To me it felt like a show for fans, it could glorify it in some people's minds.

Some fans of true crime shows have been accused of 'celebrity worship' towards figures like Dahmer. What responsibility do show creators have in addressing or discouraging this kind of behaviour, especially when their work may fuel such obsessions?

I think the creators have the responsibility to focus on the human cost of Dahmer's crimes rather than glorifying him as a figure of intrigue or horror.

How do you respond to the argument that shows like Monster could contribute to the desensitisation of violent crime, especially given how the show focuses on Dahmer's personal life and sexual relationships rather than the victims' pain and trauma?

I agree that Monster should contribute to the desensitisation of violent crimes, as it risks forgetting that the victims are human too.

What does the widespread popularity of shows like Monster reveal about society's growing appetite for sensationalised portrayals of real-life horrors? Is there an ethical responsibility to avoid portraying these killers as larger-than-life characters?

Shows like Monster highlight significant ethical responsibilities regarding how these stories are told. There is an ethical responsibility to strike a balance between engaging storytelling and respectful representation.

Do you think the portrayal of Dahmer as a complex, even 'tragic' figure in the show could lead to empathy for him, rather than the victims of his crimes? How does this affect how society deals with serial killers in the public imagination?

Exploring the complexities behind figures like Dahmer can provide valuable insights into human behaviour and psychology, it is important that such portrayals do not come at the expense of acknowledging and honouring the lives of the victims. I believe that society must strive for a balanced narrative that recognises both the psychological dimensions of criminals while also centring on justice for victims.

The Culture of True Crime and Why Are We Obsessed?

After exploring why some viewers romanticise killers, become infatuated with or become fans of criminals, it can only beg the question as to why. To answer that, as the author, diving into my own experiences of writing about and reading about true crime is imperative. As is exploring the things that I have seen in the last decade in the media, and from those around it What I have come to understand, is that there is a strange kind of comfort in true crime. While this may sound like a contradiction as there should not be anything comforting about murder – violence, or the lives that have been torn apart in the most horrifying of ways – if you take a step back and look at how we consume these stories as third parties, a pattern begins to emerge.

We're not just curious about the facts. We're hooked on them.

Serial killers have become a sort of mythological figure in our imaginations, and in our culture too. They have been turned into household names, and transformed into characters that have been interviewed, studied, filmed and dramatized by the media, and by us. Their stories have been splashed across every newspaper in the world, they are retold via streaming platforms, podcasts, Reddit threads, TikTok explainer videos, merchandise and late-night talk shows that are broadcasted live to whole nations.

Within that sea of content, Dahmer stands out above many, and he always has. This is because his story, with all of its grotesque and psychological complex details, has become one of the most infamous modern day true crime stories in history. This fact alone raises an uncomfortable, yet essential question: Why are we all so obsessed with people like him?

Some might claim that it is nothing more than simple curiosity, and others will admit that it could be out of fear. However, I think it's both of those things, and even more. True crime has given us, as the audience, a way to look into the sheer terror of what people can do in this world, without being pulled inside and affected by the horrors. This kind of psychological safety net allows us to explore the terror, depravity, evil, and danger without leaving the comfort of our couch, our bed, behind a screen or with a book in hand. So, we can confront the worst in humanity without risking anything at all. We can indulge in the horror without risking our lives. Would this be something we would risk if there was a real danger to our health? Probably not.

Watching these stories unfold, these real stories be told, we're safe. You could argue that there's something quite human about paying attention to threats, so that we can understand the danger that lurks in the most public of places, but that might not be it at all. Perhaps we tell ourselves that if we understand how it happened, we'll be safer if a murderer attempted to lure us back to his den. As a true crime fanatic, surely you would be able to spot the warning signs. You would know what to do. It's the illusion that these entertainment sources give us about our own sense of safety. While we study the dark and dangerous side of humanity, hoping to find a pattern from which we can learn from, others are being subjected to the horrors we find fascinating.

Of course, this isn't the whole story. Let us be honest with ourselves, here. Some of our fascination with the popular true crime genre is about more than just self-preservation. It's darker. Some of it is purely morbid curiosity, as it would be a rare occurrence to see these things happen on the streets. Some of it is also voyeurism, and the thrill of being afraid of something without actually putting yourself in danger. Where there is adrenaline, there is horror, and that is an addictive combination for some.

This is where things begin to get complicated. When it turns from a curiosity to a commodity, things are skewed. In modern times, true crime is not just a niche interest, it's a profitable industry to embark on. True crime essentially fuels streaming services, and tops the podcast charts, or allows YouTubers to see heights of fame they never believed possible before. It creates documentaries, reenactments, dramatizations, franchises and so much more. So, stories like Dahmer's are repackaged, rebranded to the director's vision, and then sold to mass audiences. All for a hefty profit.

This money-making scheme means that we, as the audience, no longer just want the facts. We want the sensationalism, the angles, the commentary to boot. Hungry for the never-seen-before footage, the 'chilling' titles, the actor who played the part just a little too well for our comfort. The problem with this, is that the line between storytelling and sensationalism has become so thin, it's almost completely gone.

Now, this isn't to say that all true crime projects are exploitative, and as someone who is currently writing this book for you, I'd like to believe that I have done it with a sense of retelling all angles, and without falling into the many traps other media sources do. Some of the most powerful storytelling in recent history, and in journalism has come from true crime, and when it is conducted responsibly, and factually, true crime can be a way to fight for justice, to search for answers or for change. This space can be used to amplify victims and their stories, expose failings and corruption, highlight any systemic failures and call upon professionals to make those needed changes to avoid similar incidents in the future.

However, when it is not handled with care, it becomes a revolving circus. The victims? They become the props, and their stories become the plot.

What disturbs me, and I assume, most of us, is how easily we can all forget just what we're consuming. When we sit at home and binge true crime shows, or when we listen to the graphic details while doing the housework, or commuting to the office, do we know what we're doing? When does the line between awareness and entertainment become blurred? Is there a line between empathy and consumption anymore?

When someone's worst day, their trauma, their pain and their last breath becomes a plot twist and a way to boost ratings, it is no longer content. Yet, it is packaged neatly as such, every single day. Of course, as someone who is writing a true crime book, I'm not scolding the world for their interest. But I do say this as someone who has been drawn into the fascination of serial killers too. I have watched the documentaries, read the articles, taken notes and studied timelines. I've analysed interviews, flicked through various clippings to find more and more information about a person who could commit such unspeakable crimes that it baffles the brain. But the longer I spent with Dahmer's story, and the deeper I went into Dahmer's world…

the more I felt that weight. It *should* be a heavy burden to look into someone else's horror.

So, what do we really want to get out of watching these things? It's a hard question to answer, but it's an important one. When we watch true crime shows about Dahmer, what are we hoping to feel? Do we want to cheer as the killer is put to death? Do we want to be horrified and on the edge of our seats about a real-life crime? Do we want to be reassured that murderers like Dahmer are few and far between? Or do we actually want to clutch anything that would give us feeling in a world where true crime has left us mostly desensitized? Are we just trying to feel?

With true crime stories that involve serial killers, they might offer an emotionally intense feeling that is rare to find in everyday life. It has death, mystery, cruelty and hair-raising insights into the mind of a killer that makes us believe that we're right there with the detectives in the interview room. But if we are going to give our undivided attention to stories such as Dahmer's, we owe it to the people who truly suffered from the real-life crimes to ingest the details with respect. There needs to be a willingness to reflect upon what we see, instead of just reacting to a string of carefully curated scenes with suspenseful backing music.

The problem here isn't that we are fascinated by true crime, but it is a problem when we forget that it's *true* crime for a reason. Truth be told, nobody reads or writes a book like this without being somewhat changed but it. The truth is that I don't feel entirely innocent in telling the story. This is because I largely struggled with the ethics of it all, and I had asked myself whether recounting the events that have been retold for over three decades was something that would help or would harm. While I do believe that there is a lot of value that comes from shining the spotlight on the truth behind history's most horrid crimes, I also believe that we have to take responsibility for the way we tell those facts.

So, whether this is how we frame the story, how much we decide to focus on the killer versus the victims, or any other line of focus, we have to make sure that it isn't disrespectful. As viewers and readers, we also have to take responsibility for how we engage with them. Not every story that comes through the press needs to be dramatized, and not every criminal needs to have a fanbase behind them. Similarly, not every victim should be remembered as to how they died.

If you recall the victims' section, these were respected and loved men. Men who were expectant fathers, fathers, husbands, partners, brothers, sons, nephews, friends; hoping to break into new ventures, with a spring in their step and full lives to lead. So, where does that leave us as the true crime audience? Perhaps it begins with asking different questions while we ingest these stories. Instead of 'who did it?' or 'how did the murder happen?', we should ask: "Why did this happen?" or "How do we stop future failures?". We could even ask: "Who was failed in this story?". Perhaps this means we should choose different media that prioritises the victims and their voices, instead of the persona of the killer. Maybe it also means checking ourselves when we recognise a sliver of thrill pass through us during a particularly intense scene. At this point, we could ask ourselves whether we are losing touch of what the story is about, about the real cost of this story: the victims.

Or it could be as simple as remembering that behind every true crime case is real people, real consequences, real pain and lasting issues. With that, here are my final thoughts on the social and cultural impact of the Dahmer case. Let it be known that I am not here to tell anyone to stop watching their favourite documentaries, or even from reading true crime stories. Curiosity about the unknown is a natural thing for us to have as humans. A lot of us have the desire to understand why some people go on to do awful things, but there is a distinct difference between consuming a story and then actually caring about it.

If reading this book so has made you pause for a second, and think about the lives that were lost, the system that failed so many, the people around the immediate case who are more than just a name in a headline, then that might just be enough. Perhaps reflection of these crimes is justice enough. That we are remembering a killer as something to be baffled by, repulsed by, instead of revered and sympathised with.

Yes, Dahmer's upbringing could have been the catalyst for his eventual killings, and yes, intervention may very well have stopped this from ever occurring – but two facts can be true at the same time. Dahmer may have been failed in early life, but he failed many more people when he chose to murder and orchestrate crimes so horrific that there are now numerous shows in his honour.

To end this section: Yes, we are all obsessed with true crime, and maybe we will always be obsessed with it. But whether we use this information to remember the victims, their families, and the failings, or whether we consume it for fun... that is what matters the most. If there is anything that I have learned about Dahmer whilst writing this book, it is that humanity always triumphs over darkness.

Part VI

Lessons Learned

Part VI: Lessons and Reflections

Healing and Justice

Gerald Boyle continued to practice law in Milwaukee after his infamous Dahmer case, with 'no intention of retiring'. Even after Dahmer was incarcerated and his father had retained other counsel, the lawyer used to meet with Dahmer privately, and while many people believed that he deserved to go to prison, the former lawyer always believed that he belonged at the Mendota Mental Health Institute, a Madison, Wisconsin psychiatric hospital, so that he could be studied.

He once said before passing away: "God knows what we could have learned. If we could have gotten him to Mendota, we might have found out about how to help all these other adolescents with mental health problems who are committing terrible crimes."

A Parent's Struggles

After years of standing by their son, despite being unable to comprehend why he took the lives of seventeen boys and men, the parents of Dahmer were forced to grapple with their loss, their future stigma, and their pain. While Joyce and Lionel publicly struggled in the aftermath, particularly when it came to deciding whether or not to allow their son's brain to be used for scientific research to aid in understanding more about serial killers, they did agree on their love for him, right until the end.

Lionel, who advocated for his son's psychological issues, and attempted to give his all to explaining his son and the details he held about their conversations, died on December 5, 2023, in Medina, Ohio at the age of 87. At the time, he was staying at a hospice facility which was confirmed by one of his caregivers. Jeb Muller shared that Lionel suffered a number of heart attacks in the years before his death, which was also exacerbated by the death of his second wife, Shari, in the January before.

As for Joyce, she passed away twenty-three years before her ex-husband, at the age of 64. Having suffered from a long history of mental health issues, she died of breast cancer in 2000. But before that, she had regular contact with Bill Janz of the Milwaukee Sentinel. In one telephone conversation, she shared with him that when she thinks about what Dahmer did to his victims, she can no longer breathe.

She had been a case manager at the Central Valley AIDS Team and was also the founder of The Living Room, an HIV community centre. According to her colleague: "Everybody loved her. She would do anything for her clients and for anybody really. She was just this wonderful person."

When Dahmer's crimes came to light, Joyce struggled to cope with the reality of what her son had done and attempted to take her own life by using her gas oven. Speaking about him in an interview with *Hard Copy*, Joyce later defended Dahmer, stating: "I know this sounds strange but he did not mean to hurt anyone. I still love my son. I never stopped loving my son. Jeff was a victim of a compulsion. An obsession."

She claimed: "He's not a monster. He's a human being and I think he deserves some help."

As per the *United Press International*, she was found lying face-down in her home alongside a will and a letter before being taken to hospital where she would make a full recovery. Within her will, she had stipulated that all of her belongings would be given to her son, David.

Even though her ex-husband later explained that she had not taken adequate care of her son as a baby, she revealed that she 'knew that I'd done a good job as a parent' and pointed out the 'stereotype' in society for blaming mothers for how their children turn out.

Lionel would then land another blow to her, and alleged that she had taken powerful sedatives and hormones while she was pregnant, for which he hoped medical authorities would be able to determine whether this proved to have been a contributing factor for how Dahmer became a killer.

While Lionel tried to lay blame on Joyce's parenting and her mental health struggles, Joyce argued that this answer and did not account for the complexities of being human.

Her love for her son continued long after his death, and she often gave speeches about being gay in America. After fighting for so long, her legacy remained as a woman who loved her son, and wanted to help others.

The genre of True Crime also left a lasting impact on everyone, particularly when it comes to Dahmer stories. There have been countless stories about Dahmer, and not so much about his victims. What impact does this have on us, as a society?

According to a new YouGov poll, 57 per cent of Americans say they consume true-crime content with 61 per cent of women admitting to consuming the content, 52 per cent of men admitting to doing so, and 61 per cent of women versus 42 per cent of men under the age of 65 years old confirming that they too partake in the genre.

True crime is a genre that has taken over the world. There have been more and more documentaries being created each and every year. There was the *Tiger King* series which explored the life of a man who worked with tigers, Joe Exotic, who partook in a series of illegal dealings whilst his business suffered. This all culminated in him being imprisoned for an alleged attempt of hiring a hit man to kill a rival of his. Tiger King topped the charts when it came out, and he now has a fan base.

Another series, *Don't F*** with Cats: Hunting an Internet Killer,* explored how an internet sleuth was able to catch a person who murdered animals for online entertainment, and this became a big documentary for true crime fans to dive into. There were also dramas like *When They See Us* and *Unbelievable*, as well as popular podcasts such as *Serial* and *Dr. Death.*

For Americans, and the rest of the world, obsession with the genre is not new, and you might be surprised to know that true crime literature has existed since the 1600s, but the form has shifted as time progresses. However, it is dulling our apathy towards victims. Some positive opinions of true crime appear to have decreased since 2022, when YouGov conducted a poll about true crime that included some of the same questions. Fewer Americans today than in 2022 agree that the true crime genre increases empathy with crime victims, and improves the understanding of the criminal justice system. Less people also believe that the genre helps to solve crimes that wouldn't have been solved otherwise. So, why is it so popular? There have been longstanding debates over the ethics of the genre, with questions such as whether the genre sensationalises trauma.

To this, the poll showed that Americans are split as to whether the genre is ethical or not. According to the poll, 50 per cent believe that it is ethical to consume the content, while 16 per cent think that it is unethical. 38 per cent say that it is ethical to create true crime content, whereas 50 per cent say that it is unethical. People are understandably divided as to whether their love of true crime is a good thing or whether they are playing into something bigger than themselves: sensationalising misery.

To this, Whitney Phillips, assistant professor of digital platforms and ethics, explained: "It wasn't that I set out to create a class about focusing on the harms of true crime. It was how do we use true crime to think about these really important ethical issues that everyone in the room is going to have to deal with in a professional capacity."

Dean Fido, Lecturer in Psychology, also said, as per the therapy service, BetterHelp: "As humans, we are always looking for something new and novel. Whether it's good or bad, we need something that creates an element of excitement. When we mix this desire with insight and solving a puzzle, it can give us a short, sharp shock of adrenaline, but in a relatively safe environment."

As for Charlie Tuggle, who has 16 years of experience in local television, it's a way to get justice. He told The University of North Carolina at Chappel Hill: "The murderer winds up not paying consequences. Maybe it's ineptitude by the investigators or prosecutors, or even malfeasance where people get bribed. This person committed a murder and should pay."

Counsellor Jenny Warwick told Happiful that she has her own theories on this. "People are fascinated with human psychology, particularly criminal psychology," she says. "We are often intrigued by the behaviours and motives behind criminal acts. By looking for an understanding of the motivations, upbringing, and patterns of infamous serial killers, for example, we can get an insight into criminal psychology."

But this can actually have an impact on your mental health. The Cleveland Clinic explored this topic with Chivonna Childs, PhD, a psychologist with Cleveland Clinic who said: "It can increase our anxiety because we become hypervigilant. We're always looking for the bad person. Every white van becomes the van of a killer or murderer."

Other people do not like to consume the content because something similar happened to them and it put their life and the content itself into a different perspective. *Buzzfeed* interviewed many to find out their thoughts, with one person telling the publication: "Once you experience some form of true-crime trauma firsthand in your own life, your outlook on that sort of content completely changes. You don't want to watch more of it. It's not 'entertaining' whatsoever."

Enjoying the content is also seen as a 'red flag' for one psychologist, who claims that this means that you find comfort in trauma, as you may have your own that has been left untreated. She said: "If your idea of relaxing before you go to sleep is to watch three episodes of Law and Order I would encourage you to think about 'why is trauma relaxing to me?'"

The question of why the genre is so popular is ever-present in many people's minds. But that is a very loaded question.

Humanity in the Face of Evil

When we speak about Dahmer, it is so easy to fall into the language of 'spectacle'. There are the various headlines plastered over the press, documentaries being made in circulation every other year, there is the endless retellings of his horror, and they all focus on the man at the centre of the case. The killer, and the one whose name we all know. But his story is not the story that should have the lingering impact. No, it should be about those he hurt. This book is about terrible things. It dives into violence, destruction, alcohol abuse, torture, dismemberment, rape, gruesome fantasies and so much more. But it is also about people. People who loved, who laughed, and who should still be here today.

As with many terrifying true crime cases, the victims and their names are eclipsed by Dahmer's. Too often, in these true crime narratives, the victims and their families become background characters, fillers to illustrate the depravity and how far humanity can sink before we recognise the evil surrounding us. The erasure of the victims is a second violence towards them, and it is important to talk about. Because the fact is, each one of those men had a life.

While we know of their names, we do not know their favourite songs, their inside jokes with loved ones, their peculiar habits that we all have, and their flaws. Those men had plans, and some of them were grand, or modest. Yet all of those plans were left unfinished. These people were whole, vibrant, full, and lived. Their lives are not defined by the way that they were cut so cruelly short. For once, this reflection is not about the person who murdered them. It's about them.

When we only tell one side of the story, we lose so much substance and emotion. When we talk about crimes as grotesque as Dahmer's was, it becomes very tempting to study the crime itself, and the psychology of the killer – as has been done in this book. That is where the questions begin to form. How could someone do something like this? What makes a person turn into a predator? Why did nobody stop him sooner?

While we analyse the 'how's' and the 'why's' we risk overlooking one important thing: The 'who'. The 'who' in this story matters the most. Of course, we have dived into Dahmer's childhood with such a fervour that it almost feels as though we all have some sort of understanding as to how his compulsions and fantasies were created: The mentally unstable mother who would not touch him; The emotionally and often physically distant father who taught him how to strip bones of flesh and preserve animal remains; The hernia operation which turned a happy toddler into a withdrawn boy who was afraid of his penis being removed from his body; The alcoholic teenager that was failed by the systems around him; The list could go on. But what about the ramifications of those failings?

Seventeen known victims were butchered and have been displayed on every major source of media since their deaths. Mostly, they have been used to fuel our want to learn more about Dahmer. But what about learning more about them? When you look at the victims as people, and not just names in the news, you begin to see the true scale of the loss Dahmer left in his wake. The people of Milwaukee haven't just lost lives, they lost stories. They also lost futures, fathers who did not get to see their young grow, artists who wanted to break out into the big world, models with dreams, dancers, workers, dreamers, lovers, friends, and so much more. We lost potential in people that will never be realised.

Some of the people Dahmer murdered to satisfy his need to be in total control, and his desire to use other people as a means to his end, were just beginning to live freely. They had just found their own identities. While some were struggling to navigate a world that didn't make space for their sexuality, others were striving to find stability in their lives for the very first time. Let's look at their names again.

- Steven Hicks, 18
- Steven Tuomi, 28
- Jamie Doxtator, 14
- Richard Guerrero, 25
- Anthony Sears, 24
- Ricky Beeks, 33
- Eddie Smith, 28
- Ernest Miller, 24
- David Thomas, 23
- Curtis Straughter, 18
- Errol Lindsey, 19
- Anthony Hughes, 31
- Konerak Sinthasomphone, 14
- Matt Turner, 20
- Jeremiah Weinberger, 23
- Oliver Lacy, 23
- Joseph Bradehoft, 25

Many of these men and boys were people of colour, which is a fact that is not lost on most people. This detail opened up the conversation of systemic realities that enabled Dahmer to conduct his numerous murders undetected for far too long. It also reflects just how certain lives in society are valued differently, when it comes to the eyes of institutions designed to protect them. So, to make sure that we are honouring the victims, we need to look beyond their final moments, and we also have to resist the effect of violence. When it comes to looking only at their violent end, it reduced them to a headline, or just another statistic to look at.

Of course, I did not know these men, and it is likely that you did not either. Most readers don't know the people that books are written about. But we all feel the absence of their presence, or at least, the injustice of the absence in the world. There is something so sacred about imagining having a life that goes on uninterrupted. A life that ends in the golden years, on a porch, sipping hot tea. When life is cut short, it makes us notice. It also makes us imagine who they might have become, had they had the chance to live that long.

Would they have gone on to become parents? We know that a lot of them had children, but would their partners have given birth to more? Would they have become grandparents? Would they have changed their careers, fallen in love again, moved cities or fulfilled their dreams? Maybe they would have grown into a new version of themselves that happens to all of us as we age. Sadly, we'll just never know the answer to those questions. But that doesn't mean that we don't sit and wonder. Even without knowing all this information about their stories, we can still remember them as more than being Dahmer's victims. We can all remember that they once had voices, and that those voices deserve to echo longer than Dahmer's.

Now, while we can all listen to who they were and talk about them and their hopes, we can't speak for them. Because nobody can do that now. But taking a quiet moment to speak about them with the belief that their lives mattered, might just be enough.

True crime is almost synonymous with entertainment, and it often markets itself that way. While there is nothing inherently wrong with marketing material for an audience that wants to understand the darkest parts of humanity, there is a line between engaging and consuming. There is also a line between remembering and exploiting the memories and pain of others.

I wrote about this very fact in earlier chapters but let us revisit it. When we turn real pain, real lives and real loss into plot points, we risk detaching ourselves from the very thing that makes these types of stories worth telling: the humanity. So, this section is here to slow things down a notch and to interrupt the psychological speculation you have already dived into, and the horrors of the crimes. Let us remind ourselves that these were very real people, and that every page written about their killer is a page that exists simply because they no longer can be here. That is the true costs of true crime. And this is also the cost of what cannot ever be forgotten, unless we risk turning the genre into a platform to revere murderers instead of remembering victims.

So, as we sit on our couch, on the bus, or on a beach and reflect upon this story, there is one part of the case that will never stop hurting – no matter how many times you go over the information. It is the missed chances, and the ignored warnings. These failures to listen to the cries for help of a victim who attempted to escape, cries for help by witnesses, and also from the signs Dahmer exhibited in his early and teenage years are all on society's shoulders.

While some of these men were last seen alive begging for safety to those who should have been there to protect, others were dismissed because who they were was not accepted during the time period. Some of them were also failed by a system that did not see their lives and their safety as urgent. The inaction from police, from neighbours, from anyone who could have helped, rings far louder than any headline that could be written.

Of course, it is not enough to blame just one man for all of this. He committed the crimes, that cannot be dismissed, but the silence of those around him cannot be seen as anything other than his accomplice. This silence came in many forms. There was the homophobia, the racism, the apathy and denial of what was taking place. We need to remember all of it to honour the victims and acknowledging the condition which allowed them to become victims.

Like any reader, you might be thinking about whether justice was really served in the end. Dahmer was apprehended, sentenced and then murdered in prison. So, it seems almost poetic that he met a bloodied end for what he had done to so many others. But was it true justice? After all, he served two years of his life terms before meeting his end. His murderer noted that he appeared to accept his fate. Dahmer told his mother that he did not care about what happened to him in the prison, nor did he care for his own safety. Did he want to die? Was he handed a fate he wanted for himself? Perhaps. With that, we can only come to the conclusion that no justice on Earth can undo what happened to the seventeen men he murdered. No sentence could even be long enough, and although he apologised, no apology can ever be deep enough to take away the pain he caused. But there is, however, something that we can offer. That is the memory of what happened.

After a very long analysis of Dahmer, his crimes, his life, and the lives of those he took, this book is soon to close with a thought on the impact it had on everyone, on those who cover the stories, and the impact it has on you.

Conclusion

Finally, we have come to an end to the retelling and exploration into the story. Thank you for sticking with me this far. I want to take a moment to thank everyone who was a part of this book, including the experts, contributors, numerous sources and more. I also want to take a moment to appreciate the nature of this book. It was a hard story to cover, a real story to remember, and a lasting impact on my life.

Jeffrey Dahmer's life was plagued from the beginning, and the various failures to intervene were apparent, and difficult to swallow. From a young tot born into a life without (what appeared to be) much love and support, I could easily understand how the ball began to roll on twisting his mind. But what we must never forget is that the consequences of such things caused far more hurt than what was done to the Dahmer family. There are currently seventeen families who are carrying the weight of this pain and will continue to carry it for much longer to come.

While we can speculate on just how Dahmer became the man he did, focusing on the victims should always shine the brightest. Through expert analysis, opinions and comments, a story surrounding how Dahmer may have been molded into a murderer was very interesting to be part of. The theory of nature versus nurture is something that has been widely debated, as is the criteria for who can be considered a psychopath and who may not be. The world of mental health and clinical psychology is vast, and also still continuing to grow and adapt to new terms, new issues and new ways that people present themselves.

Dahmer began his life as what was described as a happy little boy who was excited by the world around him, and after numerous issues, and an alleged molestation incident, he turned into a monster. While we can never be sure of exactly what it was that caused this, we can clearly see quite a few instances where the turning point may have occurred. His lonely isolation as a child and teenager is apparent, as was his need for love and company. But through the various failures of those around him, and the failure of himself to not seek serious help and treatment, we are all left with the grief and heartbreak.

Not only did Dahmer damage his community as a whole, but he divided the safety that people once believed they had when in the presence of police. He tarnished the memory of many boys and men, and he marked his name on their legacies. Dahmer is no hero, nor is he a man who should be obsessed over, infatuated or sympathised with. After reading through expert opinion and the retelling of his life and crimes, we can see that he was a man in need of help. However, he failed to take proactive action and instead leaned into his twisted fantasies and indulged the dark urges within him.

After taking the lives of so many within a decade, Dahmer's life came to a grisly end at the hands of a fellow criminal. Some may believe that this was his karma, and that it was a well-deserved and brutal death. Others might think that it was nothing compared to the end that he deserved to have handed to him. Opinions will always be divided in cases such as this. But perhaps we can all agree that the victims matter the most in this story, that their love, life, and futures should be at the forefront of everyone's mind after reading about Dahmer, and that he should never be able to cast a shadow over them.

After all, where there is a true crime story, there is a true crime behind it. With that, comes to an end of the story, and next, I have a few words of reflection for the readers of this book who can hopefully take this with them and ponder over it as they consider the implications of the true crime genre and our obsession with death as a society.

Author's Note

Writing about Jeffrey Dahmer was not an easy task, and nor should it be. The story above is not one that a person could tell lightly, and it is also something that cannot be told comfortably, or left behind once the final chapter has been written. For nearly a year this case has followed me. The dates, photographs and names of the victims have been with me every single day from the moment I decided to write this book, and I imagine that they will stay with me long after. The dark fascination which teeters on the edge of horror and humanity is something that many people will also feel once they have read this book. I didn't set out to become so immersed in the mind of a killer, and certainly not one whose crimes have gone on to scar so many people – yet here I am, on the other side of the project, attempting to make sense of all the information and analysis I completed.

There is a sense of duality to writing about Dahmer. On one hand, I can now understand the undeniable appeal of the case – the headline horrors, a twisted story of death and surreal destruction, and then the psychological puzzle that is, or was, Dahmer's mind. But on the other, there is a feeling of a somewhat unbearable weight. Every page of this book is a reminder that these were all real people, with real lives and loved ones and that they are no longer able to live a future, like us. All their prospects were stolen in the most unimaginable of ways. So, I found myself constantly asking: Why do we tell stories like this, and why do we also read them?

It's the allure of the darkness.

A quote which is often attributed to Friedrich Nietzsche, a German philosopher: "He who fights with monsters should be careful lest he thereby become a monster. And if you gaze long into an abyss, the abyss also gazes into you." That one quote was something that I thought about a lot whilst writing this book – and it's not because I feared that I would also become a monster, but because I believed that slowly, page by page, I was becoming desensitised by the horrors I was writing about. There's a certain kind of numbness that can so easily creep in when you spend too much time examining the worst of humanity. Even more so when you try so hard to understand it.

So, why do we read these books? There is a simple answer. Essentially, true crime stories such as Dahmer's life draw us in for a number of reasons. The first is that the information is so horrid that it's like a car crash you simply can't look away from, and the other is that we are fearful of those who look inconspicuous, and we want to know that there are those who do not lurk in the dark, but walk among us, who could do the worst to us.

The morbid fascination isn't new, and the true crime genre has been steadily gaining popularity in the last couple of decades. But what responsibility comes along with that curiosity? There really is a thin line between examining a case and glorifying crimes, and also between understanding and sensationalising. While I've attempted to walk that line ever so carefully, and respectfully, it was no simple task. It is so easy to empathise with a person who became a killer if you focus on their childhood, trauma and how preventable it could have all been. But on the other hand, at the heart of all of this, there are human lives that were taken, and they matter more than any analysis.

So, when I first took on this project, I believed that I would be writing about one man and his awful crimes against unsuspecting victims. But I very soon realised that it was about many people. First, there were the victims, who were mostly young men of colour, and that they were more than names on a search engine result when looking at Dahmer information. They were real people who were loved, and their names deserve more space than his does in this book. Their stories deserve to be told in a way that doesn't focus on their end, but rather how they lived and how they loved. Yet, we don't know them the way that we know Dahmer.

In fact, I am almost ashamed to admit that I could not have named a single victim before I began my writing. Could you have named any before watching a Dahmer show, or reading this book? These people were very obviously forgotten about in the noise of Dahmer, and it became more and more apparent as I continued to write this story. I also realised that they were much more than victims and caught myself falling into the trap of focusing on the serial killer more than those he killed. Their very real stories deserve more than to be told inside of the context of their deaths. We at least owe them that respect.

So, let's revisit the victims, who they were, and what they meant to those around them.

Steven Hicks was an 18-year-old who was interested in making friends and listening to music.

Hicks was on his way home from a music festival, which put him on a deserted road in rural Bath, Ohio. The teen had just graduated from high school, and with his parents having recently finalised a divorce, he was grappling with his father moving from the family home and his mother, against a court order, moving his younger brother out of state.

It was his father's birthday (and Father's Day) and he was going to visit his girlfriend.

Described as a kind-hearted and compassionate person who loved to help others and was always open to making new friends, Hick's memory lives on.

Steven Tuomi worked as a short-order cook and grew up in Michigan with dreams of carrying out his artistic dreams. According to those around him, he was quiet and well-liked by those around him.

Jamie Doxtator was a victim in many ways, with the youngster having been through a lot in his 14 years of life. He was a teenage runaway who wanted to escape a violent and unstable homelife and make a new life for himself. Somewhere safe, somewhere that made him feel at home. Known to the police, the Native American teenager was half Stockbridge and part Oneida, liked to play pool and ride his bike, and was described as being lively and cheerful, outgoing and that he also loved making new friends.

Richard Guerrero was of Hispanic decent and was on his way to visit a friend in Milwaukee. Loved by his friends and his family, Guerrero had his whole life in front of him.

Ronald Flowers Jr. saved another man's life after having his nearly taken from him. His act of courage is something that lives on in his story, and his willingness to put himself in the line of fire to ensure that another life is not destroyed is something that can never be taken from him.

Somsack Sinthasomphone was just a boy when he was assaulted, and having grown up in a financially struggling family, he took it upon himself to try to help out. The youngster tried to work to provide for his family, and was a strong presence in his family in the eventual court proceedings.

Anthony Sears worked at a Baker's Square and had just received the amazing news that he had been promoted to the role of a manager. With this news in mind, his family had planned a dinner in celebration of his promotion. As an aspiring model, Sears stood out from the crowd and would have made a mark on the industry.

Raymond Smith (Ricky Beeks) was dealt a trying hand in life, and his work was something that he undertook to survive. Anyone who would have had the same life, may have chosen to work on the streets too. His strength, resilience and his attempt to survive in such strained conditions can only be commended.

Eddie Smith was also an aspiring model. The striking 'African American male' with black hair and brown eyes, was known as 'Sheik' in his neighborhood because of 'the turban-like head covering he habitually wore'. His memory forever lives on.

Ernest Miller was a talented dance student who worked as a busboy at a hotel in downtown Chicago. He was incredibly close with his family and he made sure to attend every single family gathering planned.

He was known as a caring and loving person, and will always be known as such.

David Thomas was the father of a 3-year-old daughter and always made time to see her while he was in and out of the family home. He would have had so many memories of his daughter growing up and may even have become a grandfather.

Curtis Straughter is fondly remembered by his nicknames of Demetra and Curta. Those who knew him have publicly described him as a young, vivacious person who had the whole world in front of him.

He lived with his grandmother, and although he suffered the loss of his nursing job, he had dreams of becoming a model and finishing his college degree.

Errol Lindsey was very well liked by those who knew him, and was about to welcome a daughter into the world. Those who knew him described him as an upstanding and generous person who loved to make new friends. He was also very popular and was incredibly close to his mother and sister. He was the youngest of six children and worked as a plaster figure worker. He was so close with his mother, that he would always call her before going to meet with friends.

Tony Anthony Hughes will always be remembered for his want to make new friends. As a deaf man, who was also mute, he was described as 'outgoing, jolly, happy' and he 'could easily make friends'.

Konerak Sinthasomphone was a 14-year-old hard worker, who was struggling with his family's financial situation. Eager to help where he could, the teenager began to attempt to bring in money to ease the burden.

Matt Turner was also known by the name of Donald Montrell. He recently left his family home to stay at a Chicago halfway house and had high aspirations of becoming a model.

Jeremiah Weinberger was a customer service representative for a video store, and according to his roommate, he loved art and was a meticulous person who knew where everything was, dressed nicely and worried about what he wore and how he looked. He cared about how he was presented, and that is a great personality trait to have.

Oliver Lacy was a bodybuilding enthusiast who was a track racer at River Forest High School and was described as outspoken. He was the youngest of three sons and was a family man who wore his father's cross after his passing. Lacy was the proud father of a two-year-old child and was engaged to be married.

Joseph Bradehoft was the eldest of his siblings and he grew up in Illinois where he married his wife Cheryl and went on to have three young children ranging between the ages of two and seven. He was a hard worker and moved to Milwaukee to search for a job to help financially support his family back home in Minnesota. He loved sports and fishing and was also a devoted father to his children.

Tracy Edwards was a very lucky man, who was quick-witted and able to react with a speed which allowed him to survive the impossible. While he escaped, he has been plagued by the trauma ever since. However, he is the reason that there only are seventeen victims on the list, and not more. That is an achievement that nobody can take away from him.

The voices of the men above deserve to be heard, and they also deserve to be remembered. Of course, you will always remember the most shocking details first, but now you can reflect on the good times, and the hopes and dreams they once had. These men could have been anybody. They could have been a friend of yours, a relative, a colleague or passerby. All of those things matter.

Their names deserve far more space than this, and their stories deserve to be retold, again and again. While we can agree that we will never know them the way that we know Dahmer, at least we can say that we know a little bit more than we did before. The imbalance of this knowledge weighed heavily on me as I wrote this book, and it still does. Because there is always the risk of tipping the scale in the direction of the killer, or even turning the killer into a protagonist, or reducing the victims to names at the footnote.

Isn't it a painful irony when the person who committed the crime goes on to become the most famous name in the story? Of course, I took this thought with me throughout the book, and I also made a conscious effort (even in this final reflection) to remember that this is not simply a Dahmer story, but it is also a story about the people he took from the world. It's a story about a marginalised group of people, who also fell victim to the possible systemic failures, police negligence, and whose voices were not heard.

Now, people understandably want a clear answer when it comes to killers, as it is just in our nature to want to know why. As we have already explored, the questions we ask are whether or not it was his upbringing? The nature versus nurture debate is very real, and although it might seem as though it is attempting to explain away his crimes or even give him an excuse – it isn't. We all want to know what really makes a killer, and by knowing, maybe we can stop this from happening in the future.

One of my interviewees suggested the use of artificial intelligence in compiling at risk factors of those who have the potential to turn into a criminal and then using this information to single out those who are likely to be in need of intervention. I thought that it was a great idea. However, we seen realised that we might be putting those people in a box and branding them in a way which could unintentionally push them further into becoming the person we do not wish them to be. They would be ostracised, phased out of society, and made to feel as though they are inherently wrong. Of course, this might be better than having another killer on the loose; it might cause harm. So, how do we fix this? Perhaps that question is left for someone much more knowledgeable than I.

Then there is the question of whether or not he was simply born to be evil. Now, if the nature versus nurture theory is correct, that's a very unlikely scenario. But not impossible. How do we filter out those people, and once caught, what do we do with them? It's not always as cut and dry as we might like to think.

More questions come to the surface, such as whether it was a mental illness. Perhaps. Dahmer was indeed diagnosed with many illnesses after being apprehended by the police which paints the picture of a very sick, albeit sane man. Of course, this may have been helped with intervention and treatment, but was he too far gone to see the light? Nobody could ever know.

The truth of the matter is that there is rarely a simple solution, or even a satisfying solution that pleases everyone. Dahmer's life was a mess, and it was full of contradictions too. The man was soft-spoken, but he was also violent and brutal. He was intelligent, but he carried a disturbed mind. He alleged that he was remorseful, yet he was scarily methodical in his actions and words. So, trying to reduce the man to one theory or explanation would be like attempting to summarise a nightmare by using logic. Logic does not matter in this case as the pieces just don't fit as they should. Sometimes, it may just be that people simply break and cause the most harm to those all around them.

Yet, despite all of what we know, we still try to understand because it's human nature to make sense of the unknown. We are pattern seekers at heart, and we always crave an explanation that fits the bill. We do this so that we can prevent it from happening again and again. But will it work?

Sometimes we can do this, but there will always be those who slip through the cracks. There doesn't appear to be a formula as to why some people choose to kill, and others choose not to. There is also no checklist available to predict just who will cross over that line and into the darkness. So, this uncertainty is part of what makes true crime stories so haunting. After reading, listening to or watching them, we are left with more questions than answers. But did you ever think that that might be the point?

In writing this story, I have come to believe that remembering is an act of resistance against the crimes, and also against the criminals. It is a way of honouring the victims when justice has been imperfect or it has been delayed. We do this to make sure that these people are not just statistics in a report, but they are remembered for who they are. We can always reclaim their humanity away from the person who stole it without giving it a second thought. If there is any purpose of this book, it is that beyond the curtain of grim curiosity, there is always room to reflect upon the past and make changes for the future. It can also be used as a warning for what can happen if signs are ignored and intervention is lacking or delayed.

Do you know of a person who is displaying these types of behaviours? Would you call them out on it, sit with them and talk about what's going on in their lives? Or would you walk on by, muttering a little line about how they are a future Jeffrey Dahmer in the making? This is what this book is about. We can all make changes for good, and it doesn't have to be grand displays of alliance. It can be micro changes that make a difference.

While a case like this seems like it is nothing more than a terrible part of history, the truth is that it can always happen again. Copycat killers are always out there, and people who snap are just a few steps behind. The themes of this case are also well and truly alive. There was racism, homophobia and systemic neglect – things that are still with us today. This, on its own, means that the story of Dahmer can be repeated, again and again. Those failures allowed evil to happen without intervention, and whether you want to believe it or not, those failures are still present today.

Now that we are coming to an end on this book, I want to reassure you that I did not write it to scare you, and I also did not write it to glorify violence. I wrote it because these dark stories deserve to be told with consideration, and with care. This is because the people who suffered in the midst of it, and in the wake of it, deserve more than our silence. They certainly deserve more than our entertainment, social media trends, and our infatuation. There is somewhere between horror and heartbreak that we can find a lesson worth holding onto.

Now, if you made it to the end of this book, thank you for your time and for sitting with the discomfort for so long. I also want to thank you for not turning away from it, and choosing to sit in these feelings, even if they make you want to put your book on a very high shelf and cool down for a few weeks. Because remembering these crimes is something only we can do.

With that, dear reader, by the time you reach this page you will have already walked though some pretty heavy territory. You have been taken through the details, the clinical jargon, the heartbreaking insights, and delved into a criminal case that haunts people to this day. But you've made it this far, and for that, you should be proud. This kind of story is by no means easy to digest, and it isn't supposed to be.

We live in a world where these crime stories are constantly offered up to us for consumption, through the podcasts, streaming platforms, books (like this one) and more. So, in some ways, they have become out entertainment diet that we binge, rank, and debate all at the same time. Sometimes, we even have a favourite true crime show that we watch, or a murder case that is the most shocking for us. Somewhere inside of this true crime obsession are real people, and I don't want to lose sight of that. Not in this book, and not in any conversation outside of it.

So, let me be as honest with you as I can be. Writing this book changed me, and while it was not in a sensationalised or dramatic way, it changed the way that I think about these stories. It also changed the way that I look at the world, at the justice and protective systems, and at how easy it is to overlook someone who is crying out for help and for safety. It also made me more aware of what the true cost of silence is, and how quickly we can forget the victims. We always remember the name of the killer, but never remember the victims. Can you name half of them right now, even though their names are in the above chapter? Can any of us? But we remember Dahmer, and that is what truly unsettles me.

As Patrick Rogers of *PEOPLE* said, decades after he covered the case in real-time: "If only these voices had been heard earlier, the saga of America's most depraved serial offender might have been somewhat less tragic. As a reporter covering the case, and today as *PEOPLE*'s senior editor covering crime, I have learned a lesson: It's the victims who matter. "

I did not write this book because I believed the world needed another retelling of Dahmer's crimes. If anyone wanted to find out the gritty details, they could easily dive into the archives available online to find out for themselves. They could also look into the various sources of media that has covered him extensively in the last thirty years since his crimes took place. His story has been told, extensively. And it has been told again in different ways. However, I wanted to write this book because there was a quieter, and more difficult question on my mind. It was: What do we do with stories like this and what does it mean to engage with them, and then go back to our lives as if nothing had happened? What responsibility to do we carry after reading this book? I don't particularly have a neat and simple answer for this, as I don't think there is one. But I do think it begins with remembering that this story isn't fiction, and that there were real people within these pages, not just the man who has seen an immense amount of fame since his death.

I also wanted to explore the question on everyone's mind: what makes a killer? This is one of the driving forces that led me to want to work on Dahmer in particular. There have been many serial killers before Dahmer, and there have been a lot more since. But what drew me to this story in particular was the many aspects that seemed to need clarification. Was it racial bias on behalf of the police force? If you were to ask Reyes, a retired detective and judge, perhaps. Were there systemic or individual failings? Of course, he says. Was Dahmer's upbringing a significant factor in how he came to become a murderer? If you were to ask any one of the psychologists in the book, yes. Yes, it was very much so a large part of why he became a killer. What about his drinking? Yes, while adolescent years are the years for experimentation with alcohol, he took it too far. And if science has anything to say about it, it may have stunted crucial development in his brain.

Then of course, there was his opportunity. Had he not been left to his own devices for so long, he may not had been able to carry out such killings. His grandmother's basement was his safe space to begin his spree, and his apartment was his domain of terror. Being a loner was an advantage to Dahmer. The emotions a lot of these failings can bring forth is anger in a lot of people, and that's okay. If you felt sick, numb, disturbed, or even fascinated by the fluke of layered events that culminated in someone becoming a murderer, then that's okay too. But what I hope you did not feel, was an overwhelming sense of empathy.

While I was writing his formative years, I too felt sorry for a young Dahmer who needed love and support. It is only natural to feel such a way. However, as an adult? His actions were inexcusable, and entirely avoidable. I have covered true crime cases for years in the media as a journalist, and while no case has ever come close in gore, horror and length as Dahmer's did, you begin to see a pattern of events. A childhood gone wrong, a world where the person refuses to integrate into society, or simply does not know how. The stripping of so many essential support services which delays intervention and early help. There is always a pattern.

So, what do you do with this information? You can simply remember the names of the dead.

Again, I would like to thank those who contributed to this book and shared their expert insight, including Mandy Morris, Caitlin Weese, Jill Sitnick, Holly Keller, Alex Alvarez, Israel Reyes, Naomi Murphy, Fotoulla Menikou, Dr Manpreet Dhuffar-Pottiwal, Elreacy Dock, Dr Joel Frank, and Amy Bentley.

Bibliography

Video

Bad Girl (2021). *Testimonio de una víctima de Jeffrey Dahmer - Subtitulado en español.* [online] YouTube. Available at: https://www.youtube.com/watch?v=OKz7DjG62CY [Accessed 26 Jun. 2025].

Court

law2.umkc.edu. (1992). *Estate of Sinthasomphone v Milwaukee (1992).* [online] 5 March. Available at: http://law2.umkc.edu/faculty/projects/ftrials/conlaw/Sinthasomphone.html.

News Clip

Musca Law (n.d.) Florida burglary laws, Musca Law Knowledge Center. Available at: https://www.muscalaw.com/knowledge/florida-burglary-laws#:~:text=Florida%20Statute%20%C2%A7%20810.02%20defines,includes%20remaining%20on%20the%20premises

Musca Law (n.d.) Florida burglary laws, Musca Law Knowledge Center. Available at: https://www.muscalaw.com/knowledge/florida-burglary-laws

Press, T.A. (1992). Jury Hears How Unruffled Dahmer Dodged Arrest. *The New York Times.* [online] 12 Feb. Available at: http://www.nytimes.com/1992/02/12/us/jury-hears-how-unruffled-dahmer-dodged-arrest.html.

Academic Journal

Hiller-Sturmhöfel, S. and Spear, L.P. (2018). Binge Drinking's Effects on the Developing Brain—Animal Models. *Alcohol Research : Current Reviews,* [online] 39(1), pp.77–86. Available at: https://www.ncbi.nlm.nih.gov/pmc/articles/PMC6104958/.

Alcohol use and burden for 195 countries and territories, 1990-2016: a systematic analysis for the Global Burden of Disease Study 2016 GBD 2016 Alcohol Collaborators*. (n.d.). Available at: https://www.thelancet.com/action/showPdf?pii=S0140-6736%2818%2931310-2. (Accessed: 11/06/2024)

Burton, R. and Sheron, N. (2018). No level of alcohol consumption improves health. *The Lancet*, [online] 392(10152), pp.987–988. doi:https://doi.org/10.1016/s0140-6736(18)31571-x. (Accessed: 11/06/2024)

Craparo, G., Schimmenti, A. and Caretti, V. (2013). 'Traumatic experiences in childhood and psychopathy: a study on a sample of violent offenders from Italy'. *European Journal of Psychotraumatology*, [online] 4(0). doi:https://doi.org/10.3402/ejpt.v4i0.21471. (Accessed: 11/06/2024)

Hassan, A. (2025). *'The Troubled Childhood of Jeffrey Dahmer: Impact and Analysis of'*. Coursesidekick.com. Available at: https://www.coursesidekick.com/english/2560091. (Accessed: 25/06/2024)

Ing, C., Sun, M., Olfson, M., DiMaggio, C.J., Sun, L.S., Wall, M.M. and Li, G. (2017). 'Age at Exposure to Surgery and Anesthesia in Children and Association With Mental Disorder Diagnosis'. *Anesthesia & Analgesia*, December [online] 125(6), pp.1988–1998. doi:https://doi.org/10.1213/ANE.0000000000002423. (Accessed: 25/06/2024)

Mitchell, H. and Aamodt, M.G. (2005). 'The incidence of child abuse in serial killers'. *Journal of Police and Criminal Psychology*, [online] 20(1), pp.40–47. doi:https://doi.org/10.1007/bf02806705. (Accessed: 20/08/2024)

Reinisch, J.M. and Sanders, S.A. (1982). 'Early barbiturate exposure: The brain, sexually dimorphic behavior and learning. *Neuroscience & Biobehavioral Reviews'*, 6(3), pp.311–319. doi:https://doi.org/10.1016/0149-7634(82)90043-4. (Accessed: 11/07/2024)

Silveri, M.M. (2012). Adolescent Brain Development and Underage Drinking in the United States: Identifying Risks of Alcohol Use in College Populations. *Harvard Review of Psychiatry*, 20(4), pp.189–200. doi:https://doi.org/10.3109/10673229.2012.714642.

Stanzel, A. and Sierau, S. (2021). Pediatric Medical Traumatic Stress (PMTS) 'following Surgery in Childhood and Adolescence: a Systematic Review. *Journal of Child & Adolescent Trauma'*, 15(3). doi:https://doi.org/10.1007/s40653-021-00391-9. (Accessed: 25/06/2024)

Social Media

Ericthulhu (2022) Twitter post on Netflix Dahmer controversy, Twitter, 17 September. Available at: https://twitter.com/ericthulhu/status/1572997334887284745

Audio

Radio New Zealand (2016) Dr Park Dietz – the psychology of murder. Available at: https://www.rnz.co.nz/national/programmes/sunday/audio/201805933/dr-park-dietz-the-psychology-of-murder

Academic

Crouch, E., Radcliff, E., Strompolis, M. & Srivastav, A. (2019) Safe, stable and nurtured: Protective factors against poor physical and mental health outcomes following exposure to adverse childhood experiences (ACEs), Journal of Child & Adolescent Trauma, 12(2), pp. 165–173. doi: 10.1007/s40653-018-0217-9. Available at: https://www.ncbi.nlm.nih.gov/pmc/articles/PMC7163854/

Johns Hopkins Magazine (1994) The dark world of Park Dietz, Johns Hopkins Magazine. Available at: https://pages.jh.edu/jhumag/1194web/dietz.html

Book

[Author(s) unknown] (2018) p. 437. Available at: https://books.google.com/books?id=NcdiDwAAQBAJ&pg=PA437&dq=carole+anne+boone

Web Page

The US Sun:

Inside the tragic murder of Jeffrey Dahmer victim James Doxtator. 4 October. Available at: https://www.the-sun.com/news/6364243/who-was-jeffrey-dahmer-victim-james-doxtator/.

(*Who was Jeffrey Dahmer victim Anthony Sears?* 25 September. Available at: https://www.the-sun.com/news/6372126/jeffrey-dahmer-victim-anthony-sears/

Who was Jeffrey Dahmer victim Edward Smith? 6 October. Available at: https://www.the-sun.com/news/6381715/jeffrey-dahmer-victim-edward-smith/.

The Sun:

Beaumont, H. (2022). *Who was Jeffrey Dahmer victim David Thomas?...* [online] The Sun. 6 October. Available at: https://iframe.thesun.co.uk/news/20021559/jeffrey-dahmer-victim-david-thomas/ [Accessed 27 Jun. 2025].

Beaumont, H. (2022). *Who was Jeffrey Dahmer victim Joseph Bradehoft?...* [online] The Sun. 6 October. Available at: https://helios.iframe.thesun.co.uk/news/20023509/jeffrey-dahmer-victim-joseph-bradehoft/ [Accessed 28 Jun. 2025].

Bentley-York, J. (2022). *Who was Tony Hughes and what happened to him?...* [online] 22 September. Available at: https://www.thesun.co.uk/news/19882638/what-happened-tony-hughes-jeffrey-dahmer-victim/ [Accessed 27 Jun. 2025].

Bruder, S. (2022). *Was Jeffrey Dahmer in the military?...* [online] The Sun. 4 October. Available at: https://www.thesun.co.uk/news/19997893/was-jeffrey-dahmer-in-the-military/ [Accessed 24 November 2025].

Bruder, S. (2022). *Who was Jeffrey Dahmer victim Curtis Straughter?...* [online] The Sun. 4 October. Available at: https://helios.iframe.thesun.co.uk/news/19997098/jeffrey-dahmer-victim-curtis-straughter/.

Bruder, S. (2022). *Who was Jeffrey Dahmer victim James Doxtator?...* [online] The Sun. 4 October. Available at: https://iframe.thesun.co.uk/news/20002572/who-was-jeffrey-dahmer-victim-james-doxtator/ [Accessed 26 Jun. 2025].

Bruder, S. (2022). *Who was Jeffrey Dahmer victim Matt Turner?...* [online] The Sun. 4 October. Available at: https://www.thesun.co.uk/news/19997490/jeffrey-dahmer-victim-matt-turner/ [Accessed 28 Jun. 2025].

Doyle, A. (2022). *Jeffrey Dahmer Netflix show slammed by victim's family for 'retraumatising' them with violent murder scene...* [online] The Sun. 23 September. Available at: https://www.thesun.co.uk/tv/19900678/jeffrey-dahmer-netflix-show-slammed-by-victims-family/ [Accessed 27 Jun. 2025].

Hasan, K. (2022). *Who is Tracy Edwards and where is he now?...* [online] The Sun. 21 September. Available at: https://www.thesun.co.uk/news/19871794/tracy-edwards-victim-jeffrey-dahmer/ [Accessed 28 Jun. 2025].

Roback, J. (2022). *Who was Jeffrey Dahmer victim Jeremiah Weinberger?...* [online] The Sun. 5 October. Available at: https://www.thesun.co.uk/news/20009022/who-jeffrey-dahmer-victim-jeremiah-weinberger/ [Accessed 28 Jun. 2025].

Roback, J. (2022). *Who was Jeffrey Dahmer victim, Oliver Lacy?...* [online] The Sun. 5 October. Available at: https://www.thesun.co.uk/news/20019388/who-jeffrey-dahmer-victim-oliver-lacy/ [Accessed 28 Jun. 2025].

Salas-Rodriguez, I. and Quinitchett, K. (2022). *Who is in the cast of Monster: The Jeffrey Dahmer Story?...* [online] The Sun. 16 September. Available at: https://www.thesun.co.uk/tv/15230174/jeffrey-dahmer-monster-netflix-series-evan-peters/ [Accessed 27 Jun. 2025].

The Sun (n.d.) Who killed Jeffrey Dahmer?, The Sun. Available at: https://www.the-sun.com/news/6276721/who-killed-jeffrey-dahmer/

The Sun. (2022). *All you need to know about what happened to Konerak Sinthasomphone.* [online] 25 September. Available at: https://www.thesun.co.uk/news/19911735/konerak-sinthasomphone-happened/.

The Sun. (2022). *Who were Jeffrey Dahmer's victims?* [online] 21 September. Available at: https://www.thesun.co.uk/news/18506857/jeffrey-dahmer-victims/ [Accessed 29 Sep. 2022].

Who was Jeffrey Dahmer victim Errol Lindsey? [online] 28 September. Available at: https://www.thesun.co.uk/news/19941476/who-was-jeffrey-dahmer-victim-errol-lindsey/ .

Zorzut, A. (2022). *Who is John Balcerzak and where is he now?...* [online] The Sun. 23 September. Available at: https://www.thesun.co.uk/news/19895307/john-balcerzak-where-is-he-now/ [Accessed 27 Jun. 2025].

Temper a, J. & Spanfeller, J. (2022) What happened to Jeffrey Dahmer's apartment? See real photos of the building now and what happened there, Women's Health Magazine. Available at: https://www.womenshealthmag.com/life/a41335425/jeffrey-dahmer-apartment-now/

Time.graphics:

jan 1, 1978 - Murder of Steven Hicks (Timeline). [online] Available at: https://time.graphics/event/3087914

(n.d.) Public timelines, Time.Graphics. Available at: https://time.graphics/es/event/9503735

(2024). *nov 20, 1987 - Murder of Steven Tuomi (Timeline).* [online] Available at: https://time.graphics/event/3087930.

(2025). *feb 8, 1991 - Murder of Curtis Straughter (Timeline).* [online] Available at: https://time.graphics/event/3087945 [Accessed 27 Jun. 2025].

(2025). *jan 8, 1988 - Murder of Anthony Sears (Timeline).* [online] Available at: https://time.graphics/event/3087936 [Accessed 26 Jun. 2025].

2025). *jan 8, 1988 - Murder of James Doxtator (Timeline).* [online] Available at: https://time.graphics/event/3087932 [Accessed 26 Jun. 2025].

(2025). *mar 24, 1988 - Murder of Richard Guerrero (Timeline).* [online] Available at: https://time.graphics/event/3087933 [Accessed 26 Jun. 2025].

(2025). *nov 8, 1990 - Murder of Ernest Miller (Timeline).* [online] Available at: https://time.graphics/event/3087943 [Accessed 27 Jun. 2025].

(2025). *nov 8, 1990 - Murder of Ernest Miller (Timeline).* [online] Available at: https://time.graphics/event/3087943 [Accessed 27 Jun. 2025].

(2025). *sep 24, 1990 - Murder of David Thomas (Timeline).* [online] Available at: https://time.graphics/event/3087944 [Accessed 27 Jun. 2025].

(n.d.). *apr 7, 1959 - Murder of Errol Lindsey (Timeline).* [online] Available at: https://time.graphics/event/3087946.

A&E Television Networks (2017) Jeffrey Dahmer's childhood: A pail of animal bones was his toy rattle, A&E Real Crime, 14 January. Available at: https://www.aetv.com/real-crime/jeffrey-dahmer-childhood-serial-killer-cannibal-bones

ABC News Australia (2024) Fred Rose West victims remembered on anniversary, 10 March. Available at: https://www.abc.net.au/news/2024-03-10/fred-rose-west-victims-anniversary/103453858

admin (2024). *Underage Drinking Statistics | Talk it Out NC.* [online] Talk It Out. Available at: http://talkitoutnc.org/underage-drinking-facts/ [Accessed 25 Jun. 2025].

All That's Interesting (2023) The tragic life of Joyce Dahmer, All That's Interesting, 15 June. Available at: https://allthatsinteresting.com/joyce-dahmer

All That's Interesting (2024) How Christopher Scarver beat Jeffrey Dahmer to death, All That's Interesting, 16 April. Available at: https://allthatsinteresting.com/christopher-scarver-jeffrey-dahmer-death

All That's Interesting (n.d.) Carole Ann Boone: Ted Bundy's wife. Available at: https://allthatsinteresting.com/carole-ann-boone

Aly Vander Hayden (2017). *These Are The Chilling Crime Scene Photos From Jeffrey Dahmer's Apartment.* [online] Oxygen Official Site. Available at: https://www.oxygen.com/blogs/jeffrey-dahmer-crime-scene-photos.

American Psychological Association (2020). *Understanding alcohol use disorders and their treatment.* [online] Apa.org. Available at: https://www.apa.org/topics/substance-use-abuse-addiction/alcohol-disorders. [Accessed 14 May 2025]

Anderson, L. (2022). *Jeffrey Dahmer Was Arrested 4 Times Before His 1992 Murder Conviction.* [online] Showbiz Cheat Sheet. 24 September. Available at: https://www.cheatsheet.com/entertainment/jeffrey-dahmer-arrested-4-times-1992-murder-conviction.html/ [Accessed 11 Oct. 2022].

AOL, 2022:

Here's what the police found in Jeffrey Dahmer's apartment. Available at: https://www.aol.com/jeffrey-dahmers-apartment-had-11-213700334.html

Here's why people think Dean Vaughn may have been a Dahmer victim. Available at: https://www.aol.com/heres-why-people-think-dean-194200518.html

What happened to Jeffrey Dahmer's apartment building?. Available at: https://www.aol.com/happened-jeffrey-dahmer-apartment-building-213400103.html

Aoraha, C. (2023). *Jeffery Dahmer is asked by father what his most disturbing fantasy was.* [online] Mail Online. 13 September. Available at: https://www.dailymail.co.uk/news/article-12515185/Serial-killer-Jeffery-Dahmer-father.html.

AP News:

'I See Jeffrey Dahmer in My Sleep': Victim's Daughter Has Nightmares, AP News, [no date]. Available at: https://apnews.com/article/df3f5f9ed8897797e7a14e1bb666394c

(2024). '*Police Records Show Dahmer's Family Didn't Report Alleged Abuse of Son*'. [online] Unknown. Available at: https://apnews.com/article/7fc3146faf2561a8e7d91ff337615953. (Accessed: 11/06/2024)

(n.d.). *Officers Who Let Boy Stay With Dahmer Defend Actions.* [online] (Unknown) Available at: https://apnews.com/article/735e89632389f424944bf4a117c8a4da.

(n.d.). *Psychologist: Dahmer Had Drilled Head of Boy Found by Police With AM-Tyson Trial, Bjt.* [online] (Unknown) Available at: https://apnews.com/article/081e72cc128d2bfa7b9b3cf070e232f7.

Applebaum, S. (2018). 'There was always a darkness about him': My Friend Dahmer author John Backderf on growing up with a serial killer. *The Independent.* [online] 30 May. Available at: https://www.independent.co.uk/arts-entertainment/films/features/my-friend-dahmer-john-backderf-film-jeffrey-comic-book-interview-serial-killer-a8375866.html. [Accessed 4 November 2024].

NY Post:

Archive, V.A. and feed, G. author R. (2024). '*Ted Bundy's cousin dishes on the dark family history that made a serial killer*'. [online] 20 July. Available at: https://nypost.com/2024/07/20/lifestyle/the-dark-family-history-that-made-ted-bundy-a-killer/ [Accessed 3 May 2025]

Archive, V.A., Author, E. the and feed, G. author R. (2022). *Dahmer victim's mom speaks out against Netflix series: 'It didn't happen like that'.* [online] New York Post. 13 October. Available at: https://nypost.com/2022/10/13/dahmer-victims-mom-on-netflix-series-it-didnt-happen-like-that/.

Archive, V.A., Author, E. the and feed, G. author R. (2022). *Inside Jeffrey Dahmer's childhood home, where he first committed murder.* [online] New York Post. 7 October. Available at: https://nypost.com/2022/10/07/inside-jeffrey-dahmers-childhood-home-where-he-committed-first-murder/ [Accessed 10 October 2024].

Archive.org. (2025). *Jeffrey Dahmer - Serial Killer and Cannibal - Crime Library on truTV.com.* [online] (Unknown). Available at: https://web.archive.org/web/20090831100952/http:/www.trutv.com/library/crime/serial_killers/notorious/dahmer/8.html [Accessed 26 Jun. 2025].

Ashfield, A. (2022). *'Netflix's 'Monster' explores theory behind Dahmer's crimes linked to childhood surgery'*. [online] Entertainment Daily. 21 September. Available at: https://www.entertainmentdaily.com/true-crime/was-jeffrey-dahmers-hernia-operation-to-blame-for-his-violent-criminal-behaviour/. (Accessed: 03/07/2024).

Ashfield, A. (2022). *'Was Jeffrey Dahmer's hernia operation to blame for his violent criminal behaviour?'* [online] Entertainment Daily. Entertainment Daily. 21 September. Available at: https://www.entertainmentdaily.co.uk/true-crime/was-jeffrey-dahmers-hernia-operation-to-blame-for-his-violent-criminal-behaviour/. (Accessed: 17/06/2024)

Austin, H. (2022). *Monster: What Happened To The Police Officers Who Returned Dahmer's Victim.* [online] ScreenRant. 13 October. Available at: https://screenrant.com/monster-jeffrey-dahmer-police-konerak-sinthasomphone-returned/.

Ayub, S. (2023). *Who was Joseph Bradehoft, Jeffrey Dahmer victim? All the details.* [online] Tuko.co.ke - Kenya news. 20 July. Available at: https://www.tuko.co.ke/facts-lifehacks/celebrity-biographies/514434-who-joseph-bradehoft-jeffrey-dahmer-victim-details/.

Balagtas, T. (2022). *Jeffrey Dahmer's 14-Year-Old Victim: Who Was Konerak Sinthasomphone?* [online] Peoplemag. 13 October. Available at: https://people.com/crime/jeffre-dahmer-victim-konerak-sinthasomphone-police-returned-boy-home-killer/.

Balagtas, T. (2022). *Jeffrey Dahmer's 14-Year-Old Victim: Who Was Konerak Sinthasomphone?* [online] Peoplemag. 13 October. Available at: https://people.com/crime/jeffre-dahmer-victim-konerak-sinthasomphone-police-returned-boy-home-killer/.

Baltimore Sun (1994) Dahmer Victim Errol Lindsey Never Got To Meet His Daughter, Baltimore Sun, 29 November. Available at: https://www.baltimoresun.com/news/bs-xpm-1994-11-29-1994333019-story.html

Bardsley, M. (Unknown) 'Jeffrey Dahmer'. Crime Library. (Unknown) Available at:https://www.crimelibrary.org/serial_killers/notorious/dahmer/14.html. (Accessed: 12/06/2024)

New York Times:

Barron, J. (1991) Milwaukee police once queried suspect, The New York Times, 27 July. Available at: http://www.nytimes.com/1991/07/27/us/milwaukee-police-once-queried-suspect.html

Barron, J. (1991) Milwaukee police once queried suspect, The New York Times, 27 July. Available at: http://www.nytimes.com/1991/07/27/us/milwaukee-police-once-queried-suspect.html

The New York Times (1991) Officer defends returning boy to Dahmer, The New York Times, 26 August. Available at: http://www.nytimes.com/1991/08/26/us/officer-defends-giving-boy-back-to-dahmer.html

Times, S. to T.N.Y. (1991). Bone Fragments, Many Human, Are Found at Suspect's Ohio Home. *The New York Times.* [online] 31 Jul. Available at: https://www.nytimes.com/1991/07/31/us/bone-fragments-many-human-are-found-at-suspect-s-ohio-home.html [Accessed 23 Nov. 2021].

BBC News:

(2017) Why are people attracted to serial killers? Available at: https://www.bbc.co.uk/news/uk-39925965

(2022) Monster Jeffrey Dahmer: Did TV go too far in 2022?, BBC Culture, 13 December. Available at: https://www.bbc.co.uk/culture/article/20221213-monster-jeffrey-dahmer-did-tv-go-too-far-in-2022

(2022) Netflix series Dahmer 'glamorises' serial killer, says father, BBC News, 27 August. Available at: https://www.bbc.co.uk/news/entertainment-arts-62727106

BCU News (2024) Why are people attracted to serial killers?, Birmingham City University, Social Sciences. Available at: https://www.bcu.ac.uk/news-events/social-sciences/why-are-people-attracted-to-serial-killers

Beeman, A. (2021). *What Jeffrey Dahmer's Childhood Was Actually Like.* [online] Grunge.com. 26 October. Available at: https://www.grunge.com/384712/what-jeffrey-dahmers-childhood-was-actually-like/ [Accessed 12 August 2024].

Bentley-York, J. (2022). *Who was Tony Hughes and what happened to him?...* [online] The Scottish Sun. 22 September. Available at: https://www.thescottishsun.co.uk/news/9495377/what-happened-tony-hughes-jeffrey-dahmer-victim/?ref=popsugar.com&=___psv__p_48964772__m_partner__s_imdb__c_feed__t_w__r_m.imdb.com%2F_ [Accessed 27 Jun. 2025].

Betsaida, A. (2019). *'Opioid use during pregnancy alters the baby's brain'*. [online] News-Medical. 25 November. Available at: https://www.news-medical.net/news/20191125/Opioid-use-during-pregnancy-alters-the-babys-brain.aspx (Accessed: 11/06/2024)

Biggs, J. (2022). *'Jeffrey Dahmer's dad speaks out about the 'red flags' he missed in his son'*. [online] Cosmopolitan. 21 November. Available at: https://www.cosmopolitan.com/uk/reports/a42022442/lionel-dahmer-red-flags-missed-jeffrey-dahmer/ {Accessed 23 May 2025)

Biography.com Editors (2021). *'Edmund Kemper - Mother, Murders & Facts'*. [online] Biography. Available at: https://www.biography.com/crime/edmund-kemper. [Accessed 3 May 2025].

Boog, J. (1997) River of sleaze, Miami New Times, 20 March. Available at: https://www.miaminewtimes.com/news/river-of-sleaze-6378923

Booth, W. (1991) Dahmer charged in 8 more murders, The Washington Post, 7 August. Available at: https://www.washingtonpost.com/archive/politics/1991/08/07/dahmer-charged-in-8-more-murders/c3129dd2-9138-42e9-a942-bc7aafe8f40f/

Booth, W. (1991). DAHMER CHARGED IN 8 MORE MURDERS. *Washington Post*. [online] 7 Aug. 7 August. Available at: https://www.washingtonpost.com/archive/politics/1991/08/07/dahmer-charged-in-8-more-murders/c3129dd2-9138-42e9-a942-bc7aafe8f40f/.

Booth, W. (1991). DAHMER CHARGED IN 8 MORE MURDERS. *Washington Post*. [online] 7 Aug. Available at: https://www.washingtonpost.com/archive/politics/1991/08/07/dahmer-charged-in-8-more-murders/c3129dd2-9138-42e9-a942-bc7aafe8f40f/.

Breitowich, A. (2022). *'Did Jeffrey Dahmer's Childhood Turn Him Into A Serial Killer? Psychologists Unpack His Traumas'*. *Women's Health*. [online] 7 Oct. Available at: https://www.womenshealthmag.com/health/a41559253/jeffrey-dahmer-childhood-create-serial-killer/. (Accessed: 11/06/2024)

Buelow, M.C. (1991). CONVICTED MILWAUKEE CHILD MOLESTER BELIEVED TO HAVE SLAIN AT LEAST 17. *Washington Post*. [online] 26 Jul. Available at: https://www.washingtonpost.com/archive/politics/1991/07/26/convicted-milwaukee-child-molester-believed-to-have-slain-at-least-17/7a70784c-2657-4759-aa3e-ca94bc351b5f/.

Bundy (2019). *We All Come From Childhood: Jeffrey Dahmer.* [online] Quotev. 12 February. Available at: https://www.quotev.com/story/11493184/We-All-Come-From-Childhood-Jeffrey-Dahmer [Accessed 24 May 2025].

Burgess, K. (2008). *Hundreds of children under 10 hospitalised with alcohol problems.* [online] Thetimes.com. 9 November. Available at: https://www.thetimes.com/article/hundreds-of-children-under-10-hospitalised-with-alcohol-problems-320nn9597mn [Accessed 25 February 2025].

Caplan, A.L. and Pelisek, C. (2022). *He Got Away From Jeffrey Dahmer. But Tracy Edwards Couldn't Escape the Trauma, His Attorney Says.* [online] Peoplemag. (Unknown) Available at: https://people.com/crime/tracy-edwards-couldnt-escape-dahmer-trauma-attorney/.

Carter, H. (2022). *Chilling true story of Jeffrey Dahmer's unsuspecting grandmother in Netflix show.* [online] mirror. 19 September. Available at: https://www.mirror.co.uk/3am/celebrity-news/chilling-true-story-jeffrey-dahmers-28110097 [Accessed 17 May 2023].

CBS News:

(2016) Adams, C. On this day: February 17th, 1992 — serial killer Jeffrey Dahmer sentenced, CBS News, 17 February. Available at: https://www.cbsnews.com/news/on-this-day-february-17th-1992-serial-killer-jeffrey-dahmer-sentenced

(2022) Charity refuses money from Dahmer walking tour, CBS News, [date unavailable]. Available at: https://www.cbsnews.com/news/charity-refuses-money-from-dahmer-walking-tour/

(2022) Dahmer victims' sister calls walking tour evil, CBS News, [date unavailable]. Available at: https://www.cbsnews.com/news/dahmer-victims-sister-calls-walking-tour-evil/

(2022) Walking tour of Jeffrey Dahmer's neighborhood spurs controversy, CBS News, [date unavailable]. Available at: https://www.cbsnews.com/news/walking-tour-of-jeffrey-dahmers-neighborhood-spurs-controversy/

Centers for Disease Control and Prevention (2023). *Youth risk behavior surveillance system (YRBSS).* [online] Centers for Disease Control and Prevention. Available at: https://www.cdc.gov/healthyyouth/data/yrbs/index.htm.

Charley Project:

(2022). *David Courtney Thomas – The Charley Project.* [online] Available at: https://charleyproject.org/case/david-courtney-thomas [Accessed 27 Jun. 2025].

(2022). *Richard Guerrero – The Charley Project.* [online] Available at: https://charleyproject.org/case/richard-guerrero [Accessed 26 Jun. 2025].

(2025). *Edward Warren Smith – The Charley Project.* [online] Available at: https://charleyproject.org/case/edward-warren-smith [Accessed 27 Jun. 2025].

Chicago Tribune (1991) Wrongful release? Police failed to act before Dahmer attack, Chicago Tribune, 28 July. Available at: https://www.chicagotribune.com/news/ct-xpm-1991-07-28-9103230622-story.html

Chicago Tribune. (n.d.). *AFTER DAHMER: POLICE TRY TO LEARN.* [online] (Unknown) Available at: https://www.chicagotribune.com/news/ct-xpm-1992-12-13-9204230642-story.html.

Christian, E. (2024). *'Are serial killers born or made?'* [online] Rest Less. 7 March. Available at: https://restless.co.uk/leisure-and-lifestyle/art-and-culture/are-serial-killers-born-or-made/. (Accessed: 11/06/2024)

Cleveland Clinic (2023). *'Hernia | Cleveland Clinic.'* [online] Cleveland Clinic. Available at: https://my.clevelandclinic.org/health/diseases/15757-hernia. (Accessed: 17/06/2024)

Cold Case Project (2021). *The Milwaukee Monster: The Crimes Of Jeffrey Dahmer.* [online] Medium. 24 June. Available at: https://coldcaseproject.medium.com/the-milwaukee-monster-the-crimes-of-jeffrey-dahmer-5db8b245f22e [Accessed 26 Jun. 2025].

Coursehero.com. (2025). *Sample Cover Sheet Template 2016 4 -1 - JuJuan Whigham.* [online] 28 March. Available at: https://www.coursehero.com/file/p2es1s0r/July-15-Oliver-Lacy-24-A-bodybuilder-who-Dahmer-enticed-to-his-apartment-on-the/ [Accessed 28 Jun. 2025].

Crime Library. (Unknown) *Serial Killer and Cannibal- Lust, Booze & Murder.* Available at: https://web.archive.org/web/20111215115156/http:/www.trutv.com/library/crime/serial_killers/notorious/dahmer/7.html.

Crime Museum (2022). *Jeffrey Dahmer | Crime Library | Serial Killers.* [online] Crime Museum. Available at: https://www.crimemuseum.org/crime-library/serial-killers/jeffrey-dahmer/. [Accessed 3 May 025]

Crime Museum (2022). *Jeffrey Dahmer | Crime Library | Serial Killers.* [online] Crime Museum. Available at: https://www.crimemuseum.org/crime-library/serial-killers/jeffrey-dahmer/.

Dahmer (1991). *Dahmer reportedly made terror phone calls - UPI Archives.* [online] UPI. 30 July. Available at: https://www.upi.com/Archives/1991/07/30/Dahmer-reportedly-made-terror-phone-calls/1419680846400/ [Accessed 27 Jun. 2025].

Daily Mail (2024) Jeffrey Dahmer serial killer prison phone call reveals sick trophies, father speaks, Daily Mail, 5 June. Available at: https://www.dailymail.

co.uk/news/article-12518879/Jeffrey-Dahmer-serial-killer-prison-phone-call-sick-trophies-father.html

Dalton, J. (2019). *'The link is established between serial killers and animal cruelty'*. The Independent. [online] 2 Aug. Available at: https://www.independent.co.uk/news/long_reads/domestic-violence-animal-cruelty-abuse-neglect-murder-children-dogs-a9018071.html. (Accessed 23 May 2025)

Dazed (n.d.) Why do people romanticise serial killers?, Dazed. Available at: https://www.gq-magazine.co.uk/culture/article/jeffrey-dahmer-netflix

DeMaria, M. (2021). *'The Rumors About Ted Bundy's Mom and Dad Are Very Disturbing'*. [online] Cosmopolitan. 25 August. Available at: https://www.cosmopolitan.com/entertainment/movies/a27356496/ted-bundy-parents-mom-dad/ [Accessed 03 May 2025].

Deseret News (1992) Kin of victims tell judge to lock up Dahmer for life, Deseret News, 17 February. Available at: https://www.deseret.com/1992/2/17/18968211/kin-of-victims-tell-judge-to-lock-up-dahmer-for-life

DeWitt, L. (2022) A profile of Carole Ann Boone, Killer in the Archives blog. Available at: https://killerinthearchives.blog/a-profile-of-carole-ann-boone/

Diksha Sundriyal (2022). *Ronald Flowers: What Happened to Jeffery Dahmer's Survivor?* [online] The Cinemaholic. 22 September. Available at: https://thecinemaholic.com/where-is-jeffery-dahmers-survivor-ronald-flowers-now/ [Accessed 30 May 2025].

Doe Network:

(2021). *628DMWI - Richard Guerrero.* [online] Available at: https://www.doenetwork.org/cases/628dmwi.html [Accessed 26 Jun. 2025].

(2025). Available at: https://www.doenetwork.org/cases/software/mp-main.html?id=638DMWI [Accessed 27 Jun. 2025].

(2025). Available at: https://www.doenetwork.org/cases/software/mp-main.html?id=630dmwi.

Drinkaware (2022). *Alcohol dependence and withdrawal | Drinkaware.* [online] www.drinkaware.co.uk. Available at: https://www.drinkaware.co.uk/facts/health-effects-of-alcohol/mental-health/alcohol-dependence.

Dvorchak, R. (1991). *Murder in Milwaukee: Experts Struggle to Explain Dahmer's Compulsion : Crime: His behavior was always on the edge, childhood acquaintances say. But no one intervened to help him, and his problems escalated.* [online] Los Angeles Times. 11 August. Available at: https://www.latimes.com/archives/la-xpm-1991-08-11-mn-635-story.html. [Accessed 24 April 2025].

Ebrahimji, A. (2022) Netflix's 'Dahmer' is facing backlash from viewers and victims' families alike, Vox, 6 October. Available at: https://www.vox.com/culture/23375811/netflix-jeffrey-dahmer-monster-victims-controversy-backlash

Editorialge. (2024). *The Tragic Story of Jamie Doxtator: Jeffrey Dahmer's 3rd Victim.* [online] 7 April. Available at: https://editorialge.com/jamie-doxtator/ [Accessed 26 Jun. 2025].

Encyclopedia Britannica. (2024). *'The real serial killer who inspired Psycho'*. [online] Available at: https://www.britannica.com/video/did-you-know-Ed-Gein/-256894. [Accessed 3 May 2025].

Esquire:

(2022) What happened to Jeffrey Dahmer's apartment?. Available at: https://www.esquire.com/entertainment/tv/a41428868/jeffrey-dahmer-apartment-now/

(2022). *'Monster: The Jeffrey Dahmer Story' Gives Justice to Tony Hughes.* [online] 26 September. Available at: https://www.esquire.com/entertainment/tv/a41389502/tony-hughes-deaf-victim-jeffrey-dahmer/ [Accessed 24 Jun. 2024].

(2022). *What Happened to Jeffrey Dahmer's Apartment?* [online] 7 October. Available at: https://www.esquire.com/entertainment/tv/a41428868/jeffrey-dahmer-apartment-now/.

FBI (2019). *Tracking Animal Cruelty | Federal Bureau of Investigation.* [online] Federal Bureau of Investigation. 1 February. Available at: https://www.fbi.gov/news/stories/-tracking-animal-cruelty. [Accessed 12 August 2024].

FBI. (1992). [online] FBI. *'Freedom of Information and Privacy Acts'.* Available at: https://vault.fbi.gov/jeffrey-lionel-dahmer/Jeffrey%20Lionel%20Dahmer%20Part%2003 [Accessed 3 May 025]

Fennell, C. (2022) The controversy behind Netflix's Jeffrey Dahmer series, explained, Insider, 6 October. Available at: https://www.insider.com/netflix-jeffrey-dahmer-series-controversy-tiktok-romanticized-crimes-lgbtq-2022-10

Find A Grave:

(2015). *Edward Warren 'Sheikh' Smith (1963-1990) - Find a...* [online] Available at: https://www.findagrave.com/memorial/233508502/edward_warren-smith.

(2015). *James Edward 'Jamie' Doxtator (1973-1988) - Find...* [online] Available at: https://www.findagrave.com/memorial/123960816/james_edward-doxtator.

(2019). *Konerak Sinthasomphone (1976-1991) - Find a Grave...* [online] Available at: https://www.findagrave.com/memorial/9353146/konerak-sinthasomphone.

(2020). *David Courtney Thomas (1967-1990) - Find a Grave...* [online] Available at: https://www.findagrave.com/memorial/214569129/david_courtney-thomas [Accessed 27 Jun. 2025].

FreshWater Media, LLC. (2016). *Q & A: Derf Backderf.* [online] 15 September. Available at: https://www.freshwatercleveland.com/features/DerfBackderf091516.aspx [Accessed 24 April 2025].

Gale Academic Onefile. (1994) *Women: Sister of mercy - Theresa Smith's brother, Eddie, was the seventh victim of serial killer Jeffrey Dahmer. He had been strangled and his corpse sexually abused before parts of it were cooked and flushed down the toilet. So why, when Dahmer was killed, did Theresa Smith join the mourners?[online]* Gale Academic Onefile. 29 December. Available at: https://go.gale.com/ps/i.do?id=GALE%7CA170663886&sid=sitemap&v=2.1&it=r&p=AONE&sw=w&userGroupName=anon%7Ec5978755&aty=open-web-entry

Gannon, F. (2022). *Victims Spotlight: Remembering the Victims of 'Milwaukee Cannibal' Jeffrey Dahmer.* [online] Wicked Horror. 3 October. Available at: https://cdn.wickedhorror.com/features/victims-spotlight-remembering-the-victims-of-milwaukee-cannibal-jeffrey-dahmer/ [Accessed 27 Jun. 2025].

Gannon, F. (2022). *Victims Spotlight: Remembering the Victims of 'Milwaukee Cannibal' Jeffrey Dahmer.* [online] Wicked Horror. 3 October. Available at: https://www.wickedhorror.com/features/victims-spotlight-remembering-the-victims-of-milwaukee-cannibal-jeffrey-dahmer/ [Accessed 27 Jun. 2025].

Gibson, K. (2022). *'Monster: The Jeffrey Dahmer Story' : How the Serial Killer Was Caught.* [online] Peoplemag. 9 April. Available at: https://people.com/crime/how-jeffrey-dahmer-was-caught/. [Accessed 25 May 2025].

Gittins, W. (2022). *'Who was the real Jeffrey Dahmer, the serial killer who's portrayed in the new Netflix show 'Monster'?'* [online] AS USA. 22 September. Available at: https://en.as.com/latest_news/who-was-the-real-jeffrey-dahmer-the-serial-killer-who-portrayed-the-new-netflix-show-monster-n/ (Accessed: 03/07/2024).

Gov.uk (2022) 'Guidance Working definition of trauma-informed practice'. Available at: https://www.gov.uk/government/publications/working-definition-of-trauma-informed-practice/working-definition-of-trauma-informed-practice#:~:text=Trauma%20results%20from%20an%20event,as%20harmful%20or%20life%20threatening (Accessed: 17/06/2024)

Guardian TV & Radio (2022) Jeffrey Dahmer: Ryan Murphy's Netflix show is exploitative, not empathetic, The Guardian, 23 September. Available at:

https://www.theguardian.com/tv-and-radio/2022/sep/23/jeffrey-dahmer-netflix-ryan-murphy-exploitative-tv

Gurney, F. (2022). *Jeffrey Dahmer had 17 male victims – here's everything you should know about them.* [online] The Tab. (Unknown) Available at: https://archive.thetab.com/uk/2022/09/27/jeffrey-dahmer-victims-tony-hughes-konerak-sinthasomphone-errol-lindsey-275388 [Accessed 8 Nov. 2024].

Hardiman, J. (2022). *'Jeffrey Dahmer's dad thinks he knows what's to blame for son becoming a serial killer'.* [online] LADbible. 26 September. Available at: https://www.ladbible.com/news/jeffrey-dahmer-dad-reason-serial-killer-20220926 (Accessed: 03/07/2024).

Harrison, E. (2022). *The horrific true story behind the Jeffrey Dahmer serial killer series on Netflix.* [online] The Independent.5 October. Available at: https://www.independent.co.uk/arts-entertainment/tv/news/jeffrey-dahmer-netflix-true-story-victims-b2196442.html. (Accessed: 03/07/2024).

Health and Wellbeing of 15 year olds in England: Findings from the What About YOUth? Survey 2014. (2015). Available at: https://files.digital.nhs.uk/publicationimport/pub19xxx/pub19244/what-about-youth-eng-2014-rep.pdf.

Heaton, B. (2024). *'Brain rot' named Oxford Word of the Year 2024 - Oxford University Press.* [online] Oxford University Press. 2 December. Available at: https://corp.oup.com/news/brain-rot-named-oxford-word-of-the-year-2024/.

Help4Addiction:

(2023). *Alcohol and Anxiety | Help 4 Addiction.* [online] Available at: https://help4addiction.co.uk/mental-health/alcohol-and-anxiety/ [Accessed 25 Jun. 2025].

(2024). *Alcohol and Breast Cancer: Does Alcohol Increase The Risk?* [online] Available at: https://help4addiction.co.uk/alcohol-addiction/alcohol-and-breast-cancer-is-there-a-link/ [Accessed 25 Jun. 2025].

(2024). *Exploring The Links Between Alzheimer's And Alcohol | Help 4 Addiction.* [online] Available at: https://help4addiction.co.uk/alcohol-addiction/exploring-the-links-between-alzheimers-and-alcohol/ [Accessed 25 Jun. 2025].

(2024). *Exploring The Reasons Behind Teenage Alcohol Abuse | Help 4 Addiction.* [online] Available at: https://www.help4addiction.co.uk/addiction-support/alcohol-addiction/exploring-the-reasons-behind-teenage-alcohol-abuse/.

(2025). *Help With Alcohol Addiction UK | Get Advice And Guidance | Help 4 Addiction.* [online] Available at: https://help4addiction.co.uk/alcohol-addiction/ [Accessed 25 Jun. 2025].

Hinshaw, D. (2022) Jeffrey Dahmer's mother, Joyce Flint, remembered as woman of contrasts, Milwaukee Journal Sentinel, 29 September. Available at: https://eu.jsonline.com/story/news/2022/09/29/jeffrey-dahmers-mother-joyce-flint-remembered-woman-contrasts/10454514002/

History.com Editors (2009). *Cannibal and serial killer Jeffrey Dahmer is caught | July 22, 1991 | HISTORY.* [online] HISTORY. 13 November. Available at: https://www.history.com/this-day-in-history/July-22/cannibal-and-serial-killer-jeffrey-dahmer-is-caught.

HSE.ie. (2022). *Psychological dependence on alcohol.* [online] Available at: https://www2.hse.ie/living-well/alcohol/dependence/psychological-dependence/. [Accessed 3 May 025]

Hughes, G. (2022). *Jeffrey Dahmer: Through The Papers.* [online] Historic Newspapers. 20 January. Available at: https://www.historic-newspapers.co.uk/blog/jeffrey-dahmer-newspaper-analysis/?srsltid=AfmBOoqywe5bk4Tuql7nF30AYzecuP40dfXxl9id_31Iennwn2VxMGmQ [Accessed 24 June 2024].

IMDb:

(2024). *Ernest Miller.* [online] IMDb. Available at: https://www.imdb.com/name/nm1358748/.

(2024). *Konerak Sinthasomphone.* [online] IMDb. Available at: https://www.imdb.com/name/nm1360828/.

(2025). *Curtis Straughter.* [online] IMDb. Available at: https://www.imdb.com/name/nm1360921/ [Accessed 27 Jun. 2025].

(2025). *David C. Thomas.* [online] IMDb. Available at: https://www.imdb.com/name/nm1358780/ [Accessed 27 Jun. 2025].

(2025). *Edward W. Smith.* [online] IMDb. Available at: https://www.imdb.com/name/nm1362199/.

(2025). *James E. Doxtator.* [online] IMDb. Available at: https://www.imdb.com/name/nm1359392/bio/ [Accessed 26 Jun. 2025].

(2025). *Matt Turner.* [online] IMDb. Available at: https://www.imdb.com/name/nm1362225/ [Accessed 28 Jun. 2025].

(2025). *Oliver Lacy.* [online] IMDb. Available at: https://www.imdb.com/name/nm1362078/ [Accessed 28 Jun. 2025].

(2022). *Who Was Tony Hughes, Jeffrey Dahmer's 12th Victim, and Where Are His Family Today? - IMDb.* [online] Available at: https://www.imdb.com/news/ni63776549/ [Accessed 27 Jun. 2025].

(2025) 'Jeffrey Dahmer - Biography - IMDb'. Available at: https://www.imdb.com/name/nm0197213/bio/ (Accessed: 12/06/2024).

(n.d.). *Anthony Sears - Biography.* [online] Available at: https://www.imdb.com/name/nm1358770/bio/.

(n.d.). *Steven Hicks.* [online] IMDB. Available at: https://www.imdb.com/name/nm1362047/. [Accessed 24 May 2025]

(2025). *Joseph Bradehoft.* [online] Available at: https://www.imdb.com/name/nm1461435/.

Info Bites (2023). *The Mind of the Serial killer: Jeffrey Dahmer - Info Bites - Medium.* [online] Medium. 23 August. Available at: https://medium.com/@info.bites/the-mind-of-the-serial-killer-jeffrey-dahmer-4ab533b82638 [Accessed 10 October 2024]

Insider (2022) Daughter of Jeffrey Dahmer victim Errol Lindsey has nightmares since Netflix show, Insider, [no date]. Available at: https://www.insider.com/daughter-jeffrey-dahmer-victim-errol-lindsey-nightmares-since-netflix-show-2022-10

Insider (2022) Rita Isbell, sister of Dahmer victim, reacts to Netflix show, Insider. Available at: https://www.insider.com/rita-isbell-sister-jeffrey-dahmer-victim-talks-about-netflix-show-2022-9

Interactive, B. (2022). *How Jeffrey Dahmer's Alcohol Addiction Led to His Crimes.* [online] Muse Treatment. 5 October. Available at: https://musetreatment.com/blog/jeffrey-dahmers-alcohol-addiction/ [Accessed 13 October 2024].

James, E. (2023). *Retired cop describes opening Jeffrey Dahmer's fridge to see remains.* [online] Mail Online. 15 September. Available at: https://www.dailymail.co.uk/news/article-12518877/Jeffrey-Dahmer-serial-killer-detective-severed-head-new-documentary.html.

Jeffery Dahmer. (2025). *Arrest.* [online] Available at: https://jefferydahmerkillerprofile.weebly.com/arrest.html [Accessed 28 Jun. 2025].

Johnson, G.A. (2017). *High school friend recounts time with serial killer in 'My Friend Dahmer'.* [online] SFGATE. 14 November. Available at: https://www.sfgate.com/movies/article/High-school-friend-recounts-time-with-serial-12358022.php [Accessed 24 April 2025].

Kaplan, A (2022) 'What Happened To Jeffrey Dahmer's Mother, Joyce? Where She Is Now', Yahoo!Life, 10 October. Available at: https://www.yahoo.com/lifestyle/happened-jeffrey-dahmers-mother-joyce-220134534.html (Accessed: 12/06/2024).

Ke, B. (2022). *Konerak Sinthasomphone: The Jeffrey Dahmer victim police failed to protect.* [online] Yahoo News. 10 October. Available at: https://www.yahoo.com/news/konerak-sinthasomphone-jeffrey-dahmer-victim-223905041.html.

Kelly, D. (2021). *The Untold Truth Of Jeffrey Dahmer.* [online] Grunge.com. 18 April. Available at: https://www.grunge.com/385851/the-untold-truth-of-jeffrey-dahmer/ [Accessed 20 October 2025]

Kelly, D. (2024). *What Happened To The Bodies Of Jeffrey Dahmer's Victims.* [online] Grunge. 18 March. Available at: https://www.grunge.com/1537836/what-happened-to-bodies-jeffrey-dahmer-victims/ [Accessed 26 Jun. 2025].

Kill, T. (2023). *Why Did They Kill? - Who Did They Kill ? - Medium.* [online] Medium. 5 April. Available at: https://whodidtheykill.medium.com/why-did-they-kill-c8421ad75e9a [Accessed 26 Jun. 2025].

Lawes, R. (2022). *Jeffrey Dahmer stashed victim's head and genitals in work locker.* [online] Metro. 6 October. Available at: https://metro.co.uk/2022/10/06/jeffrey-dahmer-stashed-victims-head-and-genitals-in-work-locker-17519157/ [Accessed 15 Nov. 2024].

Lawes, R. (2022). *Jeffrey Dahmer survivor Tracy Edwards reveals how he escaped killer.* [online] Metro. 6 October. Available at: https://metro.co.uk/2022/10/06/jeffrey-dahmer-srvivor-tracy-edwards-reveals-how-he-escaped-killer-17511980/ [Accessed 28 Jun. 2025].

Leach, M. (2022) 'Who were Jeffrey Dahmer's family? What Joyce, Lionel and David Dahmer knew about his horrific crimes'. Now To Love, 2 October. Available at:https://www.nowtolove.com.au/news/international-news/who-are-jeffery-dahmer-family-75022/ (Accessed: 14/06/2024)

Lerner, J. (2022). *The Timeline of Jeffrey Dahmer's Victims Shows a Disturbing Pattern.* [online] Distractify. 27 September. Available at: https://www.distractify.com/p/jeffrey-dahmer-victims-timeline.

Leszkiewicz, A. (2022) Monster: The Jeffrey Dahmer Story – Netflix's new show proves true crime needs to be abolished, New Statesman, 4 October. Available at: https://www.newstatesman.com/quickfire/2022/10/monster-jeffrey-dahmer-netflix-abolish-true-crime

Leszkiewicz, A. (2022) Monster: The Jeffrey Dahmer Story – Netflix's new show proves true crime needs to be abolished, New Statesman, 4 October. Available at: https://www.newstatesman.com/quickfire/2022/10/monster-jeffrey-dahmer-netflix-abolish-true-crime

Lloyd, S (2022) 'True-Crime Expert on Whether Jeffrey Dahmer's Childhood Made Him a Monster'. Newsweek, 11 October. Available at: https://www.newsweek.com/true-crime-expert-whether-jeffrey-dahmers-childhood-made-him-monster-1747471 (Accessed: 17/06/2024)

Lloyd, S. (2022). '*True-crime expert on whether Jeffrey Dahmer's childhood made him a monster.*' [online] Newsweek. 11 October. Available at: https://www.newsweek.com/true-crime-expert-whether-jeffrey-dahmers-childhood-made-him-monster-1747471.

Los Angeles Times (1991) Milwaukee officers had entered Dahmer's apartment. Available at: https://www.latimes.com/archives/la-xpm-1991-08-02-mn-234-story.html

Los Angeles Times (1992) Dahmer found sane in grisly murders of 15. Available at: https://www.latimes.com/archives/la-xpm-1992-02-16-mn-4693-story.html

Maamodt.asp.radford.edy (2025) '*Jeffrey Dahmer*'. Radford University. Available at: https://maamodt.asp.radford.edu/Psyc%20405/serial%20killers/Dahmer,%20Jeff.htm [Accessed 1 May 2025]

Man (1991). *Complaint: Man killed victims, saved heart to eat - UPI Archives.* [online] UPI. 25 July. Available at: https://www.upi.com/Archives/1991/07/25/Complaint-Man-killed-victims-saved-heart-to-eat/3475680414400/.

Martin, L. (2019). '*The women murdered by serial killer Ted Bundy*'. [online] The i Paper. 19 May. Available at: https://inews.co.uk/culture/television/ted-bundy-victims-serial-killer-how-many-murders-zac-efron-film-286996?srsltid=AfmBOoo7ajyhWgmeJYp5mrB5-DjY4AEWkSYckNpA5kYoKh7qLyL2Q7tx [Accessed 16 Jun. 2025].

Mayo Clinic (2022). *Alcohol Use Disorder.* [online] Mayo Clinic. Available at: https://www.mayoclinic.org/diseases-conditions/alcohol-use-disorder/symptoms-causes/syc-20369243.

Mayo Clinic (2025) 'Postpartum Depression'. Available at: https://www.mayoclinic.org/diseases-conditions/postpartum-depression/symptoms-causes/syc-20376617 (Accessed: 17/06/2024)

McCann, S. (2022). *Ronald Flowers: who is Jeffrey Dahmer survivor, what he said about serial killer experience, where is he now?* [online] NationalWorld. 29 September. Available at: https://www.nationalworld.com/culture/television/ronald-flowers-who-is-jeffrey-dahmer-survivor-what-he-said-about-serial-killer-where-is-he-now-3860812 [Accessed 26 Jun. 2025].

McEvoy, C. (2023). *Jeffrey Dahmer - Murders, Victims & Death.* [online] Biography.com.15 September. Available at: https://www.biography.com/crime/jeffrey-dahmer. (Accessed: 29/06/2024)

Mclean Hospital (2024). *How Drinking Affects the Teenage Brain | McLean Hospital.* [online] www.mcleanhospital.org. Available at: https://www.mcleanhospital.org/essential/drinking-teen-brain.

McManus, R. (1995) Family seeks settlement after Nen's death, Orlando Sentinel, 22 March. Available at: http://articles.orlandosentinel.com/1995-03-22/news/9503210673_1_dahmer-racism-family

Mental Health Foundation (2022). *Alcohol and Mental Health.* [online] Mental Health Foundation. Available at: https://www.mentalhealth.org.uk/explore-mental-health/a-z-topics/alcohol-and-mental-health.

Mercury News (2025) Today in history: February 17 — serial killer Jeffrey Dahmer sentenced to life in prison, Mercury News, 17 February. Available at: https://www.mercurynews.com/2025/02/17/today-in-history-february-17-serial-kille r-jeffrey-dahmer-sentenced-to-life-in-prison/

Miami New Times (1997) River of sleaze, Miami New Times, 20 March. Available at: https://www.miaminewtimes.com/news/river-of-sleaze-6378923

Milano, J. and Milano, J. (2022). *Who Were Jeffrey Dahmer Victims? A Full Timeline Of His Murders.* [online] Alpha News Call. 12 October. Available at: https://alphanewscalls.com/2022/10/12/who-were-jeffrey-dahmer-victims-a-full-timeline-of-his-murders/ [Accessed 26 Jun. 2025].

Miller, C. (2022). *Mental health disorders and teen substance use.* [online] Child Mind Institute. Available at: https://childmind.org/article/mental-health-disorders-and-substance-use/.

Milwaukee Journal Sentinel. (2018). *Milwaukee Journal Sentinel - Milwaukee and Wisconsin breaking news and investigations.* [online] Available at: https://www.jsonline.com/.

MIND (2023). 'About Trauma'. Available at: https://www.mind.org.uk/information-support/types-of-mental-health-problems/trauma/about-trauma/. (Accessed: 17/06/2024)

Mitra, S. (2022). *James Doxtator Murder: How Did Jeffrey Dahmer Kill Him?* [online] The Cinemaholic. 27 September. Available at: https://thecinemaholic.com/james-doxtator-murder-how-did-jeffrey-dahmer-kill-him/ [Accessed 18 Nov. 2023].

Mitra, S. (2022). *Oliver Lacy Murder: How Did Jeffrey Dahmer Kill Him?* [online] The Cinemaholic. 27 September. Available at: https://thecinemaholic.com/oliver-lacy-murder-how-did-jeffrey-dahmer-kill-him/.

Mixson, C. (2012). *Writer tells you about his childhood friend: Jeffrey Dahmer.* [online] Brooklyn Paper. 19 April. Available at: https://www.brooklynpaper.com/writer-tells-you-about-his-childhood-friend-jeffrey-dahmer/ [Accessed 24 April 2025].

Moncada Storti, A.M. (2021) Remembering Konerak Sinthasomphone, Reappropriate, 3 June. Available at: https://reappropriate.co/2021/06/remembering-konerak-sinthasomphone/

Myers, B. (2022). *Jeffrey Dahmer's Repulsive Interactions With Road Kill As A Child.* [online] Grunge. 26 November. Available at: https://www.grunge.com/1113028/jeffrey-dahmers-repulsive-interactions-with-road-kill-as-a-child/ [Accessed 5 May 2023].

MyHeritage. (2019). *Joseph Bradehoft Family History & Historical Records - MyHeritage.* [online] Available at: https://www.myheritage.com/names/joseph_bradehoft [Accessed 28 Jun. 2025].

N/A. (2022). *Who was Richard Guerrero the only Hispanic among the 17 victims of serial killer Jeffery Dahmer?* [online]. News Rnd. (Unknown). Available at: https://newsrnd.com/news/2022-09-29-who-was-richard-guerrero--the-only-hispanic-among-the-17-victims-of-serial-killer-jeffrey-dahmer.BJfBZjcmMi.html

N/A. (Unknown) AP News. Available at: https://apnews.com/article/a6b7e65b1e279970ba3e5b6f45ad9095

Nast, C. (2022). *Netflix's 'Dahmer' and the Killer Who Cannot Be 'Explained'.* [online] The New Yorker. 2 October. Available at: https://www.newyorker.com/culture/on-television/netflixs-dahmer-and-the-killer-who-cannot-be-explained. [Accessed 24 April 2025].

National Institute on Alcohol Abuse and Alcoholism (n.d.). *Alcohol and the Brain: An Overview | National Institute on Alcohol Abuse and Alcoholism (NIAAA).* [online] www.niaaa.nih.gov. Available at: https://www.niaaa.nih.gov/alcohols-effects-health/alcohol-and-brain-overview.

National World (2022) Konerak Sinthasomphone: what happened to Jeffrey Dahmer's 14-year-old victim?, National World, [date unavailable]. Available at: https://www.nationalworld.com/culture/television/konerak-sinthasomphone-what-happened-jeffrey-dahmers-14-year-old-victim-who-brother-somsack-3871621

NBC Chicago. (2022). *As Jeffrey Dahmer Series Airs on Netflix, Here's What to Know About His Chicago Victims.* [online] 26 September. Available at: https://www.nbcchicago.com/news/local/as-jeffrey-dahmer-series-airs-on-netflix-heres-what-to-know-about-his-chicago-victims/2950700/ [Accessed 28 Jun. 2025].

NBC Universal (2022). *'Monster' de Netflix: Richard Guerrero, el único latino entre las víctimas del asesino serial Jeffrey Dahmer.* [online] TELEMUNDO.com.

29 September. Available at: https://www.telemundo.com/noticias/noticias-telemundo/crimen-y-violencia/richard-guerrero-latino-asesinado-por-jeffrey-dahmer-rcna49911 [Accessed 26 Jun. 2025].

NC, T.I.O. (2019). *Effects of Alcohol on Teens: Physical, Mental & Emotional.* [online] Talk It Out. Available at: https://www.talkitoutnc.org/effects-alcohol-on-teens/.

NELSON, K. (2022). *A Complete Timeline of Jeffrey Dahmer's Victims Over the Years.* [online] Men's Health. 4 October. Available at: https://www.menshealth.com/entertainment/a41468382/jeffrey-dahmer-victims-timeline-monster/.

NELSON, K. (2022). *A Complete Timeline of Jeffrey Dahmer's Victims Over the Years.* [online] Men's Health. 4 October. Available at: https://www.menshealth.com/entertainment/a41468382/jeffrey-dahmer-victims-timeline-monster/. [Accessed 1 January 2025].

Netflix (2022) Watch Conversations with a Killer: The Jeffrey Dahmer Tapes. Available at: https://www.netflix.com/title/81173345

Netflix Tudum (2022) 'Conversations with a Killer: The Jeffrey Dahmer Tapes': What to Know. Available at: https://www.netflix.com/tudum/articles/conversations-with-a-killer-the-jeffrey-dahmer-tapes-release-date-cast-news

Netflix Tudum (2022) Conversations with a Killer: The Jeffrey Dahmer Tapes Interviews. Available at: https://www.netflix.com/tudum/articles/conversations-with-a-killer-the-jeffrey-dahmer-tapes-interviews

New York Post (2015) Meet the prisoner who murdered killer cannibal Jeffrey Dahmer, New York Post, 28 April. Available at: https://www.nypost.com/2015/04/28/meet-the-prisoner-who-murdered-killer-cannibal-jeffrey-dahmer/

New York Post (2015) Meet the prisoner who murdered killer cannibal Jeffrey Dahmer, New York Post, 28 April. Available at: https://www.nypost.com/2015/04/28/meet-the-prisoner-who-murdered-killer-cannibal-jeffrey-dahmer/

News, L. (2024). *Jeffrey Dahmer Murder Timeline: Lawyer Monthly Uncovered.* [online] Lawyer Monthly. 11 December. Available at: https://www.lawyer-monthly.com/2024/12/jeffrey-dahmer-murder-timeline-lawyer-monthly-uncovered/.

NHS (2025) 'Postpartum psychosis'. Available at: https://www.nhs.uk/mental-health/conditions/post-partum-psychosis/ (Accessed: 17/06/2024)

NHS Digital (2019). *Smoking, Drinking and Drug Use among Young People in England 2018 [NS] - NHS Digital.* [online] NHS Digital. Available at: https://

digital.nhs.uk/data-and-information/publications/statistical/smoking-drinking-and-drug-use-among-young-people-in-england/2018.

NIAAA (2024). *Alcohol and the adolescent brain.* [online] www.niaaa.nih.gov. Available at: https://www.niaaa.nih.gov/publications/alcohol-and-adolescent-brain.

Nicolaou, E. (2022). *Tony Hughes' mom speaks out against Jeffrey Dahmer Netflix show.* [online] TODAY.com. 10 October. Available at: https://www.today.com/popculture/tv/tony-hughes-jeffrey-dahmer-deaf-victim-rcna50882.

Nih.gov. (2017). *Alcohol Use Disorder | National Institute on Alcohol Abuse and Alcoholism (NIAAA).* [online] Available at: https://www.niaaa.nih.gov/alcohol-health/overview-alcohol-consumption/alcohol-use-disorders.

NPR. (2017). *In New Film, 'My Friend Dahmer' Author Portrays Serial Killer As Sympathetic Outcast.* NPR. [online] Available at: https://www.npr.org/2017/11/12/563660773/in-new-film-my-friend-dahmer-author-portrays-serial-killer-as-a-sympathetic-outc.

Nucleus (2024). *'Jeffrey Dahmer - The True Crime Database Jeffrey Dahmer Cannibal and Serial Killer'.* [online] The True Crime Database. Unknown. Available at: https://www.thetruecrimedatabase.com/case_file/jeffrey-dahmer/. (Accessed: 03/07/2024).

Nucleus (2024). *Jeffrey Dahmer - The True Crime Database Jeffrey Dahmer Cannibal and Serial Killer.* [online] The True Crime Database. 21 October. Available at: https://www.thetruecrimedatabase.com/case_file/jeffrey-dahmer/.

NY daily News. (Unknown). *Jeffrey Dahmer Victims Relive Terror'.* [online] NY Daily News. (Unknown). Available at: https://www.nydailynews.com/news/crime/jeffrey-dahmer-surviving-victims-relive-terror-article-1.3626207[Accessed 13 October 2024].

Oldenquist, E. (2022). *How Much of 'Monster: The Jeffrey Dahmer Story' Actually Happened?* [online] POPSUGAR Entertainment. 29 September. Available at: https://www.popsugar.com/entertainment/jeffrey-dahmer-true-story-48962590.

Olson, S. (2022) 'Where is Jeffrey Dahmer's Mother, Joyce Dahmer?'. Seventeen, 29 September. Available at: https://www.seventeen.com/celebrity/movies-tv/a41447619/jeffrey-dahmer-mother-joyce-whereabouts/ (Accessed: 17/06/2024)

Olson, S. (2022) 'Where is Jeffrey Dahmer's Mother, Joyce Dahmer?'. Seventeen, 29 September. Available at: https://www.seventeen.com/celebrity/movies-tv/a41447619/jeffrey-dahmer-mother-joyce-whereabouts/ (Accessed: 17/06/2024)

Olson, S. (2022) 'Where is Jeffrey Dahmer's Mother, Joyce Dahmer?'. Seventeen, 29 September. Available at: https://www.seventeen.com/celebrity/movies-tv/a41447619/jeffrey-dahmer-mother-joyce-whereabouts/ (Accessed: 17/06/2024)

Online Article

Osu.edu. (2018). *Alum and 'My Friend Dahmer' author reflects on success.* [online] Osu. 23 March. Available at: https://artsandsciences.osu.edu/news/alum-and-my-friend-dahmer-author-reflects-success [Accessed 25 March 2025].

Pallavi Bhadu (2022). *Who Was Tony Hughes, Jeffrey Dahmer's 12th Victim?* [online] Popsugar. 30 September. Available at: https://www.popsugar.com/entertainment/who-was-tony-hughes-jeffrey-dahmer-victim-48964772 [Accessed 27 Jun. 2025].

Paoletti, G. (2017). *The Horrifying Story Of Jeffrey Dahmer, The Milwaukee Cannibal.* [online] All That's Interesting. 25 March. Available at: https://allthatsinteresting.com/jeffrey-dahmer [Accessed 4 Feb. 2019].

People (1994) Sins of the son, People, 17 March. Available at: https://www.people.com/archive/sins-of-the-son-vol-41-no-11/

People (2022) 'I See Jeffrey Dahmer in My Sleep': Victim's Daughter Says She Has Nightmares Since Series, People, [no date]. Available at: https://www.people.com/crime/daughter-dahmer-victim-errol-lindsey-speaks-out/

Perkins, N. (2021). *Monster: The Jeffrey Dahmer Story | Trailer, Release Date.* [online] Popsugar. 20 September. Available at: https://www.popsugar.com/entertainment/ryan-murphy-monster-jeffrey-dahmer-story-netflix-details-48234544 [Accessed 27 Jun. 2025].

Peta (2022). *Who Were the First Victims of Jeffrey Dahmer?* [online] PETA. (Unknown) Available at: https://www.peta.org/features/dahmer-bundy-and-other-killers-who-hurt-animals/ [Accessed 24 May 2025]

Piazza, B. (2022). *'Did Jeffrey Dahmer's Double Hernia Surgery Alter His Personality? Lionel Dahmer Seems to Think So'*. [online] Distractify. 27 September. Available at: https://www.distractify.com/p/jeffrey-dahmer-hernia-surgery. (Accessed: 03/07/2024).

Piccotti, T. (2021). *'Ed Gein'*. [online] Biography. Available at: https://www.biography.com/crime/ed-gein. [Accessed 3 May 2025]

Porter, R. (2022) Ryan Murphy says he reached out to 20 of the victims' family and friends for Dahmer series — 'Not a single person responded to us', The Hollywood Reporter, 28 October. Available at: https://www.hollywoodreporter.

com/tv/tv-news/ryan-murphy-says-he-reached-out-to-20-of-the-victims-family-and-friends-for-dahmer-series-not-a-single-person-responded-to-us-1235250610/

Porter, R. (2022) Ryan Murphy says he reached out to 20 of the victims' family and friends for Dahmer series — 'Not a single person responded to us', The Hollywood Reporter, 28 October. Available at: https://www.hollywoodreporter.com/tv/tv-news/ryan-murphy-says-he-reached-out-to-20-of-the-victims-family-and-friends-for-dahmer-series-not-a-single-person-responded-to-us-1235250610/

Press, A. (1991). *DISMEMBERED BODIES FOUND IN MILWAUKEE.* [online] The Washington Post. 23 July. Available at: https://www.washingtonpost.com/archive/politics/1991/07/24/dismembered-bodies-found-in-milwaukee/1651d404-6f13-4b2b-ac19-e30257ace9ca/

Public Health England (2016). *The public health burden of alcohol: evidence review.* [online] GOV.UK. Available at: https://www.gov.uk/government/publications/the-public-health-burden-of-alcohol-evidence-review.

Radcliffe, J. (2022). *What's real and what's fiction in Netflix's Jeffrey Dahmer series, 'Monster'.* [online] Journal Sentinel. (Unknown) Available at: https://www.jsonline.com/story/news/2022/09/23/whats-real-fiction-monster-jeffrey-dahmer-story-netflix/8083469001/?ref=popsugar.com&=___psv__p_48964772__m_partner__s_imdb__c_feed__t_w__r_m.imdb.com%2F_ [Accessed 27 Jun. 2025].

Radcliffe, J.R. (2022). *Jeffrey Dahmer killed 17 people before his crimes were discovered. These are the victims and what we knew about them.* [online] Journal Sentinel. (Unknown) Available at: https://www.jsonline.com/story/news/2022/09/28/jeffrey-dahmers-17-victims-and-what-we-knew-them-errol-lindsey-rita-isbell-anthony-tony-hughes/10443235002/.

Radcliffe, J.R. (2022). *Jeffrey Dahmer killed 17 people. These are the victims and what we knew about them.* [online] USA TODAY. (Unknown) Available at: https://www.usatoday.com/story/news/nation/2022/09/29/jeffrey-dahmer-victims-photos-killed/10458814002/.

Radcliffe, J.R. (n.d.). *Jeffrey Dahmer killed 17 people before his crimes were discovered. These are the victims and what we knew about them.* [online] Journal Sentinel. (Unknown) Available at: https://eu.jsonline.com/story/news/2022/09/28/jeffrey-dahmers-17-victims-and-what-we-knew-them-errol-lindsey-rita-isbell-anthony-tony-hughes/10443235002/ [Accessed 14 Dec. 2023].

Radcliffe, J.R. (n.d.). *Jeffrey Dahmer killed 17 people. These are the victims and what we knew about them.* [online] USA TODAY. (Unknown) Available at: https://

eu.usatoday.com/story/news/nation/2022/09/29/jeffrey-dahmer-victims-photos-killed/10458814002/ [Accessed 17 Nov. 2022].

Radcliffe, J.R. (n.d.). *Jeffrey Dahmer killed 17 people. These are the victims and what we knew about them.* [online] USA TODAY. (Unknown) Available at: https://eu.usatoday.com/story/news/nation/2022/09/29/jeffrey-dahmer-victims-photos-killed/10458814002/.

Ramsland, K. (2012) Women who love serial killers, Psychology Today blog, 20 April. Available at: https://www.psychologytoday.com/us/blog/shadow-boxing/201204/women-who-love-serial-killers

Ranker. (2024). '*What Jeffrey Dahmer Was Like As A Kid*'. [online] 22 April. Available at: https://www.ranker.com/list/what-jeffrey-dahmer-was-like-as-a-kid/lee-emjay. (Accessed: 11/06/2024)

Refinery29 UK (2019) How Ted Bundy met and married Carole Ann Boone, 14 January. Available at: https://www.refinery29.com/en-gb/2019/01/222617/ted-bundy-wife-carole-ann-boone-marriage-how-they-met

Rehab Clinics Group. (2019). *Why Is Alcohol Addictive (Physical & Psychological Reasons).* [online] Available at: https://rehabclinicsgroup.com/why-is-alcohol-addictive/.

Riesman, A. (n.d.). *My Friend Dahmer Author on the Boy Behind the Killer and the Movie Adaptation.* [online] Vulture. 20 April. Available at: https://www.vulture.com/2017/04/my-friend-dahmer-author-recalls-the-boy-behind-the-killer.html [Accessed 23 September 2024].

Robles, M. (2022). *Wait, so what happened to Jeffrey Dahmer's only Hispanic victim, Richard Guerrero?* [online] Annenberg Media. 21 November. Available at: https://www.uscannenbergmedia.com/2022/11/21/wait-so-what-happened-to-jeffrey-dahmers-only-hispanic-victim-richard-guerrero/.

RoC Profile: Alcoholic Beverage Consumption; 14th RoC 2016. (2016). Available at: https://ntp.niehs.nih.gov/ntp/roc/content/profiles/alcoholicbeverage-consumption.pdf.

ROSEN, M. (2005). *Woman's son 17th victim, police say.* [online] Tampa Bay Times. 17 August. Available at: https://www.tampabay.com/archive/1991/08/17/woman-s-son-17th-victim-police-say/ [Accessed 26 Jun. 2025].

Rotten Tomatoes (2022) Conversations With a Killer: The Jeffrey Dahmer Tapes: Season 1. Available at: https://www.rottentomatoes.com/tv/conversations_with_a_killer_the_jeffrey_dahmer_tapes/s01

Royal College of Psychiatrists (2024). *Alcohol, Mental Health and the Brain.* [online] www.rcpsych.ac.uk. Available at: https://www.rcpsych.ac.uk/mental-health/

mental-illnesses-and-mental-health-problems/alcohol-mental-health-and-the-brain.

Samantha.Elliott (2014). *Underage Drinking | SAMHSA - Substance Abuse and Mental Health Services Administration.* [online] Samhsa.gov. Available at: https://www.samhsa.gov/underage-drinking.

sarkar (2024). *'Jeffrey Dahmer's traumatic childhood'.* [online] Serial Killers Perspectives. Unknown. Available at: https://www.psychopathperspectives.com/jeffrey-dahmers-traumatic-childhood/ (Accessed: 03/07/2024).

Schott, G. (2022) They're making money off tragedy – Netflix's Dahmer series shows the dangers of fictionalising real horrors, The Conversation, 30 September. Available at: https://theconversation.com/theyre-making-money-off-tragedy-netflixs-dahmer-series-shows-the-dangers-of-fictionalising-real-horrors-192006

Schott, G. (2022) They're making money off tragedy – Netflix's Dahmer series shows the dangers of fictionalising real horrors, The Conversation, 30 September. Available at: https://theconversation.com/theyre-making-money-off-tragedy-netflixs-dahmer-series-shows-the-dangers-of-fictionalising-real-horrors-192006

Singh, S. (2022) Monster: The Jeffrey Dahmer Story is a grim, monotonous view of evil, The Guardian, 23 September. Available at: https://www.theguardian.com/tv-and-radio/2022/sep/23/jeffrey-dahmer-netflix-ryan-murphy-exploitative-tv

Smith, K.L. (2022). *Jeffrey Dahmer survivors: Here's what happened to Ron Flowers and the men who survived Dahmer.* [online] Capital. 27 September. Available at: https://www.capitalfm.com/news/tv-film/jeffrey-dahmer-survivors-now-today-victims/ [Accessed 6 Dec. 2024].

Smithers, D. (2024). *'Jeffrey Dahmer's dad Lionel had theory for why son became a serial killer'.* [online] LADbible. 23 September. Available at: https://www.ladbible.com/news/true-crime/jeffrey-dahmer-dad-lionel-dead-625422-20231213 (Accessed: 03/07/2024).

Sommer, T. (2018). *Meet the Rock Star Who Lives Happily in the House Where Jeffrey Dahmer First Killed.* [online] Observer. 22 February. Available at: https://observer.com/2018/02/interview-musician-chris-butler-on-owning-jeffrey-dahmers-house/ [Accessed 24 Janurary 2025].

Spanfeller, J. (2022). *Here's What The Police Found In Jeffrey Dahmer's Apartment.* [online] Yahoo Life.7 October. Available at: https://www.yahoo.com/lifestyle/jeffrey-dahmers-apartment-had-11-213700030.html.

Spanfeller, J. (2022). *Jeffrey Dahmer Killed Konerak While On Probation For His Brother's Assault.* [online] Women's Health. 14 October. Available at: https://www.womenshealthmag.com/life/a41427287/jeffrey-dahmer-victims-brothers-konerak-somsack-sinthasomphone/.

Spanfeller, J. (2022). *Jeffrey Dahmer Killed Konerak While On Probation For His Brother's Assault.* [online] Women's Health.14 October. Available at: https://www.womenshealthmag.com/life/a41427287/jeffrey-dahmer-victims-brothers-konerak-somsack-sinthasomphone/.

Spanfeller, J. (2022). *Jeffrey Dahmer's Third Victim Ran Away From Home Two Days Before His Death.* [online] Yahoo Life. 26 September. Available at: https://www.yahoo.com/lifestyle/jeffrey-dahmer-third-victim-ran-213400278.html [Accessed 7 May 2025].

Spartan Shield (n.d.) Review: Dahmer and how the media romanticizes killers, Spartan Shield. Available at: https://spartanshield.org/34362/arts-entertainment/review-dahmer-and-how-the-media-romanticizes-killers/

Spectrum News 1 (2022) Key witness reacts to renewed attention to Dahmer case, Spectrum News 1, 30 September. Available at: https://spectrumnews1.com/wi/milwaukee/news/2022/09/30/key-witness-reacts-to-renewed-attention-to-dahmer-case

Stephenson, C. (1991). *Children in Urban America - Marquette University.* [online] www.marquette.edu. 26 July. Available at: https://www.marquette.edu/cgi-bin/cuap/db.cgi?uid=default&ID=1112&view=Search&mh=1.

Sun (2022). *Police officer's horrific discovery.* [online] news. 8 October. Available at: https://www.news.com.au/lifestyle/real-life/true-stories/jeffrey-dahmer-police-officer-details-horrific-discovery-about-serial-killer/news-story/35168 10df50017e2daa9c6b91c0aab54.

Talbert, S. (2022). *Dahmer Victim Errol Lindsey Never Got To Meet His Daughter.* [online] Aol.com. 17 October. Available at: https://www.aol.com/two-jeffrey-dahmers-victims-were-163900369.html [Accessed 21 Mar. 2025].

Talbert, S. (2022). *Jeffrey Dahmer Killed Three People In His Grandma's Basement.* [online] Yahoo Life. 14 October. Available at: https://www.yahoo.com/lifestyle/jeffrey-dahmer-killed-three-people-192100776.html [Accessed 10 Jun. 2025].

Tampa Bay Times. (n.d.). *Dahmer charged in death of bay area woman's son.* [online] 23 August. Available at: https://www.tampabay.com/archive/1991/08/23/dahmer-charged-in-death-of-bay-area-woman-s-son/ [Accessed 19 May 2023].

Tempera, J. (2022). 'Jeffrey Dahmer's Dad Implied That A Childhood Surgery Triggered His Violent Acts'. AOL. 23 September. Available at: https://www.aol.com/jeffrey-dahmers-dad-implied-childhood-201300373.html?guccounter=1&guce_referrer=aHR0cHM6Ly93d3cuZ29vZ2xlLmNvLnVrLw&guce_referrer_sig=AQAAANzrJauFOfiy1IGvDSMqpW43NP39fy5mxTN_7n5vQ2adWygu_kqW-hCPqMg6EdIBf1W4Ep6V_aD7nHMwZoi0lzpMzUCCeZZ3mumvm0EHF5RnXL18FgjwInXVcbSBrsv27Z9dkALu7XmyrxScEoq0aUQgReVhHHL7ZYisuIVGkCst. (Accessed: 19/06/24)

Tempera, J. (2022). *Jeffrey Dahmer's Dad Implied That A Childhood Surgery Triggered His Violent Acts.* [online] Women's Health. 23 September. Available at: https://www.womenshealthmag.com/life/a41356522/jeffrey-dahmer-hernia-surgery/. (Accessed: 17/06/2024)

The Guardian (2022) Jeffrey Dahmer: Netflix show is exploitative TV – critic, The Guardian, 23 September. Available at: https://www.theguardian.com/tv-and-radio/2022/sep/23/jeffrey-dahmer-netflix-ryan-murphy-exploitative-tv

The Hollywood Reporter (2022) 'Dahmer – Monster: The Jeffrey Dahmer Story' review, The Hollywood Reporter. Available at: https://www.hollywoodreporter.com/tv/tv-reviews/dahmer-monster-the-jeffrey-dahmer-story-review-ryan-murphy-evan-peters-1235225967/

The Independent (2022) Netflix's Dahmer sparks debate over portrayal of real-life killers, The Independent. Available at: https://www.independent.co.uk/news/world/americas/jeffrey-dahmer-netflix-true-real-anne-e-schwartz-b2178031.html

The Jerusalem Post | JPost.com. (2025). *Meet acetaldehyde, the neurotransmitter that messes our brains on alcoho | The Jerusalem Post.* 1 January. [online] Available at: https://www.jpost.com/science/science-around-the-world/article-835640 [Accessed 24 January 2025].

The Lineup Staff (2017). '*Before the Murders: A Chilling Glimpse into Jeffrey Dahmer's Childhood*'. [online] The Lineup. 6 November. Available at: https://the-line-up.com/jeffrey-dahmer-childhood.

The New Yorker (1994) The expert who convinced a jury that Jeffrey Dahmer was sane, The New Yorker, 16 May. Available at: https://www.newyorker.com/magazine/1994/05/16/park-dietz-profile-witness-for-the-prosecution

The Tab (2022) Inside the real life apartment once owned by Jeffrey Dahmer. Available at: https://archive.thetab.com/uk/2022/09/26/inside-real-life-apartment-jeffrey-dahmer-oxford-apartments-flat-now-275256

The Washington Post (1992) Jury finds Dahmer was sane. Available at: https://www.washingtonpost.com/archive/politics/1992/02/16/jury-finds-dahmer-was-sane/7ba3ebb0-ec67-4e84-8e02-a75ee4da29bf/

thecriminalmind (2019). *Reblog by @thecriminalmind · 3 images.* [online] Tumblr. Available at: https://www.tumblr.com/thecriminalmind/184089743015/yoursonsandyourhusbands-ernest-miller-22-year [Accessed 27 Jun. 2025].

Them (2022) Netflix's Dahmer is shamelessly exploitative and exhausting, Them. Available at: https://www.them.us/story/netflix-dahmer-ryan-murphy-review

Therapistmandy.com. (2022). '*Mandy E Morris – Making The Best… Better*'. [online] Available at: http://www.therapistmandy.com [Accessed 4 February 2025].

Time (2016) How police caught Jeffrey Dahmer, Time. Available at: https://time.com/4412621/jeffrey-dahmer-cannibal-murderer-25th-anniversary-arrest/

Time Magazine (1991) The little flat of horrors. Available at: https://time.com/archive/6718295/the-little-flat-of-horrors/

To The Best Of Our Knowledge. (2018). *Separating Man From Monster.* [online] ttbook. (Unknown) Available at: https://www.ttbook.org/interview/separating-man-monster [Accessed 24 May 2025].

to, C. (2017). *Jeffrey Dahmer.* [online] Murder Wiki. Available at: https://murder.fandom.com/wiki/Jeffrey_Dahmer#Joseph_Bradehoft [Accessed 28 Jun. 2025].

to, C. (2025). *David Thomas.* [online] International Missing Persons Wiki. Available at: https://int-missing.fandom.com/wiki/David_Thomas [Accessed 27 Jun. 2025].

to, C. (2025). *Eddie Warren Smith.* [online] International Missing Persons Wiki. Available at: https://int-missing.fandom.com/wiki/Eddie_Warren_Smith [Accessed 27 Jun. 2025].

Tron, G. (2017) Here's what Jeffrey Dahmer's family thinks of their serial killer relative, Oxygen, 27 October. Available at: https://www.oxygen.com/dahmer-on-dahmer-a-serial-killer-speaks/blogs/heres-what-jeffrey-dahmers-family-thinks-of-their

Tullos, A. (n.d.) Story of boy police gave back to Jeffrey Dahmer, Ranker. Available at: https://www.ranker.com/list/story-of-boy-police-gave-back-to-jeffrey-dahmer/amandatullos

Tumblr.com. (2025). Available at: https://www.tumblr.com/datingdahmer-blog (Accessed: 03/07/2024)

Twentytwowords.com. (2025). *'Jeffrey Dahmer's Dad Says he Knows What's to Blame for Son Becoming Serial Killer'*. 4 October. [online] Available at: https://twentytwowords.com/jeffrey-dahmers-dad-says-he-knows-whats-to-blame-for-son-becoming-serial-killer/ (Accessed: 03/07/2024).

Ubiera, C.R. (2022). *Inside heartbreaking lives of Jeffrey Dahmer's victims who were slain in 'Milwaukee Monster's' lair as Netf...* [online] The US Sun. 22 September. Available at: https://www.the-sun.com/news/6284599/jeffrey-dahmer-victims-stories-netflix-drama/ [Accessed 26 Jun. 2025].

Ubiera, C.R. (2022). *Inside heartbreaking lives of Jeffrey Dahmer's victims who were slain in 'Milwaukee Monster's' lair as Netf...* [online] The US Sun. 22 September. Available at: https://www.the-sun.com/news/6284599/jeffrey-dahmer-victims-stories-netflix-drama/.

Unknown (2022) 'Who was Jeffrey Dahmer? The Notorious Serial Killer from Netflix's New Crime Series'. 5Chicago, 22 September. Available at: https://www.nbcchicago.com/news/who-was-jeffrey-dahmer-the-notorious-serial-killer-from-netflixs-new-crime-series/2947437/. (Accessed: 12/06/2024)

Vanity Fair (1991) Dahmer's inferno, Vanity Fair, 1 Nov. Available at: https://www.vanityfair.com/style/1991/11/jeffrey-dahmer-dennis-nilsen-serial-killer

Variety (2022) 'Staircase' producers detail owl theory in Michael Peterson case, Variety, 17 October. Available at: https://variety.com/2022/tv/news/staircase-michael-peterson-owl-theory-colin-firth-1235294477/

Velentzas, I. (2020). *'We Seem To Just Be Steamrolling Toward Tragedy.': An Interview With Derf Backderf.* [online] The Comics Journal. 31 August. Available at: https://www.tcj.com/we-seem-to-just-be-steamrolling-toward-tragedy-an-interview-with-derf-backderf/ [Accessed 19 Nov. 2024].

Vizaca. (Unknown). *Jamie Doxator. [online]. Available at:* https://www.vizaca.com/jamie-doxtator/

Waxman, O.B. (2016). *How Police Caught Jeffrey Dahmer.* [online] Time. 22 July. Available at: https://time.com/4412621/jeffrey-dahmer-cannibal-murderer-25th-anniversary-arrest/ [Accessed 12 Dec. 2019].

Waxman, O.B. (2016). *How Police Caught Jeffrey Dahmer.* [online] Time. 22 July. Available at: https://time.com/4412621/jeffrey-dahmer-cannibal-murderer-25th-anniversary-arrest/.

Weremember.com. (2023). *Visit Curtis Straughter's memorial page on We Remember.* [online] Available at: https://www.weremember.com/curtis-straughter/8k3s/

memories?utm_campaign=findagrave&utm_source=findagrave [Accessed 27 Jun. 2025].

Wexner Center for the Arts. (2017). *My Friend Dahmer | Wexner Center for the Arts.* [online] Available at: https://wexarts.org/film-video/my-friend-dahmer [Accessed 12 May 2025].

Wikipedia Contributors (2019). *Pyromania.* [online] Wikipedia. Available at: https://en.wikipedia.org/wiki/Pyromania [Accessed 9 May 2025).

Wikipedia Contributors (2025). '*Dissociative identity disorder*'. Wikipedia. Available at: https://en.wikipedia.org/wiki/Dissociative_identity_disorder#Causes (Accessed: 29/06/2024)

Women's Health (2022) Who is Dean Vaughn and was he a Jeffrey Dahmer victim?. Available at: https://www.womenshealthmag.com/life/a41392642/dean-vaughn-jeffrey-dahmer-victim/

Women's Health Magazine (2019) Ted Bundy wife Carole Ann Boone: what to know, 19 April. Available at: https://www.womenshealthmag.com/life/a27379040/ted-bundy-wife-carole-ann-boone/

Women's Health Magazine (2019) What is hybristophilia? Ted Bundy and the psychology of being attracted to killers, 20 May. Available at: https://www.womenshealthmag.com/health/a27397635/ted-bundy-hybristophilia-definition/

Worthington, R. (1991) Could police have saved young victim? — 911 tapes show officers were in Dahmer's place, left teen to fate, The Seattle Times, 2 August. Available at: http://community.seattletimes.nwsource.com/archive/?date=19910802&slug=1297813

Wrlc.org. (2017). *Hughes, Tony | Gallaudet University Library Guide to Deaf Biographies and Index to Deaf Periodicals.* [online] Available at: https://liblists.wrlc.org/biographies/53089?ref=popsugar.com&=___psv__p_48964772__m_partner__s_imdb__c_feed__t_w__r_m.imdb.com%2F_ [Accessed 27 Jun. 2025].

www.drinkaware.co.uk. (2022). *Teenage Drinking | Drinkaware.* [online] Available at: https://www.drinkaware.co.uk/advice/underage-drinking/teenage-drinking.

www.psychologytoday.com. (n.d.). *Alcoholism | Psychology Today United Kingdom.* [online] Available at: https://www.psychologytoday.com/gb/basics/alcohol.

www.samhsa.gov. (n.d.). *Key Substance Use and Mental Health Indicators in the United States: Results from the 2016 National Survey on Drug Use and Health*

| *CBHSQ Data*. [online] Available at: https://www.samhsa.gov/data/report/key-substance-use-and-mental-health-indicators-united-states-results-2016-national-survey.

Yahoo Lifestyle (2022) Jeffrey Dahmer killed one brother — how the serial-killer's family is coping, Yahoo Lifestyle, 26 October. Available at: https://www.yahoo.com/lifestyle/jeffrey-dahmer-killed-one-brother-211200917.html

Young, K. (2022). *Monster: The Jeffrey Dahmer Story Can Solve 1 True Crime Show Problem*. [online] ScreenRant. 20 September. Available at: https://screenrant.com/monster-jeffrey-dahmer-victims-pov-story-serial-killer-fix/ [Accessed 27 Jun. 2025].

Endnotes

1. Kaplan, A (2022) 'What Happened To Jeffrey Dahmer's Mother, Joyce? Where She Is Now', Yahoo!Life, 10 October. Available at: https://www.yahoo.com/lifestyle/happened-jeffrey-dahmers-mother-joyce-220134534.html (Accessed: 12/06/2024).
2. NHS (2025) 'Postpartum psychosis'. Available at: https://www.nhs.uk/mental-health/conditions/post-partum-psychosis/ (Accessed: 17/06/2024)
3. Mayo Clinic (2025) 'Postpartum Depression'. Available at: https://www.mayoclinic.org/diseases-conditions/postpartum-depression/symptoms-causes/syc-20376617 (Accessed: 17/06/2024)
4. MIND (2023). 'About Trauma'. Available at: https://www.mind.org.uk/information-support/types-of-mental-health-problems/trauma/about-trauma/. (Accessed: 17/06/2024)
5. Cleveland Clinic (2023). '*Hernia | Cleveland Clinic*.' [online] Cleveland Clinic. Available at: https://my.clevelandclinic.org/health/diseases/15757-hernia. (Accessed: 17/06/2024)
6. Wikipedia Contributors (2025). '*Dissociative identity disorder*'. Wikipedia. Available at: https://en.wikipedia.org/wiki/Dissociative_identity_disorder#Causes (Accessed: 29/06/2024)
7. Osu.edu. (2018). *Alum and 'My Friend Dahmer' author reflects on success.* Available at: https://artsandsciences.osu.edu/news/alum-and-my-friend-dahmer-author-reflects-success. (Accessed: 29/06/2024)
8. Myers, B. (2022). *Jeffrey Dahmer's Repulsive Interactions With Road Kill As A Child.* Grunge. Available at: https://www.grunge.com/1113028/jeffrey-dahmers-repulsive-interactions-with-road-kill-as-a-child/. (Accessed: 29/06/2024)
9. Times, S. to T.N.Y. (1991). Bone Fragments, Many Human, Are Found at Suspect's Ohio Home. *The New York Times.* 31 July. Available at: https://

www.nytimes.com/1991/07/31/us/bone-fragments-many-human-are-found-at-suspect-s-ohio-home.html. (Accessed: 03/07/2024)

10. Time.graphics. (2024). *nov 20, 1987 - Murder of Steven Tuomi (Timeline).* Available at: https://time.graphics/event/3087930. (Accessed: 03/07/2024)
11. The Sun. (2022). *Who were Jeffrey Dahmer's victims?* [online] Available at: https://www.thesun.co.uk/news/18506857/jeffrey-dahmer-victims/. (Accessed: 03/07/2024)
12. Diksha Sundriyal (2022). *Ronald Flowers: What Happened to Jeffery Dahmer's Survivor?* The Cinemaholic. Available at: https://thecinemaholic.com/where-is-jeffery-dahmers-survivor-ronald-flowers-now/ [Accessed 02 January 2025].
13. Psychology Today. (Unknown). *Women Who Love Serial Killers.* [online] Available at: https://www.psychologytoday.com/us/blog/shadow-boxing/201204/women-who-love-serial-killers. [Accessed 02 January 2025].
14. My Site. (2016). *Home | My Site.* Available at: https://www.thedoubledr.com [Accessed 03 May 2025].

Index